STUDIES IN AMERICAN POPULAR HISTORY AND CULTURE

Edited by

Jerome Nadelhaft
University of Maine

A ROUTLEDGE SERIES

STUDIES IN AMERICAN POPULAR HISTORY AND CULTURE

JEROME NADELHAFT, *General Editor*

POPULAR CULTURE
AND THE ENDURING MYTH
OF CHICAGO, 1871–1968

Lisa Krissoff Boehm

ROUTLEDGE
New York & London

Published in 2004 by
Routledge
29 West 35th Street
New York, NY 10001

Routledge is an imprint of the Taylor and Francis Group.

Library of Congress Cataloging-In-Publication data

Boehm, Lisa Beth Krissoff, 1969-
  Popular culture and the enduring myth of Chicago, 1871–1968 / Lisa Beth Krissoff Boehm.
    p. cm. -- (Studies in American popular history and culture)
  Includes bibliographical references and index.
  ISBN 0-415-94929-7 (hardback : alk. paper)
  1. Chicago (Ill.)--History--1875- 2. Chicago (Ill.)--Public opinion. 3. Popular culture--United States--History--19th century. 4. Popular culture--United States--History--20th century. 5. United States--Civilization--1865–1918. 6. United States--Civilization--1918-1945. 7. United States--Civilization--1945- 8. City and town life--Illinois--Chicago--History. 9. City and town life--United States--History. 10. Public opinion--United States. I. Title. II. Series: American popular history and culture (Routledge (Firm))
  F548.5.B54 2004
  977.3'1104--dc22

                                                                      2004000263

For Chris,
and Mom and Dad, with love

Contents

Acknowledgments

At two years old, or perhaps earlier, my parents fastened me into what was then a state-of-the-art car seat (designed for optimum views of the scenery, rather than safety) and we headed out on our first family visit to Chicago. The trip by car between our home in Grand Rapids, Michigan and Chicago, Illinois took about four hours. It would be a drive we repeated often over the years. The flat, clean landscapes of Michigan—scrubby vivid green plants and trees in the summer and gleaming, white snow with quick glimpses of Lake Michigan in the winter months—eventually folded into the scarred landscape of northern Indiana and on into Illinois. I came to know every curve of the road with time. Monthly trips were not unheard of. Certain signposts meant that we were approaching the city. My favorites were the looming and eventually abandoned brewery which even today appears in my mind's eye whenever the subject of the "Rustbelt" comes up, and the upward climb of the Chicago Skyway.

Then we would plunge into the city. First we crawled through the traffic of the Stony Island area of the city's South Side, then past the University of Chicago and the massive Museum of Science and Industry. From here you could finally see Lake Michigan, which appeared to change every day, except in its vastness. People who have never seen this second largest Great Lake cannot truly imagine its size, its twining of the inviting and the sinister, and its large, clean smell. Having grown up on the lake's eastern bank, I was glad to see it again as we rounded the corner. Yet the lake always appeared different in Chicago, in a way I could not get entirely comfortable with. When I came to live in Evanston, Illinois, the lake always seemed to be on the wrong side of me.

Trips to Chicago were a frenzy of museum going, reuniting with friends and family, and food. Western Michigan is one of the most solid and most pleasant places in America to raise a family, but the restaurant scene is less than stellar. We carefully picked our dinner reservations on each of our journeys. The most repeated and most ritualistic of our meals would be spent in

Pizzeria Due (almost never Pizzeria Uno, its older sister and the site of the founding of the famous chain) on Ontario, with our favorite—the large deep dish sausage pizza. We did not believe anything smaller tasted right, nor could anything but sausage ever really measure up. I cannot explain how I came to write this book without serving up a slice of this magnificent food. The smell alone captured my heart for Chicago.

As a frequent visitor to the city, I learned to feel that the city was mine to explore and consider. Although I would come to live in a northern suburb of the city for five years, I have felt like a little piece of me was "from" Chicago since my earliest days. This sense of belonging, accompanied by an outsider's ability to analyze place, partly explains the existence of this book. The second most important element prompting me to write this book was the enthusiasm of the students in my Chicago history courses at Indiana University, which I describe below.

I would like to thank the many people who assisted me with this project. First, I would like to thank my former dissertation advisor, John Bodnar, who supervised the project from which this book grew. I went to Bloomington, Indiana specifically to work with Professor Bodnar in 1992, and never regretted my choice. He challenged me with a number of interesting courses, and proved to be a wonderful dissertation director. Despite his numerous teaching, research, and service responsibilities he always seemed to have time to discuss the project, and provided me with rapid written responses to my chapters as I went along. Second, I would like to thank the members of my dissertation committee; Wendy Gamber, who inspired in me a great appreciation of nineteenth century history and always served as a ready and willing ear for my questions regarding research and professional issues; Judith Allen, who greatly broadened my understanding of women's history and allowed me to see first-hand how exciting research projects unfold; and David Nordloh, who skillfully introduced me to American Studies and had faith in my research and teaching abilities from an early stage.

I also would like to thank other members of the history faculty at Indiana University during my years there, including James Madison, David Pace, Steven Stowe, Irving Katz, Michael McGerr, Joan Hoff, and Derek Penslar. I believe Indiana University offered me the best possible graduate education in American history and I treasure my experiences as a student and an instructor in the university's classrooms.

Warm thanks also go out to those who awarded me grants with which to pursue this research. I would especially like to thank the family of Paul V. McNutt, who generously contributed the McNutt History Fellowship, of which I was a proud recipient in 1997. Thank you to the members of the

Indiana University Graduate School and Department of History who thought my research worthy of financial support over the years. This assistance allowed me countless trips to Chicago to explore the archives.

Thanks to those who have sat down for conversations with me about the work, or who have taken on reading parts of this book and offered up helpful suggestions. The members of the various incarnations of my dissertation study group—including Julie Plaut, Diane Pecknold, and Patrick Ettinger—provided inspiration and well-considered words of advice. Kris McCusker took it upon herself to comment thoroughly on drafts via mail, a favor for which I am very grateful. Additionally, my former University of Chicago advisor, Michael Conzen, and the Newberry Library's Jim Grossman, took time from their busy schedules to speak with me at length about the project. The students of my two courses on Chicago for the Indiana University American Studies program deserve extended thank yous—without their enthusiasm I would never have fallen in love with the subject matter like I did nor would I have begun to link together the path of the "infamous city" myth. I would especially like to thank my former student Christian Goodwillie, who gathered piles of magazine articles for me and knew how to negotiate the library like an ace.

My colleagues in the Department of Urban Studies at Worcester State College—Maureen Power, Tuck Amory, and Steve Corey—have provided a warm intellectual home for me in which to hone my teaching skills in urban studies. Although this project was close to completion when I came to Massachusetts, the collegiality of the department has been a crucial support for my work on the project's details. Colleagues Bruce Cohen and Steve Corey read and commented on sections of the book in its final stages. Administrative assistant Thressa Corazzini provided essential help with copying rough drafts of the work. Thanks to Julie Frechette, Kris Waters, and Sarah Sharbach for their friendship throughout the process. And thanks to Kimberly Guinta, Richard Tressider, and Jerome Nadelhaft of Routledge, whose hard work brought the project to fruition.

I would also like to thank the hard-working archivists and librarians of the collections I utilized for the research on this work. Getting access to a broad array of popular media about Chicago over a one hundred year period proved a much tougher task than I first surmised. Grateful thanks go out to those at the Chicago Historical Society, the Newberry Library, the University of Illinois at Chicago Archives, the Harold Washington Library, the Museum of Broadcast History, the Lilly Library, the Indiana University Research Collections, the University of Michigan Graduate Library and the Buhr Facility, the Mardigan Library at the University of Michigan-Dearborn, the Michigan

State University Library, the Oakland University Library, and the Ohio State Library.

Thanks of course also to those who provided me with lodging, food, and even entertainment in Chicago during my frequent visits. My mother-in-law Loed Boehm, cousins Steven and Susan Neumer, and friends Lynne and Harvey Golomb, Diane Pecknold and Clark Johnson, and Jamie Lewis Masco took care of me in Chicago.

My ever-lasting thank yous need to be extended to my immediate family. My brother, Jonathan Krissoff, let me stay in his apartment, even going out to buy me a new bed before I arrived. He always proved willing to see a movie with me or go out to dinner after a tough day in the archives. My sister, Sarah Krissoff, was kind enough to spend about two weeks watching my newborn son, David (whose baby smiles helped the project too!), so that I could finish up my last chapter. She gave me assistance at a crucial time. My son David, as he grew, played patiently while Mommy finished her book, and I thank him for his good-natured soul and his independence. My grandparents, Abe and Sylvia Krissoff, provided their support and understanding. Without their help, my dream of a graduate education could not have come true. My parents, Joel and Madelon Krissoff, read through chapters, shopped for old books and Chicago memorabilia for me at every opportunity, cut out relevant newspaper articles and passed them along, and allowed me to stay with them during their vacations to the city. They introduced me to Chicago at a very early age and taught me that the city could be mine, too. They of course are responsible for my love of history, research, and learning, and everything that I am. I cannot ever thank them enough for all that they have done—nor would anyone else really believe how wonderful, inspiring, and generous two human beings can be.

And especially, I would like to thank my husband, Christopher Boehm, a native Chicagoan. We met in Chicago, and the city has served as the backdrop for many of our special moments and has provided us with a never-ending site of exploration. Chris stood by me at every critical juncture of this book project. He read drafts, edited, and discussed Chicago history with me for hours. Despite his own graduate work and busy career, he has been an unwavering support system. Chris and David are the best family anyone could have.

Lisa Krissoff Boehm
Worcester, Massachusetts

2004

Introduction:
Chicago, the Infamous City

With heart at rest I climbed the citadel's
Steep height, and saw the city as from a tower,
Hospital, brothel, prison, and such hells,
Where evil comes up softly like a flower...
Whether thou sleep, with heavy vapors full,
Sodden with day, or new appareled, stand
In gold-laced veils of evening beautiful,
I love thee, infamous city!

—Baudelaire[1]

In the late nineteenth century, with gripping tales of a spectacularly destructive fire, the once far-flung Midwestern outpost, Chicago, became an integral part of the national popular culture. Chicago entered onto the national stage in a manner unlike that of any other American city. American culture fashioned for Chicago a particularly compelling national face, an intriguing image that bespoke modernity and business power yet with far from subtle undertones of crime, loosening morals, and chaotic change. As Baudelaire explains in his *Petits Poemes en Prose* collection—speaking in his case of Paris—a city could maintain both a lowly image and a fascinating one. In the United States, Chicago served for a time as the infamous city. Loved by some, reviled by others, Chicago was representative of the changes that accompanied modernity and which were not universally applauded in the United States.

Chicago is far from the first American city to have captured American imaginative attention. Large cities have fascinated and beguiled residents of the Americas since urban places began gaining a foothold on colonial shores in the mid-sixteen hundreds. As a nation came to be formed, discussions spurred by the images of cities propagated by popular culture played a role in the creation of the American identity. In the condensed view of the nation offered by the thickly settled urban landscape, viewers beheld a portrait containing both essential elements of the traditional national culture and new, discordant colors as well. Although early American leaders tended to favor rural over urban growth for their nascent country, images of urban areas—spaces of such importance to the U.S. economy and other central components of the nation—undeniably shaped the national image held by many Americans. On one hand, the close proximity in which urban residents lived provided onlookers with a targeted view of well-regarded aspects of American life and values; in a single sweep of street a viewer might take in a bustling marketplace, a church, a school, and a grouping of well-tended homes. One might see a farmer bringing his produce to town from the countryside, or peek into windows to see a minister, at his desk, preparing his Sunday sermon on predestination, or a teacher exploring geography with a slightly unruly group of boys. On the other hand, cities threatened some with their foreignness; our earliest cities served as ports of entry to international goods and increasing numbers of immigrants seeking to make homes in the New World. Change arrived daily with the tides. The newcomers disembarked and filled American cities with an increasing diversity of languages, religions, and dreams.

At the dawn of the twenty-first century, more than fifty-one percent of Americans have come to live in metropolitan regions of a million or more. Our metropolitan areas, areas that include the city proper and the counties linked to the core city by social and economic ties, are at their most populous. Yet, during the late twentieth century, our major cities have declined in population within their geographical borders. Only the census of 2000 allowed a glimmer of hope for the stabilization of population in many U.S. cities; the variety of immigrants entering the nation has again shored up the numbers of people living in our great urban centers. The metropolitan boom in the country remains largely suburban; many Americans wish to live near goods and services and reduce commute times to work, but not at the expense of giving up manicured lawns, the privately-owned swing sets, and, in many geographical regions, the nearly ubiquitous front-yard maple tree.

Although Americans' personal preferences reflect a desire to live in the quasi-rural world of the suburbs, we remain fascinated with the urban. Our nightly television news programs report on the events of urban centers; fires in the downtown areas regularly make the news, while suburban blazes receive no comment. Many local news programs begin with a panoramic view of the nearest skyline, even if the studios have long been located in a suburban outpost. Our fascination with the urban extends to the world of commercial acquisition as well. In fashion particularly, urban styles have set the trend for the nation. For example, the city-slicker style of the black or brown leather jacket remains popular throughout many regions of the United States in the early twenty-first century. In the 1990s and beyond, teenagers rushed to shop at "Urban Outfitters;" no self-respecting adolescent would don an ensemble from a clothier known as "The Suburban Shop."

The heyday of Chicago's infamous image has passed. Today, the image of Los Angeles arguably reigns as the premier battleground over the contested image of the American urban environment. Scholars now pose questions about the California city that echo those asked about Chicago during the times when it was the second largest city in America. One category of questioning involves whether or not the newest second city points the way toward the future of other American cities. Los Angeles' chaotic realities, including the 1992 riots over the police's handling of Rodney King, have brought the city to the nation's attention and have allowed its image to become an increasingly bleak one in a national public culture adverse to change and conflict. Is L.A. an anomaly, an urban experiment gone wildly wrong? Or are the sprawl, the smog, and the seemingly unending fascination with commercialism and celluloid the destiny of the other American cities? We ask if this California capital of hip is our future or an anti-model we can securely turn our backs on as we form new communities based on the back-to-basics formulation of styles like the New Urbanism.

We forget that this current bedevilment over Los Angeles has a historical precedent—the similarly vexing image of the city of Chicago. Although the image of Chicago has mellowed somewhat in the recent decades, the Midwestern center formerly reigned as the urban trouble-spot, the inherently interesting, deeply unsettling, infamous city of the late 1800s to mid 1900s. Of course some Americans have considered the Midwest—the mythical home of the farmer and the field, a geographically central district further removed from the "Old World" than the coastal areas of the United States—the embodiment of the American spirit. At times Chicago has been considered the honorary capital of the Midwest, and at other times even as the flagship city of the West. A few non-Chicagoans have even considered Chicago to be a very American or perhaps the most American of U.S. cities. But these summations proved less frequent than those that ranked the city among the nation's trouble spots between the years of 1871 and 1968. Americans felt unsettled by cities generally, and by Chicago's brashness, youth, relentless commercial drive, and connections with crime in particular. From the wrenching stories of the Great Chicago Fire of 1871, to the exotic dancers at the Chicago World's Fair of 1893, from the seemingly endless need for social services for the city's poor, to the fan dancing of Sally Rand, the bootlegging and crime sprees of Al Capone, and the riotous late-1960s, Chicago captured the nation's attention and held it fast for nearly one hundred years.

Urban historians and scholars of urban studies have been intrigued by the idea of the city and its image for some time. Urban planning has long taken on the challenge of exploring how our thoughts regarding physical forms influence our relationship with the built environment. In 1960 Kevin Lynch took on this investigation with his work, *The Image of the City*. In this look at Boston, Jersey City, and Los Angeles, Lynch contends that we ought to think about the mental images that residents form of their cities. He writes, "we must consider not just the city as a thing in itself, but the city being perceived by its inhabitants." Adding to this line of thinking, this book considers the national image of the city of Chicago. Moving outward from the way in which Lynch asks what local landmarks form urban residents' conceptions of place, this book asks what elements of popular culture have come to define a particular urban center at the national level.[2] The argument here does not look inward at Chicago to consider the thinking of its citizens in the style of Lynch's work, but asks a related question, that of how Americans generally have come to "read" Chicago. The majority of Americans had no day-to-day familiarity with Chicago's streets and shoreline, yet they still knew her in a sense. Americans came to know Chicago through the window opened by popular media. Even if their own individual experiences brought them to different conclusions, most Americans had a familiarity with media portrayals of Chicago as a shadowy city of questionable character.

A few other scholarly works have attempted to grapple with the subject of urban image-making at the national level. In *Images of the American City* (1976) Anselm Strauss, a sociologist, has written one of the few studies that examines the way in which cities are understood in American culture. Strauss argues that, "The city, as a whole, is inaccessible to the imagination unless it can be reduced and simplified." The outpouring of cultural documents which take on the city as subject, according to Strauss, are a necessary part of the quest to understand the essentially unknowable city. Kevin McNamara, in *Urban Verbs: Arts and Discourses of American Cities* (1996) explores related ground. Interested in the ways in which the urban social structure affects the construction of the self, McNamara examined the ways in which the authors of six key creative texts chose to represent modern cities and also investigated social science writings on cities at similar periods. His work becomes, then, one of the few to take on a study of the ways in which Americans understand urban society. In a manner similar to the impetus which informs this project, McNamara is motivated by a desire to "contribute to discussion about the urban present and future, because the current 'crisis of the cities' is nothing new."[3]

This work draws on analysis of hundreds of popular works on Chicago produced between 1871 and 1968. Mainstream, national periodicals, rather than those tailored for a specific audience, were preferred. Magazine articles that took on the subject of Chicago for some length proved particularly fruitful sources. They ultimately were more helpful than newspaper articles related to specific events. Most newspapers speak to a relatively localized audience—even the modern *New York Times* speaks more directly to subscribers in its region than elsewhere—and the daily changes they report seldom speak to sustained national beliefs. I literally worked through the *Readers' Guide to Periodicals,* year by year, for the entire period, reading either all of the articles related to Chicago in a given year, or covering a representative sampling.

Surveying the ebb and flow of coverage on Chicago over the years, the work focuses on times in which a new infusion of popular documents reinvigorated ongoing images of the city for Americans in a vital way. For that reason, this is not an inclusive study of all representations of Chicago in popular culture. Like all works, too, it is crafted by the interests of its author, and thus my own research and teaching philosophy figures centrally here. In both of these realms of scholarly life, I strive to insert what is missing into the dialogue. Chicago is perhaps the most frequently researched city in the United States, and the goal of the work is not to substantially repeat what has been said in other studies. I want to add unique elements—such as the origins of the O'Leary cow myth, the way the Inter-State Exposition foreshadowed later great Chicago fairs, the appeal of Sally Rand's fan dances, or the national fascination with *Playboy Magazine* to the story of Chicago. Yet I also keep in mind that many readers may not want to read shelves of works on Chicago history in order to understand my argument; for this group of readers, dates and synopses of major Chicago events are included for clarity. The work flows chronologically so that readers may come to understand how in each unfolding decade, the popular, middlebrow media continued to produce representations which reinforced the dark image of the city.

The book does not relate all of the stories or review all of the works that have come to us today as "quintessentially Chicago." Some incidents, like the Haymarket Riot and the Pullman strike, are simply too well known to rehearse in full detail here. Both certainly perpetuated Chicago's infamous image, but pre-existing works already make this point well. Other Chicago-related tales simply did not have sufficient contemporary impact to bring them into consideration here. Theodore Dreiser's *Sister Carrie*, one of most powerful works of American literature, fell rather flat upon initial publication and only later came to be regarded as one of the most outstanding pieces of American naturalist writing. Because its impact only grew over time, it has no place in the timeline of events as formulated for the book. Readers should be clear too that this book takes as its subject national attitudes towards contemporary Chicago in each time period; the book does not discuss the ways in which perceptions of events metamorphosed over the passage of years. As mentioned briefly in Chapter Two, for instance, popular conceptions of the World's Columbian Exposition have transformed over time, growing increasingly nostalgic. A work that attends to the change over time of a particular element of the city's past, such as the Columbian Exposition, would be another type of project altogether.

This book considers the image of Chicago as crafted and shaped by contemporary producers of popular culture in decades of great change for the city. The actual changes Chicago experienced, however, and its successes as a commercial center and a locus of higher education and cultural production do not constitute the book's subject. This is not a book about what happened in an actual urban space, but what kinds of discussions were going on at a national level about that place. Its mission echoes that of Michael Kammen in his 1991 work, *Mystic Chords of Memory: The Transformation of Tradition in American Culture*. His work sought not to document what is or is not "true" about national memory, but rather what these memories are and how they came to be. Kammen asserts, "the basic question that this book asks is when and how did the United States become a land of the past, a culture with a discernible memory (or with a configuration of recognized pasts)?"[4] The question at hand here is the nature of the image of the city of Chicago in national popular culture.

The work takes on the challenging task of attempting to document that the central element of Chicago's role in popular culture *does not change overmuch* during the years considered; the city persistently played a dark role in the national conversation. The book unravels the layers of documents contributing to this shared national image in consideration of the wondrous tensile strength of the infamous city symbolism. The frequency of the production of such material meant that Chicago's local boosters had little chance of successfully fighting back on behalf of their city, although they did occasionally attempt to do so.

The existence of Chicago's infamous national image is a theme which has occurred to other scholars and commentators on Chicago. Most comment on the existence of the image briefly, as if all readers had previously been informed. The off-handed and ubiquitous nature of this type of commentary on Chicago testifies to the fact that the infamous image is a deeply ingrained part of American culture. The study of the entire sweep of the near century in which Chicago played this particular role in American popular culture has not been previously attempted. Writing about a sustained image, rather than a changing one, presents theoretical hurdles to historians traditionally trained to study the continual evolution of events. Yet when the story the historian hopes to tell is one of constancy rather than the tried and true themes of change and progress, he or she ought to hold fast to the tale and attempt to tell it in its true spirit.

Documenting national public culture also presents challenges to the social historian practiced in analyzing the world from the "bottom up" rather than the "top down." Few individuals make their way into this discussion of Chicago. Popular media, the study finds, churned out such a deluge of materials in which the word Chicago served as shorthand for national anti-urban sentiment that few individuals, even the most moneyed and politically powerful of Chicago's elite, could serve successfully as the city's champion, counteracting the forces of popular culture. This work also does not take on the task of documenting how each and every different group of Americans—such as the native born, immigrant, upper class, working class, and African American groups—came to think about Chicago. Perceptions differed by race, gender, regional background, and other factors. Yet the window that popular culture offered of the world was such an integral part of the American scene by the late 1800s that few residents could escape the grasp of its explanatory power. Even when Chicago's infamous image was not the image manufactured by a person's own experiences, it was one with which they were familiar.

Cities have always provided fertile grounds for exploration in American culture. Our national attitudes towards them are riddled with tensions. On one hand, we find cities inviting samples of American culture and philosophy. On the other, we find them representative of our basest human attributes and far from celebrated national symbols. As the city physically is the coming together of a large population in a relatively small space, a conclusive reading of them is difficult. Various camps of Americans choose to interpret them differently, and the views held by individuals can range over considerable ground. Some scholars argue that since the inception of the American nation, many and perhaps the majority of Americans have been substantially troubled by the existence of large urban areas. As historians Morton and Lucia White argue, "enthusiasm for the American city has not been typical or predominant in our intellectual history. Fear has been the more common reaction." In a letter to Benjamin Rush in the early 1800s, American founding father Thomas Jefferson, great proponent of the elevating effects of farming on the democratic character, wrote, "I view great cities as pestilential to the morals, health and the liberties of man." Jefferson's sentiments and those of his philosophical heirs cast a shadow over American attitudes towards cities that has lasted up until the present day, albeit not with the strength that it did formerly.[5]

Works like Thomas Bender's *Toward an Urban Vision: Ideas and Institutions in Nineteenth Century America* have suggested that at times some of America's leading intellectuals expressed attitudes toward particular urban settings which were not entirely hostile. Bender argues that *high* culture may have reflected more favorable views of the city than have previously been admitted. Yet the present study indicates that the majority of the *popular* discourse concerning Chicago was far from positive. Through fact and fiction, an enduring myth developed and was sustained in popular culture for close to one hundred years.

Not all Americans have held anti-urban sentiments. A significant number of citizens, often city dwellers themselves, have believed urban centers to be the sites of progress. In the cities, they maintained, individuals could find the greatest possible opportunity, and come into contact with a broad array of enriching cultural experiences. Financially successful, urban boosters often believed in the tenets of Social Darwinism, or the theory that those who rise do so because of their own merit. For most of these urban proponents, the city had provided the setting for their own success, the American dreams of financial comfort that they urgently believed were available to all worthy enough to achieve them.

To what extent, then, can cities be seen as "American" places? Do they embody any part of the fundamental spirit of the United States? Do Americans feel comfortable with what U.S. cities show us about ourselves? Do specific cities play particularly important roles in this national-level discussion? In posing such questions, the long-lived myth of Chicago emerges from American popular culture. Through the years of 1871–1968, a dark legend was developed and sustained regarding the city, a legend that described the city as a threat to core American values. Chicago grew to be regarded as a place that in many ways seemed to represent what the nation was becoming—a land of immigrants, a land of unabashed capitalism, and an urban, rather than a rural, landscape. Chicago's present might have foretold the nation's future, but this particular future frightened many Americans. These Americans were afraid of change. They viewed the rapidly evolving Chicago as a challenge to the fundamental philosophical and moral underpinnings of the nation.

In unraveling the national image of Chicago, this work examines the way in which the city of Chicago became party to a verbal and visual tug-of-war between an anti-urban contingent and those who looked upon cities more favorably. The debate took place between two parties—the producers of popular culture and their readers, who tended to favor anti-urban fare, and Chicago's boosters, a group of elite who sought to strengthen the reputation of their city. Chicago proves a compelling subject with which to examine the power struggle between those who looked to the city for opportunity and those who felt something more sinister lay at the heart of American cities. The debate over what place Chicago held in national culture sparked deeply-felt outpourings from both philosophical bents. Ultimately, however, the image constructed by the cultural producers would prove much more tenacious than that of the city leaders. Because of the infectious nature of their arguments, Chicago at many points served as the national symbol of urban troubles, and at all times during the period studied here ranked highly as an image of urban discord. Between the Great Chicago Fire of 1871 and the Democratic National Convention held in Chicago in 1968, an enduring and sordid picture of the city arose, a myth of Chicago that took on important meanings for many. Chicago grew to be considered an "infamous city."

The image of Chicago set forth by the cultural producers proved stronger than that of the boosters because the reflection created in the media connected with some deeply held American beliefs. Despite the undeniable zeal of the boosters, Chicago was needed to serve as an anti-model in a national debate on self-definition. Beyond the question of whether or not Chicago could be considered "American," one can ask what, ultimately, did the term "American" mean? The study will show that anti-urban sentiments fueled the production of cultural documents that deeply scarred the national reputation of Chicago, and for quite a bit longer than urban historians have heretofore believed anti-urbanism to have remained a potent American idea. Some argue that the previous rural-urban dichotomy has been supplanted by the tensions between the suburbs and the city, and that even the suburban-urban conflict has evolved and been mitigated over time. Yet cities do still function as strong symbols in today's American mythology, often serving as shorthand for many of the nation's most pressing problems. As we begin the twenty-first century, the terms "city," "urban area," and "downtown" are hardly benign. The words often serve to evoke thoughts of racial conflict, given that in many cities, the majority of whites have abandoned their connections with the urban center. We clearly have much to learn today from uncovering the history of American anti-urban rhetoric.

This project traces the evolution of national attitudes towards Chicago, in part following the interplay between the cultural producers and the Chicago boosters. Using a wide array of popular media, and paying particular attention to magazine articles focused on general descriptions of the city, the book examines the reputation of Chicago as represented at the most mainstream level of American culture. With the disastrous fire of 1871, Chicago initially captured Americans' imaginations. The tone of the rhetoric linked with the blaze caused the city to establish the infamous image it would sustain for nearly a decade to come. In Chicago, the debate between pro-urban and anti-urban camps took root during a period of devastating disorder; the terrible Great Fire launched national interest in the city and tipped the scales unfairly towards the cultural producers. With the publication of lurid tales of the fire, the tabloid press initiated an unflattering picture of Chicago that grew over time.

In an attempt to recover from this blow, Chicago boosters formulated plans for a grand World's Fair in 1893, hoping to create a more sophisticated image for their city and compete for cultural capital with the likes of New York and Boston. Although the Columbian Exposition received praise from many quarters, the spectacle did not subdue the producers of popular culture, who increasingly cast the city in the role of the ultimate urban challenge to America's quiet, rural life. By the early twentieth century, Chicago leaders had temporarily turned their primary attentions away from boosterism and towards the implementation of real change in their city. These efforts are highly laudable. Chicago, because of the work of those involved with such cultural institutions as Hull House, the Chicago Crime Commission, and the University of Chicago, became an influential laboratory of reform. Yet the Chicagoans' inward turn came at precisely the moment when the national media's influence on American thought had grown enormously. "Yellow journalism" now swayed readers with its provocative tone, glossy magazines found their way into American homes, motion pictures began to lure crowds, and the circulation of American newspapers increased dramatically (ninefold between 1870 and 1910).

In 1933–1934, Chicagoans gave the battle of image-making one more round with their second World's Fair, A Century of Progress. With its mix of scientific exhibits and silly, Midway crowd-pleasers, fair planners hoped to beat popular culture at its own game; Chicago could be at once intellectually and culturally stimulating and a whole lot of fun. Unfortunately, Sally Rand's provocative fan dance became the talk of the fair rather than the Hall of Science.

By the 1940s, the cultural producers had seared Chicago's negative image into American popular memory. The myth of Chicago as infamous city had been strengthened from so many quarters that Chicago-based boosters could do little to effect change. Only the headline-gathering of such events as the 1965 Watts disruption and the 1968 riots in Detroit would significantly challenge Chicago's primacy as anti-urban symbol. Despite the city's violent reaction to the death of Martin Luther King and the actions by the police and anti-war demonstrators during the 1968 Democratic National Convention in the city, Chicago now had competition. Many other cities now attracted national attention with their own sordid sides. The debate between the anti-urbanists and the urban supporters remained, but the focus had shifted away from Chicago.

Between the years of the Great Chicago Fire and the Democratic National Convention of 1968, those who built popular culture erected an enduring myth of Chicago, a myth that described this city as a degradation to the American character. As David Harvey explains in *The Condition of Postmodernity*, cities, unable to be understood in their entirety, lend themselves to the fabrication of myth. Harvey writes, "A labyrinth, an encyclopedia, an emporium, a theatre, the city is somewhere where fact and imagination simply *have* to fuse."[6] Chicago's myth evolved into a tainted tale. Comprised of truths, half-truths, and out-right fallacies, the popular representations of the city set forth Chicago as one of the most, if not the most, immoral settings in the United States. Chicago became symbolic of the urban troubles of the century, its name linked with public perceptions about overcrowding, poverty, immigration, and crime—the most pressing troubles of the late-nineteenth to mid-twentieth century American city.

Like many cities around the world, Chicago cultivated a "personality" much like a celebrity. The mere mention of the name "Chicago" brought a number of standard images to mind. This set of images was shared by many Americans and could exist simultaneously with personal and/or group images of the city, even much more favorable ones. Assigning a city a more or less fixed cultural image helped people better understand a particular place. As cities grew larger, Americans found it increasingly difficult to make sense of them in any comprehensive way. So many cultures and so many histories were embodied in a city of millions of souls and a variety of spaces like Chicago. People looked for a way to grasp even a part of the metropolis, to comprehend its "gist." Thus the popularity of ascending to the top of tall buildings; where else could one better attempt to make sense of an urban center?

Chicago's public image emerged in part out of a struggle between the city boosters and the makers of popular culture, including filmmakers, television producers, novelists, poets, musicians, and journalists. The boosters sought to promote a positive image of their city, highlighting Chicago's economic and cultural offerings—and its progress. The men and women instrumental in building popular culture, on the other hand, most often chose to stress the negative aspects of the city. As sociologist Anselm Strauss explains, in the resulting visions of Chicago one can find mirrored "the tension that exists between an imagery of enterprise and an imagery of violence."[7] Like the boosters, the cultural producers might choose, for example, to speak of the power of Chicago's great commercial drive, but the cultural producers would link Chicago's commercialism with capitalistic greed, labor unrest, organized crime, violence, and the city's sex industry. Chicago's reputation pivoted then on the struggle between individuals who sought to promote their ideals of a progress based on the opportunities capitalism made possible in the urban environment and scores of popular culture developers who believed the city less than the ideal space.

The debate took hold during the Victorian era, a time in which many interested parties sought to control public expressions that appeared threatening to progress. Typically, Chicago's leaders and the institutions they controlled sought to maintain an ordered, hierarchical world in which those who rose to the top did so because of their worthy characters. These ideas, as mentioned briefly before, are the tenets of Social Darwinism, a social theory based loosely on Darwin's theory of evolution. Social Darwinism served as an explanation about why some Americans had acquired great wealth and some lived in dire poverty. According to this theory, those of true skill and talent grew wealthy and assumed leadership positions, as was their due. Social Darwinism also supposed that the nation evolved into a more and more wonderful place with the contributions of each generation.

The cultural producers highlighted the seamier sides of the city not because they were consciously out to destroy the reputation of Chicago, but because they found anti-urban themes compelling in the abstract. Most of the cultural producers held no particular spite towards Chicago. Yet they were immersed in a culture in which anti-urban sentiments ran deep. Utilization of anti-urban tenets came easily, and even for some, almost unconsciously. Interestingly, the physical location (inside or outside of Chicago) of the cultural producers often had little overall affect on the general tenor of their work. Whatever their hometown, the voices that sought to entertain and/or inform differed markedly from the boosters. The cultural producers viewed cities as troubled areas, but most did not subscribe in an orthodox fashion to the pro-rural mindset. The producers found that the darker images of the city resonated with an American public looking to place blame on "others." Anti-city and anti-Chicago invective in particular drew a wide market to the cultural producers' wares. Writers and other producers learned quickly that describing Chicago in a certain way led to the publication or distribution of their works and sold newspapers, magazines, books, and other media. Although Americans were at times outraged by some of the stories told about the Midwestern center, they were also intrigued and titillated by these same tales.

This work traces Chicago's reputation at the level of popular culture, utilizing contemporary films, television programs, and newspapers, and drawing heavily from mainstream magazines. The way in which the media shapes images of urban places has impacted national thought. As Michael Parenti, author of *Make-Believe Media: The Politics of Entertainment,* contends, while the public does not accept the constructions of the media without question, popular culture does alter personal beliefs. Parenti writes, "In modern mass society, people rely to a great extent on distant imagemakers for cues about a vast world. In both their entertainment and news shows, the media invent a reality much their own."[8] As the media provided a window onto Chicago, it formed and shaped public opinion about the city for many Americans. The image portrayed of the city in national media mattered; the image had weight and entered people's consciousnesses. Yet we should also note that the cultural producers themselves did not create their work outside culture; American culture and norms affected them as they crafted their works, making the national understanding of cities a circular rather than simply a top-down process.

Additionally, a city's national image, it must be understood, differs from an individual's own personal connection with a particular urban space. We simultaneously hold both our individual set of interactions with place and a shared cultural sense of this place's meaning or symbolism; both affect our understanding of the urban area. Even group beliefs—such as African-American or immigrant viewpoints—can coexist with ideas held by the broader culture. This work takes as its task the documentation of the evolution of this shared cultural conception of Chicago, rather than exploring individual or group perceptions.

Between 1871 and 1968, Chicago drew the commentary of a wide range of cultural producers, providing a sort of lightening rod for anti-urban language. Although many have now forgotten, at one time Chicago functioned in the national consciousness as the city of Los Angeles does today. Chicago shook free of its downward-pulling moorings through the outburst of violence in the late 1960s most often associated with Detroit. Although Detroit served as the catalyst for Chicago's change in status, Los Angeles would become heir apparent for those who needed an anti-urban focal point in the late twentieth century. Mike Davis relates this story in his book *City of Quartz*. Davis does not contend with Chicago's prior role, but does compellingly explain how Los Angeles embodies today's fears of the city. Los Angeles, according to Davis, has come to symbolize both utopia and dystopia; Americans have dreams for what it might be and nightmares about what it is. Los Angeles is a commodity in its own right, selling its own culture in films and fashion, and being sold as evil by those who oppose its existence. Similar to the debate that ranged over whether or not Chicago represented the bright possibilities of capitalism or demonstrated its uncouth missteps, Los Angeles represents the successes and excesses of capitalism in late twentieth century and early twenty-first century America.[9]

With the emergence of social history in the 1960s, many sub-sets of historical inquiry, including urban history, began to change. Contemporary urban historians increasingly seek to address the role played by urban places in national cultures and to explore the ways in which these roles are constructed and changed. Yet, to this point few works have directly assessed the shaping of a particular city's image in popular culture over a long span of time. In an age in which urban areas are often assumed to equate with such problems as infrastructure decay, drug abuse, and racism, it becomes increasingly apparent that the way in which we think about cities is very important. This project fills historiographical gaps with its assertion that understanding the evolution of the reputation of Chicago is an important part of understanding the history of this city and an important step in comprehending American views of all urban places. This story has value not only for what it uncovers about this specific Midwestern city but what it tells us about American cities generally, and what it demonstrates concerning Americans' beliefs about themselves.

Chapter One

"Do You Wonder Chicago Burned?": The Great Chicago Fire and the Launching of Chicago's National Reputation

The Great Chicago Fire of 1871 contained all the elements of a "great news story." Before the fire, Chicago received little mention in the national press; with the fire, Chicago launched a reputation for danger and intrigue that took nearly a century to overcome. The urban disaster inspired the imaginations of those who put pen to paper about it, leading them to speculate broadly about the character of Chicago in their musings concerning the fire. Prepared to view cities as threatening to American culture, the national audience found that the writings on the disastrous fire, which essentially leveled the fast growing Midwestern urban center, resonated with their world views. Given the event's rich potential for meaningful symbolism, the fire would have riveted the nation's attention even if it had broken out in more modern times. The Great Chicago Fire, which destroyed thousands of acres in central Chicago, became a spectacular media event and thrust the city into the nation's vision. As we shall see, the story had elements of nearly unfathomable disaster, class conflict, business upheaval, urban rivalry, and sexuality. The fire symbolized what was wrong with the rapid development now becoming commonplace in American cities, and provided a seemingly unprecedented opportunity for revision to, and possibly repentance for, the questionable culture of the Midwestern commercial center.

Over time Chicago developed and maintained a myth associated with what was deemed to be its character. People believed this myth helped them to know what was indeed unknowable. Unable to grasp the kaleidoscope of patterns produced in an urban space, people began to reduce some of a city's perceived qualities down into a type of shorthand. Chicago's abbreviated image cast the city in a particularly dim light, making it one of the focal points for anti-urban sentiment around the nation.

Americans startled themselves with this image of Chicago, an image quite unrelenting in its darkness at times. Americans worried that their understanding of Chicago's present foretold of a troubled future in other U.S. cities, and that Chicago represented a type of unwanted change that might eventually engulf the entire nation. In actuality, the city did reflect much of what the American people were becoming, yet it mirrored both the favorable and the unfavorable aspects of the national disposition. The city was neither the all-positive place indicated in its booster's writings nor the terrifying chasm of crime so often portrayed by popular culture. In reality Chicago had an ambiguous character, falling somewhere in-between the ratings of its rave reviewers and its sharpest critics. Unfortunately, Americans did not (and do not) deal well with ambiguity. Finding Chicago less than all good, and being afraid of change and of the cultural challenges proffered by any urban center, Americans chose to utilize Chicago as an anti-model in the debate on national self-definition. Chicago, only a youngster in the life cycle of cities, did not have the organizational apparatus or cultural clout to adequately defend itself against the American people's enormous need to take in this negative rhetoric.

Prior to the outbreak of the news stories on Chicago's great fire, Chicago had not garnered much coverage in the national media. The fire focused attention on Chicago as never before. Located outside of the American cultural production center of the East Coast, the relatively small (yet rapidly expanding) settlement on Lake Michigan had little reason to spark national interest. Although Chicago had been incorporated as a town in 1833, and established as a city in 1837, it would take the devastating fire to firmly place the city in the national consciousness. During its first four decades, Chicago received sparse coverage in the mainstream media, primarily entering American popular culture through its role as a western entrepôt—supplying needed goods to the rest of the United States through the Illinois and Michigan Canal and its railroad systems—and for its real estate speculation. In its earliest years, too, Chicago had been a sparsely settled town. Chicago housed only 200 residents in 1831—hardly a place worth mentioning. By 1870, a year before the fire, Chicago ranked as the fifth largest city in the United States, just below St. Louis. In 1870, St. Louis had over 310,000 people, while Chicago contained almost 299,000 residents. Just ten years earlier, in 1860, Chicago had had only 112,172 inhabitants, placing it ninth in terms of population nationally. Chicago's fire brought it national attention at just the moment when such attention would finally be warranted for the Midwestern city. The 1870 rankings ushered in a period of fantastic growth and unprecedented attention for Chicago. By 1890 Chicago would rank as the nation's second largest city. (If evaluating population by city borders rather than metropolitan region, Chicago remained the second largest city until the census of 1990.)[1]

So Chicago established its place in the national culture with a disaster. The fire linked the city strongly with intrigue and debacle. With the Great Chicago Fire of 1871, the city of Chicago took up the dubious role it would play in the popular culture of the United States for nearly the next century. The enormous physical damage caused by the fire and the loss of life the blaze entailed stirred interest around the nation, changing the nature of the coverage on Chicago, increasing the frequency of such stories, and leaving an indelible print on American popular images of the Illinois city. Newspapers covered the disaster thoroughly; publishers also disseminated book-length, more-or-less factually based "instant histories" of the event for the prurient interests of an American audience eager to learn more, in the months following the fire. The news was the most important American topic of discussion of its time. Dispatches from New York declared that "nothing but the fire in Chicago is talked of through our city, and the people are filled with deepest sympathy and [are] anxious for the fate of the great Western city."[2]

The Great Chicago Fire brought Chicago into the discussion of national identity and established the tone of the coverage the city would need to shoulder for the next decade. Commentary on the fire in magazine and newspaper articles, instant histories, and other popular media described the urban center as a great challenge to the morality of the nation. A particular progressive-mindedness can be considered typical to the mid- nineteenth century; the Republican party of Lincoln set forth the ideals of equality of opportunity for white males and a belief that the United States was evolving into a better and better nation. Yet the producers of popular culture found that exposing a more sordid side of the American character sold their products. Even if Americans tended to choose elected representatives who promised continual improvement to the nation, people secretly enjoyed reading stories about the many challenges to progress. As most Americans' personal lives did not contain the level of success they had hoped for, tales of the troubles of others could ease bruised spirits. Chicago, deemed by many Americans to be merely a far-away city and an urban upstart in what was otherwise perceived as the tranquil, rural life of the Midwest, provided an easy foil.

Despite the existence of excessive rhetoric, a real tragedy did lay behind the somber words. Although coverage of the fire tended toward the extravagant, the Great Chicago Fire was responsible for actual, extensive damage to the city, resulting in approximately three hundred lives lost, one hundred thousand of the metropolis' 300,000 residents homeless, and 18,000 buildings destroyed. Over 2,000 acres of the city, or three and a half square miles, turned to rubble. Early estimates approximated the property damage at 400 million dollars.[3]

On October 7, 1871, the night before the start of the extensive conflagration, a smaller yet still impressive fire started between 10:00 and 11:00 P.M., and received newspaper coverage around the country. Beginning in the boiler room of the Lull & Holmes planing mill at 209 Canal Street on the west side of Chicago's downtown, the fire devoured nearly twenty acres of the city in the area west of the Chicago River near Jackson and Van Buren (East-West streets), and Clinton and Canal (North-South streets). Firemen fought the fire for seventeen hours, finally winning the battle at 3:00 P.M. on Sunday afternoon. The blaze rendered two of the department's seventeen engines useless, and considerably tired the fire fighters. *The Chicago Tribune* of October 8 estimated a loss of approximately $700,000 due to the blaze, about two-thirds of which they assumed to be covered by fire insurance. Reporters predicted more fires to follow. *The Atlanta Constitution* eerily concluded that "the fires in the woods and on the prairies are prevailing in every direction, including Michigan, Illinois, Wisconsin and Iowa. A heavy rain alone can stop the conflagration. The country is dry as tinder." Chicago had measured only two and a half inches of rain since July, although average rainfall for the season measured eight and three-quarters inches.[4]

The second, larger fire began around 9:30 P.M. on Sunday, October 8, 1871, in or near the barn of Patrick and Catherine O'Leary, at 137 De Koven Street between Jefferson and Clinton. Dry from the months of little rain, and mainly built of wood, Chicago stood ripe for a fire, and the devastation spread quickly. Partially bungled efforts by local firefighters (such as trouble working with the signal system) did little to still the blaze, and the city lost the capabilities of their state-of-the-art waterworks early in the battle, making matters all but hopeless. By Monday night the fire had died down considerably, having already devoured most of the available tinder; only the neighborhood in the vicinity of the Clark and Fullerton intersection remained burning. But not until it rained during the late evening of October 9 and the early morning of October 10th did the fire finally end.[5]

The fire, soon known as The Great Chicago Fire, received extensive press coverage throughout the nation. Readers expressed deep interest in the disaster. The event spoke to the public's interest in urban disasters in general and also was of concern due to Chicago's far-reaching business ties. News initially traveled via the railroad, as *The Chicago Tribune* reported, "The great fire was the topic of all talk as early as 11 o'clock on Monday forenoon in every railroad town in the Northwest." Soon after, the news reached Louisville, Kentucky, becoming the "universal topic of conversation," and Cincinnati, Ohio, where businessmen ceased working in order to learn more about the fire. Detroit discovered that on October 9, 1871 "before ten o'clock in the morning, nearly all business in the city had stopped, put away that men might satisfy their excited cravings for the latest news from a sea of flames." "Great crowds" found themselves unable to break away from the news in the Michigan city, and "assembled at the bulletins and in the public places, eagerly seeking additional news from the Chicago conflagration." In Washington, D.C., concern over the fire overshadowed the upcoming elections. In Atlanta, southerners awaited "further particulars with pain and deep interest." And *The New York Herald* asserted that "nothing has occurred for years which has so stirred up the people of the metropolis."[6]

The cataclysmic news of the event prompted increases in newspaper sales. In New York, "every extra and each different edition of the evening papers were quickly snapped up, and all the occupants of the cars and stages might be seen busily perusing their columns. The shrill voices of the Gamins selling papers could be heard through all the crowded thoroughfares, crying out, 'Ere's your extry: full p'rticlars [sic] of the great fire.'" Once cognizant of the expanded market for information, newsboys raised their prices, charging twenty-five cents, fifty cents, or even a dollar for a single issue. Such techniques quickly earned the young capitalists the title "city Arabs."[7]

Over time, American popular culture came to attribute the fire to Irish immigrant Catherine O'Leary, a lantern, and a wayward cow. Recent articles have attempted to exonerate O'Leary, and have been well-publicized by the mainstream media. Amateur historian and attorney Richard Bales argues that Mrs. O'Leary and her cow cannot be responsible for the fire. Bales places the blame on Daniel "Pegleg" Sullivan, a neighbor. Sullivan appears to have been the first to have reported the fire.[8] Coverage contemporary to the fire did speculate that the O'Leary barn offered ideal protection from the wind for anyone interested in lighting up smoking materials, be it a pipe, cigar, or cigarette, on the street. Yet such knowledge cannot go much beyond speculation at this point, more than one hundred years after the fire. And attempts to uncover the origins of the blaze seemingly miss the point—the great disaster caused by the fire and the myriad of tales which then proliferated remain the central story here. Indeed, Bales' attempt to use the archival record to establish a true culprit itself attests to the imaginative power of this event after so many years. The most compelling point seems to be not who or what started the fire but why it manages to hold our interest as it does.

Scholars of Chicago history have agreed for some time that Kate O'Leary does not bear responsibility for the conflagration, yet the O'Leary story, still the subject of jokes and advertisements, has certainly persisted. We should note, however, that this long-existing tale, surprisingly, was *not* central to most of the immediate national newspaper coverage and "instant-history" pamphlets and books that first brought Chicago's calamity to the nation's attention. Most synopses mentioned the general area of De Koven Street; some wrote of the O'Leary barn and refrained from naming names. Some coverage assigned responsibility to O'Leary, but presented the story quickly and without rhetorical flourishes.

Harper's Weekly, for instance, when covering the story of the fire in late October 1871, reported the story as truthful, but did not publish O'Leary's name. Elias Colbert and Everett Chamberlin's instant-history of the fire, *Chicago and the Great Conflagration*, released shortly after the fire in 1871 and very influential in spreading the tale of the destruction, also attributed the event to O'Leary and held back her name. "The blame of setting the fire rests on the woman who milked," they explained, "or else upon the lazy man who allowed her to milk. The name of this female we shall not hand down to posterity in these pages." Popularizers of the treacherous tale, but also Chicago residents, Colbert and Chamberlin understood even this early on that making more of O'Leary than necessary would tarnish Chicago's reputation. The reporters claimed to "have no desire to immortalize the author of the ruin of Chicago" at the expense of "the noble and indefatigable pioneers" who built up the city. A local paper, *The Chicago Evening Post*, misnamed O'Leary, calling her " a woman named Scully."[9] Although anti-Irish sentiment only rarely shows up in the Chicago fire coverage, this particular error on the part of the *Post* is telling. The reporters mistook O'Leary's name, but not her ethnicity.

Other commentators attacked the O'Leary story head on, declaring it erroneous. James W. Sheahan and George P. Upton, associate editors of *The Chicago Tribune* and authors of an 1871 treatise on the fire, concluded that "the story that an attempt to milk a cow by the light of a kerosene lamp, and the rapid firing of the cow-shed, is now known to be untrue." Frank Luzerne, author of the widely circulated instant-history *The Lost City!*

found in 1872 that "the story about the old woman who went into her stable to milk her cow by the light of a kerosene lamp, which lamp said cow kicked over, is a pure fabrication. No such woman or cow probably existed, save in the imagination of some manufacturer of *canards.*" He continued to report that neighbors had testified that the family were all in bed when the fire broke out, and posited another possible theory. "The *Journal of Commerce,*" Luzerne noted, "remarks that in a high wind smokers might stop there for the purpose of striking a match [more] than at any other part in that neighborhood. A spark alighting on this tinder of hay and shingles, and fanned by the wind, would soon wrap the slight barn in flames."[10]

News of the location of the fire's origins had traveled quickly by word of mouth throughout Chicago. No one denied that the fire had begun in the O'Leary's barn. The brief references to the barn in most newspapers and contemporary books and pamphlets, however, do not seem to provide the makings of an enduring legend. Nothing about these one or two line descriptions would inspire the national imagination. *The Chicago Times'* coverage however, does reveal the roots of myth-making. I agree with Ahern that *The Chicago Times'* initial article on the fire is the source of Mrs. O'Leary's fame. Although this article did not use Catherine's name, it centered on her and went out of its way to provide inaccurate information in a manner unlike that of any other contemporary periodical.

Where then can we discover the source of this still prevalent myth? Michael Ahern, former police reporter for the Chicago-based *Morning Republican,* publicly denounced the O'Leary legend in 1915. As a child, Ahern had often purchased milk from O'Leary, and in respect for her memory he wished to speak out. Claiming to be the oldest living police reporter for a Chicago paper at the time of the Great Fire, Ahern said that he believed Jim Haynie, a reporter for the *Chicago Times,* originally "faked" the story.[11]

The Chicago Times article was the first paper to incorrectly report Mrs. O'Leary's age as seventy; she was actually only thirty-five at the time of the fire. This image of O'Leary as an elderly woman would endure for over a century. The *Times* also first provided a motive to O'Leary's actions, transforming them from accidental to intentional behaviors. The paper claimed, "Living at the place indicated was AN OLD IRISH WOMAN, who had for many years been [a] pensioner of the county. It was her weekly custom to apply to the county agent for relief, which in all cases was freely granted her." Her supposed graft continued, the paper asserted, until an old man made claims for county aid on the basis of Mrs. O'Leary's success at receiving supplies. He could not admit to abject poverty, but could be considered worse off than O'Leary, who owned a "good milch cow" and the land she lived on. "As a matter of course the agent at once cut off her supplies," the *Times* ranted on, "and when he took her to task for having deceived him, the old hag swore she would be revenged on a city that would deny her a bit of wood or a [piece] of bacon." The paper also created an enduring myth by linking O'Leary, actually the owner of six cows, with one particularly special bovine. The newspaper claimed that when its reporter met with O'Leary, "she was rocking to and fro, moaning and groaning, and crying aloud after the manner of her country-women when in great trouble. At first she refused to speak one word about the fire, but only screamed at the top of her voice, 'My poor cow, my poor cow. She is gone and I have nothing left in the world.'"[12]

The Chicago Times' reporter went to such lengths with his story in order to attract and maintain a readership for his paper. More widely read than *The Chicago Tribune* during this period, *The Chicago Times* needed a strong story for their first issue after the fire. This story needed to be particularly strong because of the long delay the *Times* took in publishing their first post-fire paper. While the *Tribune* came back to life on October 11, borrowing type from its long-time rival the *Cincinnati Commercial*, and *The Chicago Post* had put out an extra on October 9, the *Times* staff waited until October 18th for their first edition. *The Chicago Times'* staff apparently developed this scandal to peak interest in the publication and increase sales.

This article started a legend which grew up over time in American memory. While contemporary readers savvy to the *Times'* penchant for overblown language could dismiss the article upon reading it, Americans eventually forgot the way in which the story had been introduced. Only in the years after the conflagration did the O'Leary story fully capture the American public's attention. Over time many came to take the legend as truth rather than tabloid. On every anniversary of the fire, the myth gained momentum. And as she refused to speak with reporters, O'Leary encouraged newsmen to invent interviews with her.[13]

Chased by the media, O'Leary retreated into a reclusive life. She and Patrick moved around Chicago, always one step behind the rumors. Kate almost never left home, except to attend mass. In 1894, O'Leary's doctor spoke of the great pain the notoriety had caused her, calling it "the grief of her life." He added that "she is shocked at the levity with which the subject is treated and at the satirical use of her name in connection with it." In their later years, Patrick and Kate survived financially due to the monetary contributions of their son, Jim, "the stockyards gambling king," and a well-known Chicago figure in his own right.[14]

Although the earliest accounts of the fire did not solidify the O'Leary legend, the coverage of The Great Chicago Fire did establish the hyperbolic tone of news writing on Chicago which would follow the city for the next century. Most accounts, while matter-of-fact with their comments on O'Leary, chose to dramatize the story of the fire in other ways in order to draw in readers. Account after account, for instance, claimed that not only could the raging fire be termed a terrible disaster, but that it ranked among the worst disasters in history. In Atlanta, reporters stated that "the burning of Moscow with all its historic terrors seems repeated." New Yorkers found that "nothing like it has been witnessed since the first days of the Franco-Prussian war." Writers for the city's own *Chicago Tribune* took part in the over-dramatizing, perhaps with the thought that playing up the conflagration would create a heroic image for their hometown. The first issue of the newspaper after the fire set the tone for future rhetoric with its declaration, "Well Chicago has always been bent on beating the world in everything—she has done it again now. She has had the most destructive fire ever known."[15]

Books and pamphlets published shortly after the fire reflected a similar conception of the event. Edgar Johnson Goodspeed, in *The Great Fires in Chicago and The West*, published in 1871, thought the fire would "render Chicago forever memorable in the annals of history," and with his book Goodspeed did his own part in making this prediction come true. Once warmed up, Goodspeed expanded his claims. "No city can equal now the ruins of Chicago," he said, "not even Pompeii, much less Paris." Colbert and Chamberlin's *Chicago and the Great Conflagration* stressed Chicago's momentous rise in order to accent the depth of her fall, saying, "Without a peer in her almost magical growth in what seemed to be an enduring prosperity, the city of Chicago experienced a catastrophe almost equally without a parallel in history, and the sad event awakened into active sympathy the whole civilized world." *The Ruined City*, in keeping with its title, went further in its assertions about the fire's historical qualities. "NEVER," it boldly declared, "since the dreadful conflagration which laid London, the modern Babylon, in ashes, and astonished the world, has there been such a nerve-startling event, as the total reduction by the red-tongued demon of the Garden City, Chicago—certainly one of the handsomest, and one of the greatest cities of the Western World." The book *Chicago Burned: An Authentic, Concise and Graphic Account*, published in Elkhart, Indiana in

1871, echoed this tone, contending the fire to be the worst blaze ever to take place. Its authors found that:

> Never before in the annals of history can such a parallel of destruction be found. The burning of Rome, London, Moscow, New York, Portland, and Paris were undoubtedly appalling, disastrous events; but pale in significance before the awful work of devastation which has resulted in the reduction to ashes of Chicago, the city of the world—the spot on which the eyes of all nations of the earth have been fixed with mixed envy and admiration ever since she started into existence.[16]

The key claim of many of these authors concerned the extent of the physical damage caused by the flames. The authors were correct to cite the financial devastation such wreckage would cause, but often took their assertions to the outside edge of credible prose. Luzerne, in *The Lost City!*, wrote:

> Since the day when "tall Troy" crumbled away in flames, no fire has surpassed the Chicago conflagration in its terrible work of destruction. The value of the merchandise alone consumed by the flames was at least double that of the goods destroyed in the great fires of Moscow and London combined. No city ever suffered a greater pecuniary loss by fire, whether Jerusalem smitten by Titus, Rome when sacked by Alaric, or Carthage when given up to fire and sword by her Roman conquerors.[17]

Prominent personages, both inside and outside of the city, also took part in such talk. Perhaps picking up on the style of the news coverage, the Governor of Michigan, Henry P. Baldwin, maintained that "the city of Chicago, in the neighboring State [*sic*] of Illinois, has been visited in the providence of Almighty God with a calamity almost unequalled in the annals of history." And even wealthy Chicago resident William Bross, who, as we will discuss below, would become the booster most committed to spinning the fire story in a positive way for the city of Chicago, reflected the extravagant wording of the press. Part-owner of the *Chicago Tribune* at the time of the great fire, Bross perhaps intended, like the article of his paper described above, to claim greatness for his city by magnifying the extent of its disaster. Bross's words, "There has indeed been nothing like so vast a calamity of this nature in any country in the time of authentic history," and other comments of this type would ultimately backfire.[18] In stressing the city's destruction and the horrors of the fire, Chicagoans helped make a curiosity of their hometown.

Articles on the fire also likened the devastation to the events of the Civil War. Coming to a close just six years earlier, the conflict stood at the ready in all Americans' minds; all terrible events were measured by its yardstick of tragedy. Comments comparing the War Between the States to the fire came from all regions of the country. Sharing a sadness due to the losses of war, although not a political viewpoint, North and South could both lament the pain of this more recent tragedy. A reporter from Indianapolis wrote that "nothing has equaled it [the fire] since the firing on Fort Sumter." "This calamity," declared *The Atlanta Constitution*, "outside of war, perhaps is the most disastrous one of modern days." Union and Confederate were further drawn together in mourning for the losses caused by the October blaze as both regions provided financial relief for the struggling city. Confederate exiles living in London sent in contributions with the general collection, feeling sympathy for Chicago despite its Yankee past. An anonymous citizen in Nashville, Tennessee left one hundred dollars for the needy of Chicago at the *Nashville Banner* office with the note, " 'No North, no South, when our fellow men are in distress.'"[19] In some sense, then, the Chicago fire provided a degree of reconciliation between the regions so recently divided by war.

While the Chicago fire served in part to appease sectional conflict, not all authors chose to use the disaster to bring the nation together. *The Ruined City,* published in New York, even claimed that in some ways Chicago's struggle could be deemed worse than the events of the Civil War. This account concluded that "Since the memorable New York fire of December 1835, we have had no disaster of the kind in this country or on this Continent to compare with this of Chicago in the value of the property consumed, while in the number of families left houseless and destitute, it far surpasses the burnings of Charleston, Atlanta, Columbia, and Richmond during our late civil war all summed up together."[20] Perhaps these sentiments can be seen as an attempt to lessen the culpability of the North for damage inflicted upon the South during the Civil War, or to claim for the North the same type of bravery the South asserted when it confronted the numerous battles fought on its soil.

The sheer proliferation of the media coverage of the Chicago fire also inspired the comparison of the disaster to the Civil War. Ross Miller, author of *American Apocalypse: The Great Fire and the Myth of Chicago* points out that the Civil War and the Great Fire were two of the very first national media events experienced by the nation.[21] For example, New Yorkers found themselves captivated by the news flowing into their city from Chicago, admitting that "the excitement in the business portion of the city was scarcely surpassed by that of the most eventful times of the war."[22]

The producers of popular culture made the most of the city's losses. Chicago writers perhaps hoped that in exhaustively examining the horrid details and at times even stretching the truth, the city of Chicago might appear as a grander metropolis—an advanced settlement that had taken a terrible tumble. *The Chicago Tribune* again set the tone for much of the later discussion. Highlighting the city's impressive rise even as it catalogued her devastation, the *Tribune* writers explained that "the vast extent of territory is nearly as desolate and empty as it was 50 years ago." Outside of Chicago, other periodicals followed suit. One admitted that "the imagination stands appalled at the magnitude of the terrible calamity now visiting Chicago."[23]

Chicago lay in ruins, wrote its assessors, like a romantic European city. James W. Sheahan and George T. Upton, authors of *The Great Conflagration*, painted the scene with a sentimental brush, writing unblushingly, "Dark nooks and deeply-shaded recesses, which by daylight would lose their secrecy, and be nothing but waste blanks, are in the evening full of the charm and mystery of darkness. Fancy peoples those secluded spots with the creatures of her imagination, and they seem fitting homes for ghoul and afrit —creatures who lurk among the ruined tombs and devour the belated wanderers there." Apparently some felt the city equally mysterious in the morning. Edgar Johnson Goodspeed recounted, "Under the light of the sun, wandering among the ruins of a day, the beholder cannot dispel the illusion that he is the victim of some Aladdinic dream, and that he has been transported with the speed of light, by the genius of the lamp or ring, and set down among the ruins of the Titanic ages."[24] Ironically, by being forced to begin anew because of the devastation, the relatively young Chicago gained a patina of age through the fire. Although rebuilding the infrastructure of the urban center would make it even newer physically, Chicago had gained a well-known past. Unfortunately, in claiming this particular past, Chicago established a enduring connection with devastation and scandal. The American public grew accustomed to using Chicago to feed their prurient interests.

The fire undeniably caused excessive physical damage to the city. Yet, despite the heightened rhetoric, the blaze was not in fact the worst in terms of loss of life for 1871, nor even the worst for that day. Also on the evening of Sunday, October 8, the town of Peshtigo, Wisconsin caught fire, and the conflagration continued until Friday, October 13. Peshtigo was "totally destroyed" by this disaster; in the town and in neighboring Sugar Bush eight hundred people died as a result of the fire. According to Karen Sawislak,

author of *Smoldering City: Chicagoans and the Great Fire, 1871–1874,*
however, Peshtigo's fire failed to capture the nation's attention as it was
caused by "nature" rather than human error.[25] Most Americans, of course,
had not heard of Peshtigo, so its news held little cachet. In addition, city
disasters played better with a national audience already primed to revel in
urban misadventure.

Both the instant-histories and newspaper coverage of the event set aside
a few pages for stories of other contemporary fires across the United States
and abroad, as well as fires throughout history. The work *Chicago Burned*
acknowledged, "Chicago is not the only place that has been visited by this
great destroyer of life and property. From Wisconsin and Michigan comes a
cry of desolation and misery that makes us sick at heart. All along the shores
of Lake Michigan and Huron the suffering is intense. Whole towns have
been destroyed and nothing remains of them but the horrible black ruins
that are to be seen on every side." Beginning with the first issue of *The
Chicago Tribune* issued after the disaster, the mainstream media carefully
documented other great historical fires, noting the Charleston blazes of
1838 (1,158 buildings and forty five acres burned), 1845 (nearly the entire
city destroyed), and 1868, the Quebec fires of May and June 1845 (2,800
buildings ruined in all), the San Francisco fire of 1851, the Portland, Maine
fire of 1866, and the infamous London conflagration of September 1666
(depleting 436 acres and five-sixths of the city). Fires in the city of Chicago
itself, occurring in the years of 1857, 1859, 1866, and 1868 were also
discussed.[26] Instead of minimizing the impact of the 1871 fire, however, the
discussions of these blazes instead magnified this latest urban destruction.
Presentations of these earlier events in the instant-histories, usually in a back
section of the works, were designed to make Chicago's disaster appear all the
more devastating. After comparing the various fires, writers concluded that
the Chicago blaze ranked first in terms of tragedy.

Reporters made the most of the chaos inspired by the fire, portraying a
scene of utter confusion. Chicagoans, the observers concluded, appeared
psychologically damaged by the disaster. "The panic is increasing," said *The
New York Times* on October 9, "and the people seem almost crazy with
alarm." *The Detroit Free Press'* correspondent on the scene spoke of the "in-
describable noise" of the fire itself and "the hurly burly" in the street as firemen rushed about. "Wails and lamentations of the homeless, houseless
people filled the air," the subsequent edition explained, "like one great cry
of distress to the heavens. Men wept or raved like lunatics, women fainted
away, children ran hither and thither in their night-clothes, and the awful
picture was colored anew by the fresh flames leaping up from roofs

untouched but a moment before." A native Chicagoan, Mr. Lockwood, provided his personal reminiscences of the fire to *The New York Sun*. Lockwood stated that Chicagoans gathered on the lakefront in order to flee the heat of the fire in the cold waters, acting "more like dead than living men." *The New York Herald* felt that fire stripped Chicagoans of their humanity altogether. *The Herald* reported that "fifty thousand men, women, and children huddled together like so many wild animals; helpless children asking for bread, heart-broken parents, who knew not which way to turn or what to say." One work of contemporary history vividly explained that before the demon of fire "the proud city's populace scattered and squirmed like so many little ants."[27]

In order to make the report palatable to a wide variety of readers, authors often worked the plight of Chicago's women into their accounts. Hundreds of premature births were attributed to the shock of the disaster. Writers made countless references to the lack of clothing worn by women running from their homes unexpectedly. These unclothed women had two main effects. First, on some level they inspired sympathy with the city; many readers could comprehend the comparison between Chicago and an innocent maiden whose dignity had been compromised or a mother breast-feeding her offspring. Frank Luzerne undoubtedly hoped to encourage a sympathetic response when he wrote, "Mothers, slightly enrobed, and carrying tender babes, were crying bitterly, while others cherished their young babes at their panting breasts and were silent in their overpowering agony."[28] Second, and probably more forcibly, however, these images of women served to downgrade Chicago's reputation. Here stood a city, the authors insinuated, where young girls could not feel safe. Here lay a city that provided the unclothed bodies of its women for the entertainment of the rest of the nation.

Some women, the readers learned, emerged from their homes fully ablaze, and had to remove their burning clothing publicly in the street. After rescuing three hundred dollars from her home, and returning inside for yet more valuables, a wife fled back outside with her clothing on fire. "The only way that her husband could save her," explained the report, "was by tearing off her clothes; not a shred of clothing being left on her. Her nakedness, however, was finally covered with a blanket." If this was yet not enough to satisfy the reader's voyeurism, the author went on to say that "her eldest daughter was in the same plight." In "A Thrilling Scene: A Lady Braving the Flames with Her Child," from the Englewood, Illinois *Telegram*, a presumably lucky rescuer saved a nude woman whose "garments nearly completely burned off." If not entirely naked, a number of women entered the streets scantily clad; one man admitted that he had a particularly fine recollection of " a very pretty girl, who must have had barely time to leave her bed ere the room took fire, as she was clad in nothing but her night clothes and a thin shawl." Author Frank Luzerne even provoked his readers with the story of mischievous cross-dressing Gussie, who found herself forced to wear her brother George's pants when fleeing because of her "careless" attitude towards organizing her own clothes.[29]

Stories of particularly sad or odd reactions to the fire were reprinted in more than one periodical or instant history. Many accounts spoke of confused mothers mistaking small wrapped bundles for their infant children as they fled, leaving their babies to die in the ruins. Often repeated as well was the tale of a young girl with burning long hair, on which well-meaning citizens threw whiskey in an attempt to put out the flames. Another infamous figure, a middle-aged woman hauling heavy bundles through the Chicago streets, had lost her mind, and sang a Mother Goose rhyme as she wandered, "Chickery, Chickery, Crany Crow/I went to the well to wash my toe!"[30]

Reporters attributed part of the apparent chaos of the fire to the mixing of classes caused by the blaze. Driven from their homes, rich and poor, white and black, Scandinavian, Irish, and English found themselves together. "Thousands of persons and horses inextricably commingled," explained *The Ruined City*, "poor people of all colors and shades, and of every nationality, from Europe, China, and Africa, mad with excitement, struggled with each other to get away."[31]

The mainstream media claimed the confusion of the fire provided license for a wide variety of vices. Edgar Johnson Goodspeed wrote that "it was a time when the worst forces of society were jubilant, and all the villains had free course." Colbert and Chamberlin, probably fashioning the most colorful account of the temptations of the ruin, stated:

> Villainous, haggard with debauch and pinched with misery, flitting through the crowd, collarless, ragged, dirty, unkempt, were negroes with stolid faces and white men who fatten on the wages of shame; gliding through the mass like vultures in search of prey. They smashed windows, reckless of the severe wounds inflicted on their naked hands, and with bloody fingers rifled impartially, till, shelf, and cellar, fighting viciously for the spoils of forays. Women, hollow-eyed and brazen-faced, with foul drapery tied over their heads, their dresses half-torn from their skinny bosoms, and their feet thrust into trodden-down slippers, moved here and there, stealing, scolding shrilly, and laughing with one another at some particularly 'splendid' gush of flame or 'beautiful' falling in of roof.[32]

While women lost their clothes or their sanity in the conflagration, men turned to drink. Saloon-keepers, knowing that the fire would soon consume their wares, threw open their doors to the public for last-minute parties. Some Chicagoans simply helped themselves to alcohol by breaking into abandoned bars. *Harper's Weekly* felt that the men seemed "to have the same impulse that leads sailors on a sinking ship to drown their terrors in the delirium of intoxication." Drunkenness brought death to those too senseless to out-run the rapidly moving destruction. The many references to intoxicated behavior made buffoons of male Chicago residents. Even local papers encouraged the characterization. One stated, "Drunken men staggered among the crowds, apparently possessed of the idea that the whole affair was a grand municipal spree, in which they were taking part as the duty that should be discharged by all good citizens."[33]

The media presented Chicago as a place with almost unlimited possibilities for disaster. In the face of unthinkable horror, the cultural producers insisted that Chicago residents still found a way to make matters worse by becoming drunk or committing crimes. A national weekly magazine proclaimed that "armed patrols... needed to guard the helpless from robbery and the baser passions of desperate ruffians, who, under cover of the general panic and disorganization, sought to inaugurate a new reign of terror." Chicagoans allegedly robbed, raped, and murdered during the chaos of the fire. Of course, in keeping with the rhetoric of excess, reporters deemed these violations of law the worst ever experienced by any city. Chicago's own *Lakeside Monthly* magazine stated, "Before daybreak the thieving horror had culminated in scenes of daring and robbery unparalleled in the annals of any similar disaster." Many sources claimed that incendiaries roamed the streets and that self-appointed vigilantes had executed up to fifty people for reportedly starting fires. A local paper urged, "We hope that whenever a citizen can catch an incendiary attempting to fire a building, he will shoot him on the spot. This is the best way to dispose of such wretches at a time like this." Most likely journalists concocted these tales of incendiarism to please audiences; evidence seems to suggest that no such events occurred. Carl Smith, author *of Urban Disorder and the Shape of Belief*, the 1995 study that devotes a section to the 1871 fire, concludes that none of the cases can be verified.[34]

One of the most prevalent complaints about lawlessness connected to the Great Chicago fire involved the mercenary attitudes and even outright thefts attributed to the city's deliverymen during the conflagration. Fleeing from their homes, the frightened populace turned to those with carts and horses to help them haul family members and belongings to safety. A good number of these businessmen, according to later articles, demanded exorbitant rates for their services, discharged one family's goods to carry items for higher paying customers, or stole family heirlooms under the pretense of moving them. These incidents were recounted as morality tales for readers; in Chicago, the quest for money had gone too far. Goodspeed related, "This class of people made great profit out of the calamities of their fellow-citizens. Their pockets may be heavy to-day, but their consciences, if they have any, should be still heavier." During the fire, express drivers charged anywhere between five and one hundred and fifty dollars for use of their carts. This led, post-disaster, to the Mayor's proclamation prohibiting hackmen from charging more than their regular fares.[35]

Because of the public's belief that the city teemed with crime, the city undertook extraordinary law enforcement measures. Within two weeks of the fire, hundreds of extra policemen began duty. Chicago Mayor R. B. Mason called upon Lieutenant General Philip Sheridan, along with several companies of regular soldiers and volunteers, to guard Chicago beginning October 11th. The military reigned in Chicago for nearly two weeks. Along with security, Sheridan dispensed supplies to those hit hardest by the fire. John M. Palmer, Governor of Illinois, vociferously protested Sheridan's presence. Citing objections to army rule in his state, Palmer lobbied President Grant and others in Washington, D.C. to have the forces removed. Although most contemporary sources on the fire praised Sheridan's efforts and deemed such a level of protection necessary, the troops' presence heightened the connection between Chicago and disorder in the public eye. With the shooting and death of Prosecuting Attorney and former editor of *The Evening Post* Thomas W. Grosvenor on October 20, 1871 by young militia member Theodore Treat, Sheridan's protection perhaps appeared more dangerous than stabilizing. On October 23, Mayor Mason relieved Sheridan of his command over Chicago.[36]

The perceived level of chaos in Chicago led to repeated comparisons between the city and hell itself. One observer of the disaster reported that "he could feel the heat and smoke and hear the maddened Babel of sounds, and it required little imagination to believe one's self looking over the adamantine bulwarks of hell into the bottomless pit." Goodspeed contended that the night sky of the smoldering ruins "glowed like the canopy of hell and threatened universal ruin." For some, the fire seemed to hearken the end of the world. *The New York Sun* found that more than one witness exclaimed "This is the day of judgment! This must be the end of the world!" as they watched the devouring flames. "God only can save the city from utter destruction," warned *The Ruined City*. And in fire-inspired poetry, like N.S. Emerson's "Call for Help for Chicago," the fire was portrayed as the devil.[37]

Believing that Chicago's fiery fate could foreshadow events in other American cities, citizens looked for lessons in the ruins. On the most practical level, Americans looked to better fireproof their buildings, and to increase water supplies. Yet the lessons also assumed a more metaphorical and religious demeanor. Observers noted that sites of vice burned in the con-flagration—brothels, saloons, gambling halls, and theaters. Was this merely coincidence? Reverend Robert Collyer, of Chicago's Church of the Unity, found the metropolis guilty of a wide variety of sins, and of harboring "a criminal population almost equal to that of London, which is the worst on the face of the earth." Colbert and Chamberlin assumed a different tack, ar-guing that the fire had perhaps been a sign of all that Chicago had achieved, yet noting that perhaps the city had succeeded too quickly. They wrote, "What if these fires should be but one of a series of events, designed by the Great Ruler of the universe to prevent man from progressing too fast or too far, in his forward march toward the perfection of knowledge, and of that power which knowledge confers upon its possessors?"[38]

The Indiana publication, *Chicago Burned*, warned that Chicago's experiences demonstrated the futility of accumulating material wealth. "We learn from all these disasters," it concluded, "what a poor place the earth is to put our treasures in." Publisher Alfred L. Sewell equated the destruction with biblical proclamations, saying, "He smote Chicago not only for its own ultimate good, but also as a warning and a lesson for all other cities, if not for all mankind. That this will be the effect, is already evident. He has said that 'pride shall have its fall,' and that 'the lofty shall be brought low'—and He has enjoined us also not to place our trust in riches."[39]

The most common exhortation concerning the cause of the fire centered on Chicago's lack of humility. Oftentimes, authors characterized Chicago as a shameless woman. Cities, like ships, frequently were referred to by female pronouns, but cultural producers, in an uncommon twist to this gendering of cities, proclaimed Chicago's womanhood of a particularly unchaste type. In the same *Chicago Times* issue that launched the O'Leary legend, the reporter opened with a seemingly prophetic biblical passage. "Saith Holy Writ," he proclaimed, "The merchants of the world are waxed rich through the abundance of her delicacies. How much she has glorified herself and lived deliciously, so much sorrow and torment give her; for she saith in her heart, I sit a queen and am no widow, and shall see no sorrow. She shall be utterly burned by fire." *Chicago Burned* urged all its readers to build up their souls rather than their reputations. The book stated, "Politicians have worshipped their offices, and merchants their business, and painters their pictures, and musicians their attainments, and architects their buildings, and historians their books; and how often have they seen their works perish!"[40]

Chicago might be able to recover, other cities conceded, if she could cast off this burden of pride. *The Cincinnati Commercial* predicted that Chicago would "arise from her ashes a grander city than ever, chastened by her calamity, and by experience grow less confident in startling rapidity of progress, and have more content with gradual returns and solid gains." Murat Halstead, the editor of *Commercial*, believed that the city would rebuild in plain brick rather than ornate ironwork, donning the clothing of a more sober city than the Chicago of the past.[41]

The best-selling novel of the 1870s, Reverend Edward Payson Roe's *Barriers Burned Away*, first published in installments in *The Evangelist* beginning at the end of 1871, envisioned the fire as a lesson in Christian piety. So popular that it was continually reprinted until after 1900, the book exposed many Americans to the argument that Chicago's fire had provided a needed cleansing to the urban center.[42] Like Theodore Dreiser's *Sister Carrie* of a generation later, Payson's protagonist Dennis Fleet came to Chicago full of plans. As he embarked for the city, Dennis believed that "the world was all before him, and Chicago, the young and giant city of the West, seemed an Eldorado, where fortune, and perhaps fame, might soon be won."[43] Dennis managed to elude the temptations of the wicked city and ultimately became a successful artist after holding a series of humble jobs.

Dennis fell in love, despite himself, with the beautiful-yet-cold German aristocrat, Christine Ludolph. Christine embodied the get-ahead Chicago business ethic; she and her father wished to make enough money to be able to return to Germany and maintain the family lands. An atheist, Christine believed that those who claimed religion in her city fooled only themselves. She stated, "Here in Christian Chicago the will of God is no more heeded by the majority than the Emperor of China, and the Bible might as well be the Koran." Yet in surviving the fire, Christine learned humility and the joy of helping others as she tended to an elderly woman overwhelmed by the confusion. On the shore of Lake Michigan, Christine broke down and earnestly prayed to God for the first time in her life. This newly acquired religion allowed Dennis and Christine to marry, and presumably to live "happily ever after." In Roe's fictional conception, Chicago had a wicked past, but could hope for redemption if Christian souls like Dennis and Christine managed to prevail. Roe, a pastor from Highland Falls, New York, bet on the side of the many Chicagoans who were convinced that Chicago could rise again.[44]

Predominately local voices made up the contingent of those who worked to beat back the onslaught of negative media coverage with more positive arguments. Unlike Roe, these writers did not predict a moral face-lift for their city, as they were not concerned about whether Chicago had suffered from any ethical laxity in its pre-fire period. They argued instead that Chicago would soon return to its former physical and financial strength. *The Chicago Evening Post* explained that Chicago, as the nation's "representative city," had to be rebuilt. The claim that Chicago was representative would be a theme that others would take up from time to time during the next hundred years, and is something further chapters will explore. When those inside the city made this claim, the representative-ness was seen as a positive attribute. In the *Chicago Evening Post*, this attribution signaled the writer's belief in Chicago's pioneer spirit and optimistic business sense. In three to five years, Chicagoans ambitiously (and correctly) challenged, their city would resume its post-fire demeanor. The effusive *Chicago Times* uttered, "We have here won one of the grandest conflicts known to history, and although our defeat is without parallel, we shall marshal out the remnants of our routed but not demoralized armies and shall march once more to victory." Most influential on national fire coverage and the historical memory of the conflagration, however, were the now famous words of *The Chicago Tribune*. The paper urged, "CHEER UP. In the midst of a calamity without parallel in the world's history, looking upon the ashes of thirty years' accumulations, the people of this once beautiful city have resolved that CHICAGO SHALL RISE AGAIN."[45]

Competition between cities, particularly emerging American cities, was fierce during this period. The battles between urban centers for financial investments and population led a few urban newspapers to forecast ruin for Chicago. Perhaps the fire would allow for a reordering of the urban hierarchy. *The St. Louis Republican* believed that the fire might enable St. Louis to make a bid for Chicago's trade. *The Cincinnati Commercial* felt that other cities would at least temporarily divert much of Chicago's business. A New Orleans paper proclaimed Chicago's financial rulership at an end. "The magical growth and stupendous wealth of this great interior metropolis was, in the main, due to geographical, commercial, and other causes, which no longer exist in their original force," it stated, making the prediction that St. Louis would now replace the Lake City. To the New Orleans author, St. Louis' growth appeared sure and solid, while Chicago had supposedly grown through speed and unsubstantiated speculation.[46]

Most urban spokesmen, however, predicted that Chicago would overcome its predicament. Considerate commentators felt that showing a degree of concern for the city was the appropriate public response. Observant business people in other regions must have realized that, whatever their boosterish loyalties, a fall for Chicago could mean a decline in the fortunes of the many non-resident investors in Chicago's economic expansion. A man speaking for Milwaukee, Wisconsin, a longtime competitor for Midwestern trade, admitted to no feeling of rivalry with Chicago despite the two cities' long and acrimonious history. The businessman challenged, "It is nobody but a narrow-minded fool that will talk of Milwaukee being benefited by this calamity to Chicago. What is your misfortune is ours too, and that of the whole Northwest. As for trade, we haven't goods enough to serve a single day of Chicago's trade." Even some in St. Louis, a city known to harbor outspoken critics of Chicago, spoke rapturously of Chicago's golden future. *The St. Louis Democrat*, perhaps feigning tenderness for its "sister city," stated:

> It is a dreadful blow to a swiftly growing city but they are mistaken who think it will prove fatal. Chicago has been the world's wonder in her rise, and she is now the world's sad wonder in her almost unprecedented calamity. She will now astonish by the rapidity and success of her recuperation. One year hence will witness orderly arrays of new and grander piles in place of those that are now smouldering [sic] in the blackness."[47]

More established cities also spoke of their hope for Chicago's quick rejuvenation. In this catastrophic time, people from other urban centers sought to overcome jealousies. *The New York Herald* flattered the ruined city, conceding, "Our Chicago friends were not without good reason for speaking of their own city as a possible rival to New York."[48]

How can we explain these claims of predicted success for Chicago? When the preponderance of stories about the Great Fire highlighted the weight of the city's enormous struggles, why these proclamations of regrowth? The commentators felt compelled to make positive statements for the most practical of reasons—they knew that the financial futures of their cities depended on Chicago's. For all of the metropolitan rivalry of the late nineteenth century, many writers understood how economically interdependent these urban centers had become.

With the news of the fire, the American market did falter. New York stocks tumbled, particularly Western Union Telegraph (given the physical damage to telegraph facilities in Chicago). On Wall Street, brokers tried to remain hopeful, but stock prices lost ten percent of their pre-fire values during the trading day of October 9, picking up slightly at the close of the day. Members of the New York produce market also expressed concern, and the traders "refrained from pelting each other jocosely with little balls of dough, and stood in small knots and discussed the sufferings of the homeless people of the Queen City of the West."[49] All over the nation, people had invested in the booming Midwestern city, and wondered if the fire would devastate them financially. Investors worried that Chicago businesses would fail to repay their loans; merchants worried that Chicago businessmen would delay in placing orders for more goods. Despite the initial slump in the market, national business soon recovered. The Great Chicago Fire, in spite of Chicago's importance to the national economy, did not lead to an economic debacle.

Due to the hundreds of millions of dollars in assets lost to the conflagration, the nation fretted about the strength of its insurance houses. In Providence, Rhode Island, for instance, insurance companies were "very much excited over the great Chicago fire, nearly all of them having risks of large amounts in Chicago." Boston insurance concerns lost over half a million dollars; some insurance companies based in Chicago closed altogether. Early reports in Chicago placed the local companies' losses at approximately twenty-five million dollars, with tallied assets at close to four hundred million dollars.[50]

The wealth of positive commentary concerning Chicago's business future perhaps did work to shore up its finances. While individual investors inside and outside of the city collapsed, Chicago businesses did begin to regroup immediately after the fire. While the makers of popular culture wanted to make money off the fire by selling their "thrilling" stories to the prurient public, they did not wish to simultaneously kill financial investments in Chicago businesses. They succeeded in balancing the two concerns in part because Americans could indeed conceive of an infamous city as financially lucrative. Americans did not consider "scandalous" and "sound investment" contradictory.

Along with supportive commentary, cities provided financial and material contributions to the burned city in an attempt to protect the national economy and relieve suffering Chicagoans. All over the country, Americans held meetings in order to coordinate local relief efforts that would total in the millions of dollars. In Columbus, Ohio local bakeries and the penitentiary commissary baked bread and cooked meats for the Chicago homeless. In Cincinnati, the Allemania Jewish Society cancelled their ball and sent their foodstuffs to Chicago. Railway companies provided free transportation out of Chicago, as well as free shipment of relief goods into the city. The state of Illinois paid Chicago back the nearly three million dollars the city had expended on the Illinois and Michigan Canal project (which linked the Great

Lakes with the Mississippi River and officially opened in 1848) in exchange for a lien on the canal. The state also relieved Chicago of approximately three million dollars in taxes.[51]

According to the media, the contributions at times took the form of personal sacrifices. An Irish lad in Springfield, Massachusetts reportedly sold his toy whip, his favorite plaything, for ten cents in order to provide help for Chicago. One young girl sent all of her clothes to Chicago through her school's fund drive. A railroad executive supposedly returned home to find his wife, clad in fine silk, preparing supper. She had given all of her other clothes, their son's clothes, and her husband's clothing, to the needy of Chicago. Even the family's pickles were missing, for "the poor souls in Chicago would relish them so much." While the businessman admired his wife's spirit, he inquired, "Do you think we can stand an 'encore' on that Chicago fire?"[52]

The amount of generous gifts given the city prompted Mayor Mason to utilize the city's Relief and Aid Society as a coordinating committee. Run by "honest" businessmen rather than Chicago politicians, the society, established in the late 1850s, attempted to distribute aid only to applicants they deemed worthy. The society's screening process must have eliminated many Chicagoans, because the Relief and Aid Society still held thousands of dollars in donations for fire victims two years after the blaze.[53]

In a matter of days, writers dubbed the outpouring of relief unparalleled. *The Detroit Free Press* found Chicago's calamity "the occasion of one of the most magnificent displays of sympathy and charity that the world has ever beheld." Poet Henry M. Look of Pontiac, Michigan described the sentiments in rhyming verse, writing, "Destruction wasted the city,/But the burning curse that came/Enkindled in all the people/Sweet charity's holy flame." Similarly, poet N.S. Emerson mused that the world "gave and gave, and still had more/To give from Love's exhaustless store." Chicagoans responded to the aid with thanks. The earnestly devout William Bross, Chicago's fire spokesman and consummate booster, stated, "Strong men in Chicago weep at midnight, not over their losses of thousands, aye, many of them even millions, but with joy and gratitude at the noble charity you have shown us. God will reward you for it, and our children and children's children shall bless you."[54]

Also in a more positive vein, both local and national commentators occasionally took up the figure of the phoenix, the Egyptian mythological bird that arose from its own ashes and began its life anew, as a mascot for Chicago's recovery. Unlike the phoenix, Chicago had not been around for hundreds of years when it had to start again, but the comparison seemed appropriate. Like many of the powerful post-fire images, this symbol first took shape in the pages of *The Chicago Tribune*. The paper exclaimed, "So Chicago, aided by the sympathy and already tendered assistance of her friends in other parts of the country, joined to the indomitable and elastic energy of her own people, will be builded again, solemnly yet determinedly, upon the still smoldering ashes of her late glory, and become known as the Phoenix City—an appellation to which her somewhat obsolete one of Garden City will readily give place." In using this legend, the *Chicago Tribune* provided precedent for the city's miraculous rebirth. William Bross, editor and part-owner of the paper, took the claims even farther. Not only would Chicago regenerate, "Phoenix-like," but also she would be "more glorious than ever before."[55]

William Bross tried to influence the coverage of the Chicago fire through a number of speeches and contacts with prominent people. Bross, first setting eyes on Chicago in October 1846, moved to the city permanently in 1848. Primarily of Huguenot origin, he had been raised as a Presbyterian in the Delaware Valley. A graduate of Williams College in Massachusetts, Bross came to Chicago with considerable intellectual skills. He first ran a bookstore, but finding he enjoyed reading books better than selling them, entered into the newspaper publication business. In partnership with Chicagoan J. Ambrose Wight, Bross purchased the religious paper, *Herald of the Prairies*, and printed the newspaper and the *Chicago Tribune* on the city's first power press. When Wight and Bross determined the paper could not support both their families, Bross sold his share to Wight and began the *Democratic Press* with John L. Scripps in 1852. In 1857–1858, the *Democratic Press* and *Chicago Tribune* merged. From 1865 to 1869, Bross also served as the Lieutenant Governor of Illinois.[56]

Bross, the author of two booster histories of Chicago (built of articles culled from his newspapers), *The Railroads, History and Commerce* of 1854 and *History of Chicago* of 1876, became Chicago's most tireless spokesperson after the fire. Most importantly, while traveling to Buffalo and New York City the Thursday after the fire to get materials for the *Tribune*, Bross gave a number of pro-Chicago speeches and interviews. Bross and his family lost their home in the conflagration, and the Tribune building, built to be "fireproof," did not withstand the blaze. But Bross presented an unflappably optimistic face to the public. He made claims early on as to the unstoppable energy of Chicago and its inevitable rejuvenation. The morning after the fire he saw all around him "evidence of true Chicago spirit. On all sides men said to one another, 'Cheer up; we'll all be right again before long'; and many other plucky things. Their pluck and courage was wonderful. Every one was bright and cheerful, pleasant, hopeful, and even inclined to be jolly in spite of the misery and destitution which surrounded them and which they shared. One and all said, Chicago must and should be rebuilt at once."[57]

On his trip, Bross spoke to the Buffalo Board of Trade, where he gave an account "of the extent of the fire, the relief that had been sent, and of the certainty that the city in a very few years would rise from its ashes in all its pristine vigor." Bross reasoned that Chicago's re-growth was linked with the idea of Manifest Destiny; as the nation would inevitably spread west, its western gateway city, Chicago, must return to its former power. In New York, two reporters for the *New York Tribune* interviewed Bross, the first prominent eyewitness to visit their city. The resulting article appeared in the *Tribune* on October 14. In the interview, Bross urged New York financiers not to abandon Chicago. Bross persuaded:

> New York is the senior and Chicago the junior partner of the great firm which manages the vast commercial interests of our nation. By a dispensation of Providence which the wisest could not foresee, the means in the hands of the junior partner have been destroyed. Will the senior partner sit by and see the business of the firm crushed out when he has the means to establish it on a scale more gigantic and profitable than ever before?[58]

Bross also met with a friend who worked for the *Springfield Republican*, and the president and secretary of the Connecticut Mutual Life Insurance Company, Chicago's largest creditor. On October 17th, Bross spoke to the New York Chamber of Commerce. His remarks were copied or summarized in many New York morning papers, and in the papers of other American cities. For the Chamber of Commerce, Bross highlighted the economic opportunities available in the fallen city. The fire had leveled distinctions between businessmen; whoever could offer the least expensive goods would prosper. Bross encouraged young men everywhere to hurry to Chicago to seek their fortunes. 1920s Chicago historian Lloyd Lewis asserts, "Everybody agreed that Bross' beating of the tom-toms induced tens of thousands to seek Chicago as a home for either themselves or their dollars."[59]

But even Bross' concerted efforts could not substantially change the unflattering rhetoric concerning Chicago generated by the cultural producers. The material, which detailed the chaos of the fire scene and the wayward character of Chicago, spoke to a readied part of the American personality. The scandalous story of the blaze proved popular with a nation primed to link great troubles to the urban environment. In the end, a good many Americans concluded that Chicago had burned because the city had, at some level, deserved the punishment. The city's rapid growth and seemingly insatiable drive to make money worried Americans trying to hold onto a disappearing rural way of life. The Great Chicago Fire of 1871 launched the style of popular expression that would color Chicago's national reputation for almost a century. With the fire, Chicago became a city in which drunkenness and crime could barely be controlled, and in which young innocent women were at risk. The city's disaster pointed the way towards America's final destiny—the pits of hell—if the tides of progress were not stalled. Americans found themselves utterly captivated by the news of Chicago's scandalous fire, but not surprised. Edgar Johnson Goodspeed expressed many of these issues in an anecdote: "A girl carrying her sewing machine to four different points...was forced from each by the advancing [fire] fiend. At last an expressman seized her treasure, and in spite of all her efforts drove away with it. Said the impoverished girl, 'Do you wonder Chicago burned?'"[60]

Chapter Two

"The New City of the New World": *Fin-de-Siecle* Chicago and Its Fairs

Fin-de-siecle America was a place of great change. Just catching their breath after the traumas of the Civil War, Americans found themselves in a rapidly evolving era. Immigrants poured into the country, some of whom posed a challenge to the predominantly Protestant and northern European heritage of the nation. Between 1860 and 1890, ten million immigrants entered the United States; most of these people settled in cities. And as the American economy industrialized and corporations grew in size, the urban areas grew even larger. Between 1890 and 1920, eighteen million more immigrants entered the United States. Many of these "new immigrants," hailing from southern and eastern Europe, settled in urban locations. The nation, predominantly rural for over one hundred years, became a nation of urbanites. In 1880 nearly one-half of the population of the northeastern states lived in settlements of four thousand or more, and by 1890 one-third of all Americans lived in settlements of twenty-five hundred or more.[1] A great change was taking place; a change which upset Americans' conceptions of themselves. Where there had once been a Protestant, rural and agricultural nation, a new type of republic took root, based on industry and large corporations instead of farms, cities instead of country, and a polyglot population instead of a more homogenous, Anglo-Saxon one. This transformation unsettled many Americans.

Historians of turn-of-the-century America speak of the power of the status quo in American life, and the loss perceived by long-settled Americans during these tumultuous years. Alan Trachtenberg, in *The Incorporation of America: Culture and Society in the Gilded Age*, explains that the meaning of the word "America" itself became a point of conflict. Focusing on the ways in which American life became increasingly "incorporated"—more bureaucratic, hierarchical, professional, and secular—Trachtenberg argues that incorporation abruptly pulled the nation away from its traditional values. Pondering the rise of the frenzied cities, many Americans mourned the increasing abandonment of what they perceived to be their old way of life, wondering if they could hold on to any of its pieces. Could the crowded cities possibly provide sustenance to the national psyche in the way that rural America had? Trachtenberg writes, "If the frontier had provided the defining experience for Americans, how would the values learned in that experience now fare in the new world of cities—a new world brought into being as if blindly by the same forces which had proffered the apparent gift of land? Would the America fashioned on the frontier survive the caldrons of the city?"[2]

Fin-de-siecle America glittered and sparkled, but its glistening shine did not entirely obscure the cultural questions which lay below the surface. Mark Twain's name for the peculiar period, the "Gilded Age," implied both this sheen and an underlying rot. Other cultural commentators of the day also spoke to the confusion and what they considered a loss. Historian Frederick Jackson Turner addressed the 1893 American Historical Association meeting at the World's Columbian Exposition in Chicago, speaking on "The Significance of the Frontier in American History." Turner believed the availability of great swathes of what he considered unused land (the claims of Native American peoples did not interest Turner) in the United States could be seen as instrumental in the building of the American individualist character and the spirit of democracy. With the publication of the 1890 census and its finding that no unbroken line of frontier remained in the American West, Turner concluded that a formative period of American life had come to an end.

Turner's pronouncement correctly refracted views held by the American people of the time, thus the frequency with which Turner's work is invoked by historians of the United States in their explanation of the period. Of course, we now understand the idea of the frontier as a myth; the United States was not an uninhabited expanse lying in wait for the plans of white Americans. Native Americans had utilized the continent for thousands of years. But the death of deeply held beliefs about oneself and one's nation, even when based in part on erroneous assumptions, cannot come without pain. As historian Henry Nash Smith argues, Americans clung to their republican beliefs of the virtuous yeoman farmer despite significant changes in their society. He writes, "One of the most significant facts of American intellectual history is the slow and inadequate fashion in which the momentum of the new forces was appreciated, or, to put the matter another way, the astonishing longevity of the agrarian ideal as the accepted view of Western society." The trust in the agrarian way inspired an equal distrust of urban areas and industrialization. The republican belief centered on the democratic opportunities of farming; everyone, it seemed, had a chance to do well on the rich American soils of the West, so there would be no glaring distinction between rich and poor as had been so obvious in European agricultural regions and cities. "The Western farmer had been told that he was not a peasant but a peer of the realm;" Smith muses, "that his contribution to society was basic, all others derivative and even parasitic in comparison; that cities were sores on the body politic, and the merchants and bankers and factory owners who lived in them, together with their unfortunate employees, wicked and decadent."[3]

Perhaps the most important commentary on Turner's argument in the course of American historiography, Henry Nash Smith's work, *Virgin Land: The American West as Symbol and Myth*, speaks of the power of this American belief in the frontier. Smith explains that "one of the most persistent generalizations concerning American life and character is the notion that our society has been shaped by the pull of a vacant continent drawing population westward through the passes of the Alleghenies, across the Mississippi Valley, over the high plains and mountains of the Far West to the Pacific Coast." Smith terms this generalization "the myth of the garden." The myth had been central to the arguments of many important American thinkers. These prevalent republican ideas sprang from a long-standing western philosophy on the advantages of agriculture. Smith writes:

> The agrarian doctrines of Jefferson and his contemporaries had been developed out of a rich cluster of ideas and attitudes associated with farming in European cultural tradition: the conventional praise of husbandry derived from Hesiod and Virgil by hundreds of poetic imitators, the theoretical teaching of the French Physiocrats that agriculture is the primary source of wealth, the growing tendency of radical writers like Raynal to make a farmer a republican symbol instead of depicting him in pastoral terms as a peasant virtuously content with his humble status in a stratified society.

The western garden, Americans believed, offered opportunities for an independent livelihood—the connection between farming and markets yet to be fully recognized—and it was America's "Manifest Destiny" to spread over the continent. Smith explains that "this image of this vast and constantly growing agricultural society in the interior of the continent became one of the dominant symbols of nineteenth-century American society—a collective representation, a poetic idea (as Tocqueville noted in the early 1830s) that defined the promise of American life."

Understanding the deep conviction concerning the frontier helps us to understand the values of turn-of-the-century Americans. We comprehend that these values were based largely on myths, myths couched even more on fancy and cultural misunderstanding than Smith imagined. Smith, although he realizes that conceptions about the West are part of a grand American folklore, defines the West himself as "the vacant continent beyond the frontier." Today, historians emphasize the fact that Turner's frontier had already been in use by Native Americans; even tribes that were not settled agriculturists utilized the land in complex ways, such as hunting and gathering or burning tracts of land to provide game animals with a park-like area in which to forage. Additionally, many areas that appeared to be relatively "free" of previous settlers had been claimed by Native American tribes, before newly transmitted diseases ravaged native populations. The colonialists of European-origin did not understand the natives' methods of land use and considered the New World real estate shamefully underutilized. European colonists also interpreted the mortal illnesses affecting the Native Americans as a sign from God encouraging European settlement of the land.[4]

The belief systems of the European colonists provided the backdrop for the fear of the growing urban nature of the United States that plagued many in the late 1800s. The rapid pace of the metamorphoses of American society caused considerable emotional upheaval to the observers of the day. One of the chief public witnesses to the pain of this changing society was Josiah Strong of the American Home Missionary Society. In 1886, Strong wrote his treatise *Our Country*, which in part testified to the trauma of the altered American way of life. Strong contended that one could trace these disruptions to the city, saying, "The city is the nerve center of our civilization. It is also the storm center." Fearful of the accumulation of wealth stemming from the newly formed corporate world, Strong maintained, "It is the city where wealth is massed; and here are the tangible evidences of it piled many stories high. Here the sway of Mammon is widest, and his worship the most constant and eager. Here are luxuries gathered—everything that dazzles the eye, or tempts the appetite; here is the most extravagant expenditure." Strong's attitudes toward urban areas stemmed from a long line of anti-urban writings, writings extremely influential to American thought. The Bible's story of Sodom and Gomorrah provided an ancient example of urban chaos. Englishman John Bunyan's *The Pilgrim's Progress* (1678), read by generations of Americans, contrasted the "blood-red city of man" with the "white, shining city of God." Bunyan's book, according to historian Alan Trachtenberg, ranked with the Bible as the best read book in America from the late seventeenth century until the Civil War, and was widely read even after this time.

T.J. Jackson Lears, author of the persuasive *No Place of Grace: Antimodernism and the Transformation of American Culture, 1880–1920*, explains that part of the Americans' distrust of cities also stems from the nation's English Whig ancestry, which passed on the idea that every republic would eventually be destroyed by its own successes. "The flourishing of trading centers," Lears writes, "inevitably bred [according to the English] an irresponsible leisure class and a vicious urban mob." Lears states, "In republican mythology, the virtuous husbandman had long been counterposed to the corrupt cosmopolitan." The rise of the city in America corresponded to an increased perception of dislocation from "true" experience; people felt more and more as if they were observers of, not actors in, their communities. This led, according to Lears, to a backlash against societal changes, to a protracted antimodernist spirit. In this new nostalgic philosophy, "the city became an emblem of modern unreality."[5]

Unfortunately for Chicago's boosters, its stupendous growth in the late nineteenth century, coupled with its rise to fame just as public interest turned from matters of civil war to questions caused by immigration and incorporation, made the Midwestern city the perfect target for anti-urban sentiments. Between 1870 and 1890, Chicago grew from the fifth to the second biggest city in the United States.[6] As the fastest growing city in the United States, Chicago became the focus of growing doubts about urban places. As the West had been a place of particular importance to the American people—its "free" land seen as a safety valve for eastern cities and its agricultural opportunities considered by many to be the heart of the American personality—the western city Chicago proved especially egregious. According to American thinking, the West was to be an agricultural environment, not an urban one. Author Henry Loomis Nelson labeled Chicago "the new city of the new world" in the pages of *Harper's Weekly*.[7] But the new was not often highly regarded in an America wary about its future.

With the increasing presence of poor southern and eastern European immigrants in the nation's cities, middle class and elite Americans worried about their continued ability to craft American culture. As "their" cities filled with strangers, the previously comfortable classes scrambled for ways to retain their cultural rule. As Lawrence W. Levine, author of *Highbrow/Lowbrow: The Emergence of Cultural Hierarchy in America*, contends, many of these financially secure citizens looked to escape from the realities of the present into a nostalgic vision of the past, and in some instances attempted to use any manipulation of culture they had left at their disposal for social control. Robert H. Wiebe's *The Search for Order, 1877–1920* makes a similar argument, finding that in the upheaval of the period, many tried to use their organizational abilities to take control of the messages of their new society. Wiebe explains, "They tried, in other words, to impose the known upon the unknown, to master an impersonal world through the customs of a personal society. They failed, usually without recognizing why; and that failure to comprehend a society they were helping to make contained the essence of the nation's story."[8]

In Chicago, the wealthier citizens (upper and middle classes) sought to use their long practiced tactics of cultural leadership for a number of purposes: they wished to set forth an image of an organized urban center in order to reinforce their leadership over the lower classes, to build a "highbrow" world in which they could momentarily hide from the pressures of change and to present a tailored image of their particular city to the world in an attempt to lessen the impact of anti-Chicago rhetoric. The first and second of these aims have previously been well-documented by James Gilbert's *Perfect Cities: Chicago's Utopias of 1893* and other works of Chicago history. The third goal—confronting the image of Chicago manufactured by anti-urbanists—has not yet been adequately explored.

Although immersed in the culture which mourned the passing of the supposedly nutritive rural landscape themselves, Chicago's elite wished to strengthen the reputation of their city. Surely, they, like a number of others, found celebrating the achievements of the city more in tune with the central concerns of their lives than fretting over the loss of the rural. Even if they had agreed in part or in full with pronouncements like those of Turner, they did not wish their own city to be seen to symbolize the new threats to American integrity. The city's leaders wished to present the material and cultural attainments of their hometown as an antidote to the building wave of anti-Chicago sentiment in popular culture. In *Fin-de-siecle* Chicago, two events, the on-going Inter-State Industrial Exposition of 1873–1890 and the mammoth spectacle of the World's Columbian Exposition of 1893, became tools with which to fight for authority over Chicago's meaning.

The fire, which emblazoned Chicago's name on the minds of most Americans and linked the city for nearly a century with the perceived calamities of urban life, did not irrevocably dash the Chicago boosters' dreams for their city. As soon as the heat from the Great Chicago fire began to cool, Chicagoans publicly claimed that they would rebuild, and that the new city would even surpass the old. Large-scale physical disaster had occurred, but the great Chicago spirit remained, and was even invigorated by the disaster.

William D. Kerfoot, businessman, in one of the most well-known moments from the fire's aftermath, hung a sign outside a rude shack built over the ruins: "All Gone But Wife & Children & Energy." The *Chicago Tribune* owner William Bross publicly claimed to have maintained unwavering strength while watching his own house burn. Although Bross lost both his home and the *Tribune* building to the flames in just a few hours, he asserted that, "I indulged in no useless sorrows, and, as I saw my home burn, simply resolved as in the past, to do my duty each day as it came along as best I could. I had begun life with no patrimony, save strong arms, willing hands, and I hope, an honest heart, and I could do so again."[9]

Chicagoans predicted a quick return of metropolitan vigor. "The great calamity which has fallen upon our city, as overwhelming as it is, has not broken the spirit of our citizens," remarked a Chicago writer, continuing, "She will arise from her ashes, with an energy that will eclipse all her former efforts, and speedily regain her former position."[10] This positive outlook is illustrated in Chicagoans' attitude regarding their sewer system, of all things. Beginning in 1889, area engineers had begun a project to divert the flow of the Chicago River away from Lake Michigan rather than towards the great lake in order to improve the quality of Chicago's drinking water. Chicagoans pumped their water from the lake through a technologically advanced system. The Chicago River functioned as a sewer for the city and reversing the river's flow kept the waste from the site of the drinking water intake. Although those living south of the city were not particularly pleased with this new development, it made Chicagoans proud. Braggadocio stemming from the engineering feat worked its way into assertions that Chicago could also overcome the difficulties posed by their burned business district. A city capable of making the Chicago River "run up hill," as the saying went, could achieve just about anything.

Chicagoans seemed to have unflappable belief in their city's ability to recover. Only a few days after the Great Chicago Fire, a man in the grain business was said to have been confronted by a zealous Chicago booster while completing his trade at a railroad yard. According to the booster, a representative of the *Chicago Tribune*, the grain shipper offered to give up his train car to another businessman, saying, "You can have that car. I had it partly loaded for Chicago; but there is no Chicago now." Unable to restrain his urban loyalties, the booster then stepped forward. "Wait a little," he insisted, trusting the tenaciousness of his hometown, "and see if there isn't a Chicago." Similar spirit comes through in a telegram sent from Chicago on October 11, 1871, just after the fire, to New York, by a Chicago business. The telegram directs:

Send two cases steamboat cards, $500 worth Faber's pencils, $300 worth Eagle pencils, One case each, 5 and 6, in German S.S. pencils, One cask Arnold's quarts, $18,000 worth of school books, assorted, 200 gross Gillott's 303 pens, 100 gross Gillott's 404 ones, 50 gross Gillott's 170 ones, 100 gross Estabrook's pens, assorted, One cask, Arnold's pints and half pints.

Mentioning nothing at all about the recent calamity, and speaking only of business, the telegram exemplified the undaunted nature of the Chicago character and was considered fascinating enough to warrant reprinting in both the *New York Tribune* and the *Chicago Evening Post*.[11]

While people across the country were busy worrying about keeping the problems of Chicago away from their backyards, Chicagoans considered the quickest possible ways to reshape their public image and physically rebuild their city. They wanted to call attention to the rebirth of their city after the fire, a rebuilding so substantial that the area's residents took to calling their city "New Chicago." The first large-scale effort to battle negative images of the city spurred by the fire was the Inter-State Industrial Exposition. Held yearly between 1873 and 1890, the fair lasted approximately two weeks during each run. The city utilized the empty exposition space for other cultural events throughout the year. Although of great significance to the Chicagoans of its day as a symbol of rejuvenation, the exposition has largely been forgotten by twentieth century urban historians.

Noted architect W. W. Boyington designed the Inter-State Industrial Exposition Building, reminiscent of London's Crystal Palace of 1851 with its iron framework and glass window-walls. The Chicago version of the glass building, historian Ross Miller points out, was made of opaque glass rather than the translucent glass of the Crystal Palace and similar exposition structures in Paris and Vienna (built in 1867 and 1873 respectively). Miller concludes that the opaque quality of the glass and the conventional roof of the building offered a solidity that the more playful European designs failed to provide, a solidity more in keeping with attempts to stabilize post-fire Chicago's shaky public image. Completed in 1873, the structure stood on the lake front site which would later be the home of the Art Institute of Chicago. Measuring two hundred by eight hundred feet, it stretched between Monroe and Jackson streets on Michigan Avenue, Chicago's premier address. Conceived in part as a memorial to the fire, the building stood on land that contained buried fire debris. But the structure spoke more directly to the progress made since the fire than the actual tragedy. Boyington and the exposition organizers considered the building to be a model for a new type of temporary architecture, a style that could influence future designers.[12]

The Inter-State Industrial Exposition marks the beginning of Chicago's fascination with the use of fairs as public relations devices. Although the well-attended River and Harbor Convention of 1847, two Sanitary Commission fairs during the Civil War, state fairs, United States fairs, and numerous national political party conventions had been held in Chicago before the fire, these events had not stemmed from the same high-minded local booster spirit which would drive Chicago's larger spectacles—the Inter-State Exposition, the World's Columbian Exposition (1893), and the Century of Progress (1933–1934). A handful of county and state fairs held in Chicago were in fact so linked with risky real estate speculation that the organizers of the Inter-State felt obliged to testify to the credibility of their event. Some of these small-scale fairs had been staged simply as ruses to interest buyers in dubious land deals. The guide to the first year's fair soothed, "The present enterprise is earnest and honest in its endeavor, there are not speculators in it, no member of the board of directors sells any ground or has any contract."[13]

As a grand scheme to rewrite Chicago's public image, The Inter-State Industrial Exposition proved unsuccessful. Although some fair planners were level-headed enough to admit that the first year's Inter-State might not be "justly styled 'International' or even 'Inter-State,'" they hoped later editions of the event would bring outside recognition to Chicago. Most exhibitors throughout the fair's history were Chicagoans. Although the planners claimed to be happy with attendance of less than one hundred thousand visitors a year, this limited attendance spoke to the local flavor of the fair. The Inter-State did not generate enough positive press to qualify it as an urban advertising device of national scale. Although its boosters claimed that "the general appearance of the Exposition, is by far, more impressive and pleasing than that of anything of the kind every [sic] gotten up in this country," the fair was known to few outside Chicago. The industrial fair sparked almost no coverage in the newly popular national magazines and national papers. Most of the out-of-town visitors probably learned of the event through some sort of personal contact with the businesses displaying goods at the fair or through the tens of thousands of free posters the exposition officials distributed to the railroad lines leading into Chicago. Certainly the Inter-State, like its successors the Columbian Exposition and the Century of Progress, succeeded in one of its underlying goals—bringing increased revenues to area businesses during times of economic difficulty. Revenues came from the sale of goods at all three major Chicago expositions as well as the ancillary services offered to out-of-town fair goers, including lodging, meals, and transportation. But as a means to influence the general public's opinion of Chicago, the Inter-State fair proved ineffective at best.[14]

The fair organizers believed that the Inter-State fulfilled a need that existed even before the city's calamity—a need for space to display and sell commercial goods. The achievement of this desire showed the nation that Chicago was back on the track of urban progress. The fair spokesman claimed:

> The need of an exposition has long been apparent to the people of Chicago. The growth of the city was wonderful beyond precedent, and it seems as if, in the rush of rapid accumulation, some of the important details of a metropolis were neglected; but now that we have risen to the undisputed point of being the great city of the West—the little twin-sister of the national metropolis in fact—that our stability is unquestioned, that we have been weighed in the balance of fire and not found wanting, the importance of having some distinct and emphatic exponent of our wealth and commerce becomes an absolute necessity, and the great 'Inter-State Exposition of Chicago' is the result.[15]

The Inter-State Exposition grew out of the efforts of the Woolen Manufacturers' Association to establish a permanent annual fair for textiles in the Midwest. The group had previously adopted a system of migratory expositions, but this had become cumbersome. In February of 1873, the association, led by its president George S. Bowen, along with Chicago area manufacturers of different types, led unofficially by James Nowlan, met in Chicago's Gardner House. They discussed the possibility of combining efforts to organize a broad-based industrial exposition. Enthusiasm for the idea caught on quickly; by late February, after only two meetings, the group established fixed plans. On March 1, a resolution was offered and accepted that the exposition open in the fall of 1873, in a building to be built on the lake front, with capital stock for the event set at $150,000. Subsequently, planners raised the stock to $250,000. Just eight days after the initial resolution, the Chicago Chamber of Commerce met, officially naming the fair "The Inter-State Industrial Exposition of Chicago," and securing articles of incorporation. By April 10, the corporation named its first board of directors, including hotel owner Potter Palmer as President and *Chicago Tribune* editor and then Chicago Mayor Joseph Medill as one of the Vice Presidents.[16]

Because of the swiftness and sure-footed organization of the exposition, it epitomized the spirit of the city for many Chicagoans. The exposition guidebook proclaims, "It, itself, is the history of Chicago in miniature—it rose up in a day, and it is magnificent in its conception and its accomplishment. The exposition is a monument to that peculiar energy which amazes the world and confounds our contemporaries." Where less than two years earlier nothing but ruins could be seen, an architectural wonder shot up in less than four months. "If any further evidence was needed to convince the stranger of the indomitable pluck, enterprise, and energy of the people of Chicago," the exposition guide to Chicago explained, "a visit to the Exposition Building is all-sufficient for that purpose." Building began on June 16th and was completed on September 25.

Architect W.W. Boyington took on the project at very short notice, and the contractors agreed to have the building ready for occupancy by September 15. The contractors earned a $1,000 bonus for every day earlier they finished, and paid a fine for every day they extended the work past the deadline. The land used for the space had been donated to the city by the national government for use as a public park; the City Council initially passed along rights to the exposition for one year, and renewed the privilege each year. The building which housed the World's Fair Congresses (of the World's Columbian Exposition) and became home to the Chicago Art Institute later replaced the exposition building. [17] By the early 1890s, the once dazzling Inter-State building had begun to fall into disrepair. Designed to last only one year, the building grew unsafe with continued use. In 1890 Judge Murray F. Tuley issued an injunction, closing the exposition building temporarily. Boyington's building was razed to make way for the new structure in 1892.[18]

In keeping with the Chicago tradition of maintaining every possible bit of numerical data associated with a metropolitan event, fair organizers counted the building supplies used in their new structure and printed their findings in exposition guides. Surely it would be "of interest to our readers," they insisted, to know that "1,716,000 bricks; 4,200 cubic feet of stone; 3,000,000 feet of lumber; 1,500 squares of tin, each 10 by 10 feet; 133 tons of bolts, nuts and plates; 4,600 feet of galvanized iron cornices; 1,000 feet of galvanized iron conductor-pipe; 7,000 feet of glass in the windows; 5,000 feet of sheet glass in the ventilators, and 27,000 feet of ribbed glass in the sky-lights" went into the building.[19]

The building offered display space of 230,000 square feet within its walls, with an additional 20,800 square feet in two free-standing exhibition sheds. A large center ring lamp with sixty gas burners provided light for night events. Restaurants were located within the exposition for the comfort of visitors. Open every day except for Sunday from 9 A.M. to 10 P.M., admission was $.50 for adults and $.25 for children on weekdays, and $.25 for adults and $.15 for children on Saturdays. Fair authorities categorized goods for display into eight groups: fine and liberal arts, objects for dwell-ings and personal wear, minerals, raw materials, instruments and machin-ery, products of the farm, food and tobacco, and natural history. In response to a growing disinclination on the part of manufacturers to submit their products to award committees (the awards being considered crass by some), the executive committee of the exposition decided against competition for prizes among the exhibitioners.[20]

In addition to conceiving of the fair as a way to display goods, the ex-position organizers understood that the event could change the national im-age of Chicago. They worried that other Americans believed their city to be a financial risk, a speculative bubble ready to burst at the slightest provoca-tion. The fire, as attested to by the chaos on Wall Street when the news broke, had damaged Chicago's business reputation. The Inter-State Exposi-tion, they hoped, would demonstrate Chicago's continued financial health. According to the exposition boosters, Chicago's continued successes were in the hands of the highest of powers, a force that had designed the city so as to maximize its economic fortunes. The organizers wrote:

> Chicago is simply the inevitable result of a prophetic intention. When God dropped the lakes into their places, and unfolded the millions of acres of the bursting West beyond them, and pressed his finger at the base of the great lake, indenting a river mouth, He—speaking with rev-erence—He meant business. As surely, by the law of gravitation the ap-ple fell before Newton's eyes, so surely was a great city to rise at the river's mouth and the base of the lake, to be the great clearinghouse be-tween the producers on the west of it and the consumers of the entire East.[21]

The Inter-State Exposition formally opened on September 25, 1873 with 25,000 people in attendance. Newly elected Chicago Mayor Lester Legrant Bond, Illinois Governor John L. Beveridge, and Senators John A. Logan and Richard Oglesby gave welcoming speeches. The crowds were pleased with a number of the building's pleasing curiosities, including an ori-ental pagoda devoted to selling candy, a central fountain, an elevator, and the 165 foot glass dome in the center of the space.[22]

Perhaps most intriguing of all the exposition exhibits, the fine arts sec-tion of the fair, received high praise from Chicagoans and even a few on-lookers from outside the city. Much of the high style of the collection came from the work of art agent Sara Tyson Hallowell, just twenty-seven years old at the opening of the Interstate. Hallowell brought impressionism and the "modern art" of the day to Chicago. The 1873 Exposition featured the paintings of Whistler, Sargent, Chase, Eastman Johnson, Rousseau, Daubigny, Corot, Millet, and their followers. The most popular attraction of the collection, a work by Edward Armitage of the Royal Academy of London, and presented to Chicago by the owners of the *London Graphic* for display in the city's new city hall, portrayed Chicago as an unclothed woman. A fair guide book described:

> Hence he portrays a vigorous Chicago entirely stripped of her beautiful clothing of purple which the last vestige is seen still smoking, and, though losing all of her possessions, yet she has escaped from personal injury. America has partially raised the fainting form, has administered a stimulating cordial, and, as though she had done all in her power, now turns to Britannia, who comes to her aid with vigor and fresh strength.

The 1890 Exposition was perhaps the most remarkable of Hallowell's Inter-State exhibits, featuring paintings by Monet and Pissarro, as well as a pastel by Degas. New York art critic Montague Marks of *Art Amateur* supported Hallowell's work over the years, believing the shows equal or beyond that of similar events on the East Coast. In 1885 Marks insisted, "Largely due to the personal efforts of that extremely intelligent and energetic lady, Chicago this year has anticipated New York, Boston and Philadelphia in exhibiting the important American pictures from the last [European] Salon."[23]

The Inter-State Exposition opened each year between September and October in its specially-designed structure. In the fair's dormant months, other events took place in the lake front building, including the 1880 and 1884 Republican national conventions. The Republicans nominated James Garfield there in 1880, and Grover Cleveland in 1884. The 1885 renovation by architects Adler and Sullivan took place at the behest of real estate tycoon Ferdinand Peck, who wanted to improve the acoustics of the large hall so that a summer music festival featuring New York's famous maestro Theodore Thomas could be staged in Chicago. Adler and Sullivan added six thousand seats to the hall, and made changes so that each instrument could be heard distinctly. The success of the Thomas engagement led to the construction of Adler and Sullivan's Auditorium Theatre, conceived of and built between 1886 and 1889, across Michigan Avenue from the exposition.[24]

On a much larger scale, Chicagoans staged the world's fair that would commemorate the four hundredth anniversary of Christopher Columbus' arrival in the western hemisphere, and would advertise the attributes of their city to a wide American and international audience. The World's Columbian Exposition, held a year after the true anniversary of Columbus' voyage (1893), signified triumph over the disastrous fire for its Chicago planners, as well as a chance to show-off local and national progress. The Columbian Exposition would testify to the great achievements of the American people since Columbus' arrival in the Western Hemisphere. The location of the fair in Chicago seemed to indicate that Chicagoans could legitimately link their city to the central story of American progress. Henry Steele Commager terms the event the watershed moment of American history because of the way it marked a time of great change. He explains:

> On one side lies an America predominantly agricultural; concerned with domestic problems; conforming, intellectually at least, to the political, economic, and moral principles inherited from the seventeenth and eighteenth centuries... On the other side lies the modern America, predominantly urban and industrial; inextricably involved in world economy and politics...; experiencing profound changes in population, social institutions and habits of thought to conditions new and in part alien.[25]

Despite its importance as an American event, however, the exposition did not, in the last analysis, provide the level of cultural capital hoped for by its local sponsors. The World's Columbian Exposition fell between a series of scandals for Chicago, and the event seemed at the outset the answer to the boosters' prayers for a powerful way to advertise their city's attributes. The scandals Chicago experienced in the late 1800s are well known; a recitation of the unflattering images of the city created in their wake need not be explored at length here. 1886 brought the Haymarket Affair, the disastrous bombing and resulting violent melee that brought the deaths of seven policemen and several civilians. Although authorities never determined the source of the bomb, they tried and convicted eight anarchists for the murders. The event sparked an international debate over worker's rights, free speech, and capital punishment. Chicago's image suffered. And in 1894, workers laboring for Pullman's palace car manufacturing plant protested against wage cuts and high rents in their company town, and went on strike under the leadership of Eugene Debs and the American Railway Union. This event further linked Chicago's name with conflicts between rich and poor, and recent immigrants versus more long-standing American population groups. Despite the hopes of Chicago boosters, the elaborately conceived fair did not cast the sufficiently impressive cultural legacy necessary to reverse Chicago's increasingly negative image. While the efforts by the boosters on behalf of their city draw our attention for their intensity, the story of the Columbian Exposition, like that of the Interstate Exposition, is more noteworthy for its underlying intentions than its ultimate affect.

Calls for a Columbian celebration came from many different quarters across the United States and the Americas, dating back as far as the Philadelphia Centennial Exposition of 1876. Inspired by the Centennial, Carlos W. Zaremba of Mexico sent out circulars to foreign ministers in Washington in 1884; Zaremba gathered some positive responses for a fair in Mexico City but could not inspire momentum for fair organization. Alexander D. Anderson, secretary of the board of trade of Washington, D.C., spoke of the desirability of such an affair in an interview with the *New York Herald* in 1884. In Missouri, where interest in hosting an international exposition ran high, a convention of western states met to consider the possibility of a fair.[26]

Dr. A.W. Harlan, the first to write to publicly on the fair in Chicago, authored a letter to the *Chicago Times* in early 1882. In 1885, Edwin Brown and George Mason brought the idea of holding a world's fair in Chicago to the directors of the Inter-State Exposition. The Chicago *Inter-Ocean* published an editorial endorsing the idea. By 1888, Chicago Judge Henry M. Shepard started a movement to launch a fair; members of Chicago's elite club scene met to make plans, but their interest and commitment soon waned.

Chicago's final and successful push came from Mayor De Witt C. Creiger, who, acting on the suggestion of local newspapers and some of the city's elite, read a message to the city council on July 22, 1889 calling for the formation of a group to lobby the federal government for the right to hold a world's fair. The city council, voting to support Creiger's initiative, named a panel of one hundred prominent Chicago personages. At the mayor's suggestion, the city council expanded the organizing committee to two hundred and fifty-six Chicagoans. Other cities formed similar groups in order to win the chance to remember the deeds of Columbus, but Chicago pushed forward with its characteristic buoyant booster spirit. The fair committee resolved that "Men who helped build Chicago want the Fair and having a just and well-sustained claim they intend to have it."[27]

In August, an executive committee of thirty-five was chosen out of the large organizing committee. This committee formed the basis of a corporation, formally titled the "World's Exposition of 1892." On August 15, 1889, the Secretary of State of Illinois granted articles of incorporation and the right to solicit subscriptions for world's fair stock to Mayor Creiger and six Chicagoans from the executive committee.[28]

But, as the 1894 *Campbell's Illustrated History of the World's Columbian Exposition* explained, the fair "was not secured for the city of Chicago without struggle, or for that matter a series of struggles." Congress would decide which American city would ultimately win the right to hold the exposition. The rivalry provoked by the race dismayed many onlookers in its fierce nature. Francis A. Walker, writing for *Forum*, commented, "To me there appears something contemptible in inducing cities to bid against each other for the supposed profits of holding such an exhibition." [29]

Chicago, New York, St. Louis, and Washington, D.C. emerged as the leading contenders for the fair site. The main battle, however, clearly lay between New York and Chicago. National public opinion during the early years of the competition favored New York. Many Americans remained unable to conceive of the young and inland Chicago, so recently devastated by fire, as an appropriate showcase for American achievement. Public commentators deemed Chicago too provincial to merit serious consideration; neither did many feel it capable of attracting enough international business interests to its doors. Captain Charles King, great-grandson of Senator Rufus King of New York, wrote of the improbability of Chicago as the chosen city. New York could claim experience as a fair host as well as many years of American cultural leadership. In an 1891 edition of *Cosmopolitan*, King recalled, "Who that witnessed the destruction of New York's beautiful Crystal Palace in '59 would have dared to prophesy then and there that the World's Columbian Exhibition [sic], the greatest of the Century, would be opened in 1893, not in the Empire City, but in that far-away frame-shanty metropolis, spreading like dandelions over the prairies of Illinois."[30]

A local publication, *The Chicago Record's History of the World's Fair*, published in 1893, concurred. "New York's acknowledged position as the metropolis of the western hemisphere and the commercial center of the country gave it an advantage in the contest which very many persons believed would render it invincible," the instant-history admitted. Chicago's inland position hampered its claim to win the fair, as did its "supposed provincialism," and its "rawness and lack of resources and culture." And industrialist Andrew Carnegie remembered in 1894 the way in which the East had balked at Chicago's bid. Writing in the world's fair issue of *Engineering Magazine*, Carnegie mused:

> When it was decided that the discovery of the country by Columbus should be celebrated, it seemed to be taken for granted at first that there was but one proper place for the ceremony. Soon, however, a second claimant intimated its advantages, but the East was slow to realize that there was anything to be said for the western city. The people of the eastern Atlantic States travel far too little westward. The mention of Chicago as a possible site generally created a smile on the face of the citizens of New York.[31]

Congress held the legal power over the selection of the world's fair city. The various interested states took action in both the Senate and the House of Representatives. Prospective cities had bills submitted on their behalf; Senator Shelby M. Cullom of Illinois introduced a bill in the Senate on December 19, 1889 that would make Chicago the capital of the Columbian festivities, and Congressman George E. Adams brought a similar bill to the House on December 20. The Senate bill made its way to a special fair committee, while Adam's bill was referred to the committee on foreign affairs. A pro-Chicago lobbying body was formed, with ex-congressman George R. Davis serving as chairman and Mayor Creiger as the nominal head. According to the *World's Columbian Exposition Souvenir*, the fight for the fair became "the most spirited ever witnessed in the halls of congress [*sic*]."[32]

The lobbying efforts resulted in the presentation of protracted arguments before the Senate special committee. St. Louis representatives presented their case on January 8, 1890. Speaking for his city, Col. Charles H. Jones insisted, "Were the nation's capital to be located now, in the light of existing conditions, and having in view the spread of the territorial area, the trend of population, and the development of transportation facilities, we think St. Louis would hardly have a competitor for the choice." He calculated that the population within a five hundred mile radius of St. Louis exceeded that of New York and Chicago, and steadfastly refuted charges that his city had miserable summer weather. St. Louis was not hotter than Chicago, Jones claimed. Another speaker, the Honorable E. O. Stannard, insisted that with St. Louis' unique combination of Yankee and southern character, all would feel at home.[33]

The spokesmen for Washington, D.C. emphasized that their city, already the nation's capital, best represented the nation as a whole. John W. Douglas, president of the Board of District Commissioners, provided opening remarks for Washington before the Senate committee on January 10 and explained his belief that "this being a great International Fair it should be sustained and carried on by the General Government at the capital of the nation." As Washington, D.C. had the smallest capital resources of any of the four final competitor cities, D.C. representative Alex Anderson put forth his committee's plan to fund the fair with national monies.[34]

Chicagoans argued for the selection of their city on January 11. Mayor Creiger praised the metropolis, saying, "In the short space of eighteen years, Chicago has grown to this imperial magnificence, and she now stands the highest type of all characteristics which have made this nation what it is, boldly claiming recognition." While New York had had two hundred years to mature, Creiger instructed his Senate listeners, Chicago had achieved greatness in the fifty-three years since its incorporation. Impressively, she had survived the ravages of fire. Railroad mogul and Chicagoan E.T. Jefferey also added his analysis; he enumerated all that Chicago offered a potential world's fair, including skilled engineers, several suitable sites, adequate funding, more railroad connections than any other city, cool weather, great public spirit, and a familiar setting for international businesses.[35]

Although rancor between the four contestant cities had reached high levels in local newspapers before the Senate debates, the Chicago representatives, like those of the other cities, tried to do what they could to soothe ruffled feathers in this formal setting. Creiger insisted, "There is no rivalry between the Empire City of America—New York—and the Empire City of the Great West—Chicago." His comments brought applause. Additionally, the Mayor added, "Gentlemen, we do not forget to accord to the other gateway to the Mississippi Valley—St. Louis—her advantages, but in so doing we ask [that] your judgment shall not be swerved from that marvel of the nineteenth century—Chicago!"[36]

Animosity between New York and Chicago had run deep during the months of preparation for the final battle. The *Chicago Tribune* had referred to New York as the "meanest city in America." In perhaps the most biting indictment, Charles A. Dana of the New York *Sun* had informed his readers to ignore "the nonsensical claims of that windy city [Chicago]. Its people could not build a World's Fair even if they won it." Dana spoke not of Chicago's weather, but of the Chicago boosters' tendency to thickly praise their hometown. Dana characterized them as full of hot air, or "windy." With this commentary, Dana settled upon Chicago the sobriquet—windy city—that it would bear until the present day. While the performances before the Senate were staid in comparison with the antics of the papers, Chicagoan Thomas Bryan felt compelled to defend his home against the attacks of New York in his testimony. "To the imputation to-day, and often before," Thomas said, "that whilst New York has moved forward with dignified and majestic step, Chicago has been sedulously occupied in 'brass-band and trumpet blowing performances,' allow me to say that the truth is precisely the reverse, as a comparison of the official circulars will show."[37]

New York, the nation's largest city, had its merits presented last. Following Chicago's presentation on January 11, the Honorable Chauncey M. Depew of New York downplayed the tensions of the last months. His remarks, while perhaps not entirely genuine, allow for an informative glimpse of his sense of the positive attributes of the competing cities. Depew insisted:

> While there has been some chaff and ridicule and raillery and pleasantry
> in the discussion of the claims of Washington and St. Louis, of Chicago
> and New York, I can say for New York that there has been no feeling
> other than the warmest, the kindest, and the most respectful for those
> other cities and their ambitions. We appreciate the public buildings and
> unequaled situation of Washington; the history, the location in the Mis-
> sissippi Valley and the future of St. Louis; and the commerce and trade,
> but in all the elements which constitute a great city, of art and culture,
> of Chicago.[38]

Depew, who would later offer the dedicatory address for the World's
Columbian Exposition in Chicago, took time to defend the distinctive elements of his city. The population of New York exceeded that of Chicago;
inside Manhattan, he claimed, lived three times the number that lived in Chicago. New York's location on an island made it ideal for visitors; the com-
pact land mass was easy to get around. New Yorker James Wood added that
New York reigned as a marketplace. "Other cities are the markets for certain districts only, as Chicago for the Northwest, St. Louis for the Central
West, etc., but New York receives from all," Wood said.[39] Although few
stated it outright, the trade generated by a world's fair was an important
component of its function. Wood was right to cite New York's high level of
commerce, but he had inaccurately portrayed Chicago, which could claim
world-class trade status by this time.

The final decision regarding the placement of the fair was to be made by
the House of Representatives. On the fateful day, February 24, 1890, the
House chamber "was crowded almost to suffocation." On the first ballot,
305 votes were cast, Chicago capturing 115, New York 50, St. Louis 61,
Washington 58, and Cumberland Gap 1. Chicago won the matter on the
eighth ballot with 157 votes to New York's 107, St. Louis' 25, and Washington's 18. National periodicals retold the story of this final vote over and
over again in their pages. One wonders, would the moment have been so often referred to if New York had claimed the prize? The remarks reveal underlying disbelief; clearly the underdog had won the day, but the process by
which this had occurred proved mystifying.[40]

Celebratory Chicagoans greeted the nearly one hundred members of the
city's Washington delegation upon their return home. Among the revelers
paraded the Chicago-based chapter of the Sons of New York, complete with
banners and placards representing every county of their previous home
state.[41] Across the country, some raised voices of protest against the government's choice. Others expressed the sentiment that this recognition of Chicago was long over-due.

In looking back at the history of Chicago's first world's fair, we must remember that historical memory is influenced by the concerns of the present day. Today, the World's Columbian Exposition primarily invokes thoughts of a positive tone. As we begin the twenty-first century, the quaint architecture of the fairgrounds appears inspiring. The event itself, a watershed in its own time, symbolizes the American Victorian period—an era of great nostalgia presently. Antique collectors now hunt for Columbian Exposition memorabilia. Clara Burnham's 1894 world's fair story, *Sweet Clover*, finds a popular audience once again as a work of romantic fiction. But the concern of this work is to evaluate the image of Chicago in national popular culture over a period of one hundred years—tracing the attempts of local boosters to mold the image of their city, and following the reaction to these attempts in popular culture. Of course, any method that attempts to evaluate past culture is tinged with present-day values, as much as we might try to filter them out of our work. But closely analyzing what cultural critics contemporary to an event have to say about it is much different than overtly applying our own opinions. Although we might remember the World's Columbian Exposition with fondness, the event cannot be considered entirely successful at the task of raising the nation's esteem for Chicago.

On April 25, after months of campaigning, Chicagoan's dreams of acquiring world recognition for their city became reality as President Benjamin Harrison signed the act officially declaring Chicago the fair site. Due to the late date of the decision, the act stipulated that the fair be held in 1893 rather than the correct Columbian anniversary of 1892. Although the boosters' dreams of winning the fair had been met, Chicago's difficulties were not over. Even this initial legislation contained hints of the struggles to come, struggles well-broadcast in the fair reports published by the local and national media. Harrison's proclamation required that "satisfactory proof has been presented to me that provision has been made for adequate grounds and buildings for the uses of the World's Columbian Exposition, and that a sum of not less than $10,000,000 to be used and expended for the purposes of said Exposition" before the federal government would grant final permission to hold the fair. Hubert Howe Bancroft's massive history of the fair, published in 1893, explained that "though somewhat stringent in its conditions, the terms of the act were accepted [by Chicago's local commission], not, however, without forebodings of evil from undue influence on the part of the National Commission."[42]

Initial world's fair tensions included disputes over authority between the National Commission, supposedly representing the nation's interest, and the Local Commission, representing Chicago's concerns. The creation of the national oversight committee displayed a lack of confidence in Chicago's organizational abilities. The existence of the two governing bodies complicated the already prodigious project. Confusion reigned over the authorities of the respective commissions. One important source of discord was the question of contact with potential exhibitors—which commission would wield this important control? National media quickly reported on the controversy. A reporter for *Harper's Weekly*, in November of 1890, found the array of national and local bodies "bewildering." Although the journalist admitted that "order has been gradually evolving out of the somewhat chaotic order of things," he worried about the "lack of clearness, also, as to the extent of the authority of the National Commission." The act of Congress creating the National Commission indicated that the body should "generally have charge of all intercourse with the exhibitors and representatives of foreign nations." The national group understood this statement as designating them the power over all fair exhibitors, while the local group read this as a command over foreign exhibitors only.[43]

Another site of contention involved the national organization's role as liaison between the fair and the federal government; the organization would ultimately be the judge of the fair's "character," deciding whether or not the affair warranted governmental approbation. As mentioned, the National Commission had to approve plans for the fair site and the provisions for buildings, as well as certify that all necessary fair finances were in place before President Harrison would give the fair his final go-ahead and would invite foreign nations to participate in the event. On November 25, 1890, the National Commission did grant its certification to the Chicago body, stating that it had met the conditions of Harrison's original April 1890 decree. Harrison issued a proclamation on December 24, 1890, announcing the official opening of the fair for May 1, 1893 and the closing for not earlier than the last Thursday in October, 1893.[44]

The National Commission consisted of two commissioners from each state, one a Democrat and one a Republican, with two official state alternates. Thomas W. Palmer of Michigan served as the national president. Palmer had built a fortune as a real estate and lumber speculator in Detroit, and had served Michigan as a state senator and as a U.S. senator. Palmer resigned his appointment as United States Minister to Spain when placed on the national fair commission.[45]

The Director-General of the entire World's Columbian Exposition, chosen by the local committee and accepted by the national body as its leader on September 15, 1890, was Colonel George R. Davis. Davis led an executive committee of twenty-six members, half Democrats and half

Republicans, representing the National Commission. The executive body would sit permanently in Chicago, so as to be better able to direct the fair than the larger National Commission. Born in Massachusetts in 1840, Davis served in the Union Army during the Civil War and then settled in Chicago. Davis worked with the local militia until he won a seat in Congress as a Republican in 1878. At the time of his appointment as Director-General, Davis was serving as Treasurer of Cook County.[46]

On April 4, 1890, stockholders of the World's Columbian Exposition in Chicago elected forty-five local citizens to serve as the directorate of the Local Commission. Later in April, the directory members chose their own leaders from among their ranks: Lyman J. Gage, Vice President of the First National Bank of Chicago, as President of the commission, Thomas B. Bryan, attorney and a previous president of a Chicago-based Sanitary Fair, as First Vice President, hotel mogul Potter Palmer as Second Vice President, and A.F. Seeberger, head of a wholesale hardware firm, as Treasurer. The Local Commission gave Gage a salary of $6,000 yearly, Bryan a salary of $12,000 yearly (to compensate him for a law practice he could not presumably live without), and Seeberger a salary of $5,000 yearly. The wealthy Potter Palmer would serve without a salary.[47]

A writer for *Harper's Weekly*, one of the most widely circulated periodicals of its day, stated, "The impression conveyed to the casual observer hitherto by the movements of those officially concerned with the Fair has been that of a lot of people suddenly given a task to perform without any definite conception as to how it was to be done." Men from one body were sent to gather information already in possession of another group, reported the paper, and such bureaucratic bungling led to the swift resignation of the Local Commission Vice-President Thomas Bryan, although he had been a committed fair supporter from early in the process.[48]

Realizing the negative light in which comments of this kind cast Chicago's endeavor, editor J.B. Campbell of the *World's Columbian Exposition Illustrated* attempted to discount rumors of bureaucratic unrest. "Too much has been made by inconsiderate persons of the apparent lack of harmony between the Local and National authorities of the Exposition," commented the Chicago magazine, continuing," That some friction exists cannot be denied. Neither is it desirable to be in a position to deny it. There never was an exposition given at which similar disputes did not arise." Chicago's own nationally distributed cultural journal, *Dial*, conceded that one might rightly criticize the fair management on many points (which the magazine did do), but also weakly complimented the organizers on their lack of "jobbery" and their "self-sacrificing devotion" to the planning.[49]

The jumble of administrative committees led to significant questions over the jurisdiction of various aspects of the fair and considerable repetition of tasks. In response to the confusion, national and local officials agreed to form a jointly-run body, the Board of Reference and Control. Eventually, even the Board proved too unwieldy, and the Council of Administration, composed of only four members, took up ultimate authority. H. N. Higinbotham and Charles H. Schwab of the local directory and George V. Massey and J. W. St. Clair of the national commission served on the Council. This coordination led to some decrease in friction between national and local concerns. Yet untrusting government officials still ordered the formation of a special Congressional body to investigate the fair on the issue of national-local problems.[50]

Given that the world's fair was to represent an anniversary important to the national government (and indeed historically significant to all the Americas), the United States government understandably involved itself in matters of fair organization. Primarily, however, the Congress' continued interest in the most mundane aspects of the fair reflected a distrust of Chicago fair officials, and a continued disbelief that this seemingly backwater town had the cultural resources to produce such an important spectacle. Congressman John Candler, a representative of Massachusetts and an earlier critic of the fair organizers, headed a committee to investigate the exposition management in 1891. Suspiciously, of all the possible states to be represented on that committee, two unsuccessful applicants for the job of hosting the fair, New York and Missouri, had delegates. The group came to Chicago on November 14, 1890, and presented their report to the House of Representatives on January 17, 1891. Speaking with the *New York Times*, New York Congressman Roswell P. Flower, a committee member, expressed "The first thing I propose to learn, if possible, is who is running this fair. The next thing is how the commission is spending the money appropriated by Congress."[51] Although the investigation added to the tinge of dishonor coloring the exposition, the final "Candler Committee Report" chastised the National Commission's management techniques rather than that of the Local Commission. The Congressmen found the National Commission to be operating outside its purview, taking up powers not originally in its jurisdiction, but rather under the authority of the local body.

Money issues remained a persistent source of tension between the national and local representatives, despite the Chicagoans unprecedented initial fundraising. Chicago's strong financial commitment to the endeavor had been a key element in its winning the right to hold the fair. An 1892 guidebook to Chicago pointed out the importance of Chicago's spirited and generous business community, saying, "This is one of the reasons why Chicago secured the Fair: it was a case where 'money talked.'" In the application stage, Chicagoans' hopes had been threatened by lack of money; finance sub-committee chairman Lyman J. Gage had gathered pledges of $2.5 million, but he knew this sum could not fulfill the needs of an elaborate fair. Luckily a newly organized sub-committee with Otto Young as chairman managed to find pledges of $5 million through a carefully organized solicitation process that targeted each Chicago trade group individually. Wealthy Chicago businessmen gave generously; palace railroad car maker George Pullman alone contributed $100,000 to the endeavor.[52] These extensive pledges had impressed Congressional decision makers, swaying their votes for Chicago.

Chicago added to the financial pot by issuing bonds for an additional $5 million. However, even during the period of fair construction it became clear that such sums were not adequate. Chicago asked Congress for a loan of an additional $10 million, on the grounds that the affair was a national, rather than a local, event. Congress disagreed with this analysis, however. Although President Harrison concurred that such an amount was not egregious, the Congressional members distrusted Chicago. A new bill would have allowed the Treasury to coin $5 million in souvenir coins for the exposition, the coins to be passed on to Chicago for resale. After opponents in Congress filibustered this bill, a new act authorizing the minting of $2.5 million worth of coins was introduced and was passed by the House in the summer of 1892. Local officials guessed that up to seventy percent of the coins would be kept by their purchasers as souvenirs.[53]

Heated debates over whether or not officials of the World's Columbian Exposition could open the fair on Sundays also degraded the reputation of the event and of Chicago itself. As we shall see, Christians remained divided on the subject; some supported closing and some considered closure to be a misreading of Christian scripture. The debate brought an unwanted type of attention to the upcoming fair. Many Americans expected something of this nature to befall the scandalous Chicago. In May of 1893, a *Harper's Weekly* cover portrayed crowds unsuccessfully trying to enter the exposition grounds. The controversy no doubt contributed to the low attendance during the first months of the fair. A variety of orthodox Christian groups, including the evangelical American Sabbath Union and the Columbian Sunday Association, appealed to fair officials to keep the gates of the exposition closed. Initially the decision seemed to rest with the local officials; indeed, many national officials wanted to shift responsibility for this public relations hot-potato onto the local group. During the Fifth Session of the National

Commission, during September 1891, the national body resolved, "That, whereas, the question of opening or closing the doors of the National Fair on Sundays is one which belongs to the Chicago Board of Directors; and whereas, this Commission, under the Act of Congress, can only exercise supervisory power," they would only confront the question if they absolutely could not avoid it.[54] In this instance, the national advisors board willingly abdicated authority.

However, the act authorizing the minting of the world's fair souvenir coins stipulated that the fair close to the public on the Christian Sabbath. Pressure from religious groups led to the addition of the closure clause to the act. Beset with financial difficulties, the local directors had to accept the limitations of this new bill. The directors looked hopefully towards the 1892–1893 session of Congress; perhaps the hindrance could be lifted then. Although the closure order did remain, the weight of this proclamation was tempered by Congress' subsequent decision in March of 1893 to withhold approximately $570,000 of the $2.5 million appropriation[55]; the withholding, apparently an attempt to force the local commission to pay for exhibitors' prizes (what body ought to fund these awards being in dispute), seemed to nullify the Sabbath closing mandate.

Campbell's Illustrated History of the World's Columbian Exposition, an "instant-history" of the fair, asserted that, "perhaps no question, which has grown out of the location of the Columbian Exposition, has attracted more attention and feeling than that of the Sunday opening of the gates and the admission of visitors." Jackson Park, site of the Columbian "White City" (named for its whitewashed Beaux Arts structures), had been open to Sunday visitors since its creation. During the building of the "White City," home of the major exhibitions of the fair, Sunday visitors had toured the construction, eventually even paying admission to see the sights on the Lord's Day.[56]

Debates raged over the proper course of action. Carefully detailing the pro-closure position, Professor Herrick Johnson wrote for the Christian magazine, *Our Day*. Johnson attempted to discredit the argument that working-class Americans, many of whom labored on Saturdays, would benefit from a Sunday fair. While Sunday openings might increase overall gate receipts, Johnson stated, he asked whether this expanded fair access was the desire of actual working people, or only those who claimed to speak for them. Johnson argued that Sunday visits to the fair would require exposition employees to labor, an outcome most of their fellow workers would abhor. Kindly employers would of course offer half-day vacations during the week while the fair ran, Johnson concluded. Foreign visitors would find the

Sunday openings strange, as they went against the beliefs of the nation. "There could be no more magnificent exhibit made to the assembled nations by this distinctly American city than an ideal American Sabbath," Johnson preached. And as for the often-repeated argument that the fair crowds, unable to pursue their true object, would fall into more vicious pursuits, Johnson could only scoff. He wrote "It is like antidoting [sic] the brothel by opening the whiskey saloon, and antidoting the whiskey saloon by opening the beer saloon, and antidoting the beer saloon by keeping men at Sunday labor."[57]

A wide variety of journals and spokespeople disputed such arguments. The Chicago cultural magazine, *Dial*, the comic magazine *World's Fair Puck*, and the *World's Columbian Exposition Illustrated* stood up for Sunday access, along with such figures as Samuel Gompers, Eugene Debs, and Elizabeth Cady Stanton. [58] The *World's Columbian Illustrated* pointed out that Sunday fairs would not be equivalent to the week-day versions—the machinery would be stopped, sales of displayed goods would be prohibited, and the numbers of employees would be kept to a minimum. *The World's Fair Puck* complained that given the current attitude of many in government, it would be made a crime to look at the Niagara Falls on Sunday; it would have to be fenced off, and all who peeked would be arrested. The magazine also joked, "The Hebrews seem to be more liberal than the Christians are. They have not yet clamored to have the Fair closed on Saturdays." *Puck* featured a full-color cartoon depicting international visitors watching Americans taking part in activities located outside the fair grounds—the antics of Buffalo Bill (who staged his show in Chicago during the fair), the pleasures of saloons, and beautiful dancing women—diversions presumably less well-suited to Sunday than those within the exposition. And in a publication paid for out of his own small salary, Chicago minister Reverend Henry C. Kinney asked "If this opening be a sin, as some say, would it be such a sin as would be equally as destructive to body or soul, as, say, theft, adultery, drunkenness, or bearing false witness?"[59]

Writing in the Christian journal *Arena*, Bishop J.L. Spalding put forth the idea that Christian Sundays centered on rest rather than unending worship. He wrote, "The essence of the observance of the Sunday consists in these two things: in worship and in rest from servile work. To ask men to remain all day long in church would be absurd." With a true day of liberty, Americans would learn to be grateful to Jesus. With more than a dollop of anti-Semitism, Spalding explained that the Christian Sabbath differed substantially from the prohibitive, "irrational" Jewish Sabbath and the Puritan Sabbath. The Puritan version incorrectly revived Jewish practices, according to the Bishop. "The Lord's Day was the symbol of victory," offered Spaulding, "of joy, peace and gladness, on which thoughts or practices suggestive of gloom and mortification [apparently his views of the rabbinical teachings] were wholly out of place."[60]

Bishop Henry C. Potter echoed Spaulding's sentiments, writing in the pages of *Nation* and *Forum*. Christ practiced Sunday differently than the Puritans; Christians could spend an appropriate and respectful Sunday in libraries, museums, or galleries, Potter asserted. Some worried that once Christians made concessions on Sundays they could never stop. Yet Potter said that knowing just where to stop could be considered the essence of Christian liberty.[61]

Reverend James De Normandie of Boston also published views against the closure of the event. Like Spaulding and Potter, De Normandie believed the Christian Sabbath to be about rest rather than restriction. "We are not under the laws of Moses, but the grade and truth of Jesus Christ," he scolded, continuing, "The authority of all commands, of all laws, is simply the proportion of eternal truth we find in them." With fair closure, people would become frustrated and turn to crime. De Normandie warned that the *Wine and Spirit Gazette* believed "a golden harvest is expected by the liquor-dealers of Chicago from the closing of the Fair on Sunday."[62] Elder Frederick W. Evans of the Mt. Lebanon congregation of Columbia County, New York, argued that all days of the week were equally holy. Evans considered the Sunday closure idea the result of old-fashioned attitudes. Linking his argument with the thinking that informed the fair's honoree, Christopher Columbus, he colorfully declared:

> For untold ages, the wise of this world thought the earth was flat. One man arose who said it was round, and that it turned around. The Christian Priests arrested, imprisoned and tortured him to death, just as they have arrested, imprisoned and killed the King of Tennessee [a Tennessean tortured for plowing his fields on a Sunday], who kept the true Sabbath, Saturday, and plowed his field on their Sabbath. Either open the World's Fair upon the seven Sabbath days, or close it upon the seven Sabbath days, and tax the Church and State 50,000 Balak Priests to pay the outlay and all the losses to the Exhibitors.[63]

The legal wrangling over the right of the exposition to operate on Sundays reveals the depth of the confusion over who ultimately bore authority for the event. On May 6, 1893, a stockholder of the World's Columbian Exposition company, Charles W. Clingman, made a formal demand that the fair open on Sunday; if his demand was not met, he would begin injunction proceedings against the exposition. During May 7, the first Sunday after the fair opened, Clingman demanded entrance to the fair grounds, but was rebuffed. He then filed an appeal in the state courts on May 14, declaring his rights as a stockholder violated. At the same time, a district attorney filed a federal injunction against Sunday openings. On May 17, the local directory, looking for a way to keep the fair open, voted to refund nearly $2 million of the souvenir coin monies to Congress and voted to open the grounds on Sundays. On Sunday, May 28, the fair stood open for visitors. Clingman's successful petition helped strengthen the legality of this move. Although the federal courts granted the injunction to close the fair on Sundays on June 8, the Cook County Circuit Court of Appeals cancelled the injunction on July 17. When fair organizers closed the gates again on July 23 in response to low Sunday attendance (potential fair guests could, of course, hardly keep the openings and closings clear enough to plan their visits), the Illinois State courts fined the directors for violating the Clingman petition. After this, the World's Columbian Exposition executives kept the fair open every day, even though Sunday attendance, often fifty to sixty percent lower than other days, left something to be desired.[64]

Another sore point between the national and local commissions involved the fair site. Many local officials pushed for placement of key fair buildings just east of the northern edge of the downtown on the lake front, while national officers believed a centralized placement in southern Jackson Park to be best. This conflict between the national and local leaders, publicized in articles like the *New York Times'* front-page "A Clash of Authority: Two World's Fair Committees in Juxtaposition," brought the credibility of the event down a notch or two.[65] After a protracted debate, the fair directors agreed to a physical plan for the World's Columbian Exposition. The central buildings of the fair, including its focus the "Court of Honor," found their home in Frederick Law Olmsted's beautifully redesigned Jackson Park, located south of downtown on Lake Michigan. The fair's concessions spread out down the narrow road, the Midway Plaisance, which sliced in close to the new University of Chicago just west of Jackson Park. The Midway Plaisance, often shortened to "Midway," hereafter leant its name to the concession/amusement areas of other fairs. The fair's fine arts building took up a lake front site north of the fairgrounds and just east of Chicago's main business area. And the southern park system's Washington Park, located at the western end of the Midway Plaisance, had some minimal usage as well.

Despite these troubles, the Columbian Exposition was not without enthusiastic supporters. Many touted the educational affects of the grand displays. Judge Benjamin Butterworth of the National Commission, in a speech on the status of the fair to a contentious House of Representatives in 1891, believed that "each intelligent visitor will have his mind sown with seed that may produce a rich harvest in the coming years." Chicagoans Teleford Burnham and James F. Gookins predicted that the fair would offer a great learning opportunity for all Americans. They wrote that the fair would be a place that "the high minded youth—the hope of the Nation [*sic*]—no matter from what State [*sic*] he comes, or how limited his purse, can easily attain these inestimable advantages, and at the same time study his fellow-men and their achievements, and thus learn at once the wisdom of the present and the past."[66]

Many proclaimed the exposition a site of educational opportunity. Noted Chicago novelist Henry B. Fuller proclaimed, "The 30th of October, 1893 [the last day of the fair] will be Chicago's graduation day. And the World's Columbian Exposition will be found to be no mere 'business college,' qualifying us narrowly for a narrow life and its narrow purposes, but a real and broad university—one to advance us in the arts, the sciences, the amenities, the humanities." Looking back at the fair, the booster editor J.B. Campbell concurred that "in a sense the Columbian Exposition was a vast cosmopolitan university." *Harper's Weekly*, although at times critical of the fair, also referred to it as, "that great university to which all can go for an admission fee of fifty cents." Steel magnate Andrew Carnegie raved, "Everyone who was privileged to spend days and evenings in windings in and out, through and among the palaces of the White City, and especially to saunter there at night when footsteps were few, has the knowledge to treasure up he has seen and felt the influence of the greatest combination of architectural beauty which man has ever created."[67]

The World's Columbian Exposition boasted of a tightly-run office of publicity, designed to stimulate positive press on the fair wherever possible. Established in December 1890, the department's staff of journalists, led by newspaperman Moses P. Handy, produced prodigious amounts of copy. The publicity department had four main goals: first, to advertise the aims of fair in order to encourage U.S. states and foreign nations to participate, second, to advertise the potential benefits of the fair, third, to write of the attractions of the fair, and fourth, to let the world know about the achievements of Chicago.[68]

By soliciting the names of prominent foreigners from diplomats, the department garnered a list of twelve thousand people living abroad to whom they sent weekly updates on the exposition. The office also sent the newsletter, *World's Fair Notes*, to ten thousand newspapers in the United States and seven thousand in other nations. Understanding the fair's physical structure to be its most noteworthy attribute, the department sent out one hundred thousand copies of a watercolor of the fair grounds by Charles Graham. Two thousand copies of the carefully structured fair guide, *After Four Centuries*, printed in a variety of languages, were widely dispersed. The publicity group kept track of the number of words written on the fair by sources around the world, and estimated that of the nearly five million words published on the exposition prior to May 1892, two million came from the pens of the department staff.[69] Certainly, the department could claim responsibility for much of the news of a pleasant tenor regarding the fair. However, even this great booster machine could not eradicate coverage of the tensions brewing between the national and local groups of fair organizers and other stains on the exposition.

Of all aspects of the Columbian exposition, the event's architecture garnered the most effusive praise. The Beaux Arts style structures, designed by supervisor Daniel Burnham's collection of architects from around the nation, were iron and steel frames covered with a plaster material called "staff" and white-washed. These buildings, while temporary, nonetheless created a historical atmosphere for visitors. Although the inside of the buildings were in effect nineteenth century versions of today's extended shopping malls, and very real indeed, the buildings' facades transported fair guests into a world of fantasy. Writing in *Engineering Magazine*, Henry Van Brunt, who himself designed for the fair, praised the structures, saying that they "expressed in terms of architecture the highest civilization of our times." Journalist M.A. Lane bestowed high laurels on the buildings, proclaiming, "With one or two exceptions, the buildings of the exposition are all among the most extensive structures with any pretensions to architectural beauty ever designed by man." Some architects of the day, however, complained that the majority of the writing on the buildings came from non-architects, a trend which stimulated undue appreciation for the designs.[70]

Although the great majority of the fair guests were pleased with what they saw on the exposition grounds, the fair proved to have only a mixed effect on the overall reputation of Chicago. Chicago boosters yearned for a newly cast image for their city, one that forever vanquished the troublesome tales of the Great Chicago Fire and linked the city with the nation's cultural leading lights, New York and Boston. Yet even the most highbrow of the fair's offerings, the extensive musical performances under the leadership of renowned conductor Theodore Thomas, came off badly. The planned opening concert by Poland's famed pianist, Ignace Jan Paderewski, faced attack by piano exhibitors at the fair as well as the National Commission. Paderewski always performed on his Steinway piano, but Steinway had no exhibit at the event and other piano manufacturers objected to Paderewski's prominent usage of his instrument. The piano exhibitors, with the National Commission and many Chicago papers at their side, found this violated their purchased rights to display their goods. Although the performance took place as planned on May 2, the near cancellation of the concert made a mockery of the fair's cultural pretensions. Chicago had lost points in precisely the field she had been hoping to gain them in this instance. Once again, the city appeared to be the leading center of no-holds-barred capitalism. Not even the concerns of this national celebration could quiet those worried about advertising their products. *Dial* editors announced, "The incredible insults that were...heaped upon him [Paderewski] must make many an outsider wonder if Chicago be a civilized city after all." The May 15 issue of *World's Fair Puck* depicted a frenzied Paderewski, his much-adored long locks flying, attempting to play on all the exhibitors' pianos simultaneously. The caption read, "A Peaceful Solution—At the Next Worlds' Fair Paderewski will play on all the pianos at once." The *Dial* lamented in June of 1893, "The disgraceful way in which, acting as the tools of a few unimportant piano manufacturers, certain members of the Chicago newspaper have recently attempted to attack Mr. Thomas and to asperse the sincerity of his motives, provides the history of music at the exposition with its one discreditable chapter." After his troubled presentation of Paderewski, Thomas fell ill for several days. [71]

Outside of this negative incident, on the whole Theodore Thomas' attempts to bring high-minded musical entertainment to the fair received little media coverage. Thomas' eighty-five piece Exposition Orchestra, formed two years before the event opened and considered the most technically skilled orchestra in the United States, drew limited crowds at the fair. Born in Germany, Thomas had come to America at ten years old in 1845. A violinist, Thomas turned to conducting and garnered attention as an orchestra leader. In 1889 Chicago businessman C. Norman Fay invited Thomas to Chicago to lead the country's first permanent orchestra. Thomas replied, "I would go to hell if they gave me a permanent orchestra." But although the Chicago Symphony Orchestra formed by Thomas became one of the chief cultural prides of Chicago, his Exposition Orchestra and his musical direction drew attacks from local newspapers. Visitors, it seems, did not take well to Thomas' very serious concerts, and his choice of largely Germanic composers had failed to inspire fairgoers. The dispersions eventually led to the conductor's resignation from the exposition. After Thomas' resignation, fair officials also threatened to dismiss its contracts with the fair musicians.

Thomas despaired of ever entertaining children or working-class Americans, whose musical tastes seemed to tend toward more accessible music.

Perhaps Americans were not ready to take in a full program of classical music as their recreation. Clover Van Tassel, protagonist of Clara Louis Burnham's romantic novel, *Sweet Clover: A Romance of the White City*, witnessed Thomas' failure to connect with the fair crowds. Burnham reports the scene clearly, yet adds her own twinge of mockery for the limited tastes of the mainstream American. In the novel, Clover watched "pleased hopefulness give way to apathy in many faces, as strange harmonies and dissonances fell upon uncultivated ears. She noticed one patient-faced countryman who waited through two numbers, evidently discovering nothing but a wilderness of sound. He then examined his programme, and not finding 'After the Ball' [a popular 1890s tune] on it, arose and departed from the hall more in sorrow than in anger."[72]

While some of the commentators referred to above had lauded the educational achievements of the fair, others, particularly those aware of the offerings of the exposition's lowbrow Midway, expressed concerns about the fair's overall affect. The Chicago *Dial*, usually broadly boosterish in tone, criticized the fair's attempts at public education. Writing in September 1893, even before the fair had concluded, one *Dial* writer admitted, "Amusement, of cheap and even vulgar sorts, is being substituted for education, because most people prefer being amused to being instructed." Fair organizers surrendered their initial highbrow aims, the reporter chided, for the stilted devices of the country fair—including an actual greased pole for fairgoers' climbing pleasure. The author stated, "Such pleasing novelties, announced in great variety from day to day, are converting the Exposition, as far as it is possible, into a huge circus (the [Midway] Plaisance furnishing the sideshows), and mark a process of degradation aptly described by its sponsors as that of 'barnumising [*sic*] the Fair.'"[73]

According to many accounts, the exhibits and concessions of the Midway Plaisance—including the Street of Cairo, the Working Man's Home, and the Irish Village—became the most readily accessible fair memories in the minds of numbers of visitors. The Midway, physically and philosophically separated from the White City, offered a home to all for-profit fair exhibits. The Midway grew out of an idea for a museum-like display of anthropological exhibits, known as Department M to fair planners. Although first headed by American Folk-lore Society president and Harvard professor Frederic Ward Putnam and categorized by the Smithsonian's G. Browne Goode, financial difficulties soon led to the appointment of entrepreneur and showman, twenty-two-year-old Sol Bloom, as Midway director.[74]

The depression, which hit the United States in 1893 just as the fair opened, compounded the initial monetary miscalculations on the part of the fair organizers. Although the fair prolonged Chicago's financial stability beyond that of many other American locales, the depression did affect fair investors and visitors. Bloom's flair for the eccentric became even more valuable in this climate. Bloom, born to Orthodox Jewish parents in Pekin, Illinois, had traveled to Paris for the 1889 Exposition Universelle and had signed a contract there to tour a group of Algerian performers—sword swallowers, dancing women, and other acts—in North and South America.[75] The group would entertain enthusiastic crowds in 1893.

The final incarnation of the Bloom-run Midway Plaisance differed greatly from the first round of plans. Fair organizers originally fretted about whether or not to allow paid concessions and exhibits of "lower" cultural value to participate in the Columbian Exposition at all. During the meeting of the National Commission in September of 1891, the officers decided that publicity concerning the existence of theatrical shows requiring extra fees on the fairgrounds damaged the overall reputation of the event. They resolved, "That it is the sense of this Commission that when the gates to the Fair are opened in 1892, the admission fee collected at the entrance should entitle the visitor to see everything on exhibition within the enclosure. In other words, there should be no side shows of any name or nature—theatres and snake charmers alike must be barred out."[76]

Under Bloom's stewardship, the Midway evolved into exactly what the national commissioners had most feared; the Midway had both theaters and snake charmers. Fairgoers flocked to Bloom's Midway; photographs of the amusement center always show it packed with crowds. Americans felt at ease on the Midway, which openly catered to their desires. While the White City also spoke to American materialism with its elaborate commercial and industrial displays, the Midway's sale of exotic scenes—the Javanese, the Dahomey—and its offering of adventure—including dancing girls and Ferris wheel rides—more openly commodified the fair experience in a way which struck Americans as familiar. Historian James Gilbert explains, "For just as commercialism and consumerism lay at the very heart of the White City that so ostentatiously disguised their existence in its artistic exteriors, so in the chaotic competitiveness of the Midway lay a kind of order imposed by the marketplace itself, which transformed each exhibit from the curious and unique into the accessibly exotic."[77]

"High-minded" cultural observers like the *Dial* did not approve, but many fairgoers found they wanted to spend a great deal of time on the Midway. Perhaps its lack of rigorous intellectual stimulation drew the crowds. While visitors compared the White City to a university, the Midway recalled the years of childhood instruction. A *Harper's Weekly* commentator believed this watered-down education the best possible means to instruct the great crowds of fairgoers. "It is well, therefore, that these [people] should be provided with the kinds of things that are likely to please them," the journalist wrote, "for there are many men and women in the world who will only take instruction incidentally, as children do in kindergarten."[78]

Contemporary voices admitted that the Midway offered a memorable experience to fairgoers. *Frank Leslie's Weekly* proclaimed the Midway "the great attraction of the fair." A booklet dedicated to the exhibit called the "Street of Cairo" predicted, "When the Columbian Exposition shall have become a thing of the past and its memories hazy with the flight of time, if there shall be one spot which shall remain brighter than all the rest, that one will be its beautiful Cairo Street, in the Midway Plaisance." Andrew Carnegie repeated a common opinion when he stated that "the favored traveler who had done the sights of the world was disposed to jeer at the Midway Plaisance, but I doubt if any department of the exhibition gave as much pleasure and even instruction to as great a number as this unique feature did to the vast majority who cannot hope to travel abroad." Even the often critical artist/journalist Frederic Remington concluded "The Midway is an engaging place. If it were less commercial it would be great."[79]

As the least respectable forms of entertainment proved the most memorable of the fair, and as these entertainments required additional fees from fair visitors, the Chicago booster's hopes that the fair would advertise the city's post-fire cultural achievements and free the city from its earlier reputation as a city of real-estate speculation and materialistic concerns fell flat. Fair planners had only transformed the Midway from anthropological exhibit to a long concession strip out of financial need. But in making what they considered a compromise between underlying fair goals and financial realities, the directors ultimately surrendered much of the control over the memory-making capabilities of the fair. Without the Midway's allure, fairgoers would have had memories only of Daniel Burnham's White City, Frederick Law Olmsted's flowing water-ways, and the museum-like, albeit market driven, displays of goods within these building's innards. Admittedly, visitors could still have found less high-brow entertainments outside the Columbian gates; such entertainments as Buffalo Bill's Wild West show, the ubiquitous Chicago saloon, and a wide variety of burlesque shows all were quite easily located by travelers. But the official sanction of the questionable entertainments of the Midway permanently connected them with the fair. The Columbian Exposition and its host Chicago formally presented popular entertainments within the fair, thus condoning the blatant sales pitches of the sideshows, the degrading, imperialistic exhibits of cultures—including Dahomey, Javanese, Native American, and Eskimo—and the virtually unprecedented displays of female sexuality.

On the Midway, the exhibitions dedicated to Cairo, Algeria, Turkey, Java, and others presented shows of dancing women. Many of the North African and Middle Eastern women performed dances which became known as *danse du ventre*, the French colonial term for women's dances in these regions. In later years performances of the *danse du ventre* type were more commonly known as "belly dances." Extremely popular during the 1889 Paris exposition, the dancing acts became the most frequented displays of the 1893 Chicago fair as well. The Street of Cairo, thanks in part to the charms of its female dancers, made more money than any other Midway concession. References to the varieties of dancing women are frequently found in the writings of fairgoers. Julian Hawthorne's published 1893 recollections of his visits to the Columbian exposition include several sections dedicated to dancing. He described the careful, graceful poses of the Javanese women at length. Hawthorne expressed fascination with their sexual appeal, yet looked at them with an imperialist's supposed cultural superiority. He commented, "They do not impress one like real people at all, and yet you know they are alive. They remind me of a new and beautiful sort of insect in human form—a splendid beetle, perhaps." In speaking of "that renowned performance known as the stomach-dance," Hawthorne confided, "if you go in there, as you certainly will, in your good time, and with trusty and discreet companions,—you will see the female abdomen execute such feats as never before entered your wildest and most unrestrained imaginations to conceive."[80]

Fair publicists assured the public that all attractions of the Midway were perfectly respectable, but tourists were not entirely convinced by these claims. Frederic Remington mused, "Cairo Street contains the theatre where the women dance in such a shockingly interesting way. It is best not to dwell on this thing. It has been sat upon by the people who best know what is proper or not, and one only goes there in order to verify their judgment." Perhaps a typical tourist, a young woman named Calista Webster Jones, in a letter to her parents during June of 1893, worried about the respectability of the shows her fair escorts might take her to see. "I am just going with the rest to the entertainment—or wherever they take me," she conceded, warning, "& I tell them if they take me to anything bad they will have it to answer for." Old Aunt Love, a character from Burnham's *Sweet Clover*, fled from the Midway. She described walking away from the Midway and into the White City as a joy; when "you know in what seemed like one step, you've passed out o'darkness and into light."[81]

The appropriateness of the dances for crowds containing women and children became a subject of debate in the local press, much to the delight of concession operators dreaming of increased revenues. On July 23, 1893, someone claiming to be a Chicago dancing master informed the *Chicago Tribune* of his horror at the sight of the dancers. During August, the fair's Board of Lady Managers, led by the very wealthy Bertha Honoré Palmer, investigated the quality of the attractions after they receive a "tip" from Anthony Comstock. As a result of the women's tour, Director-General Davis ordered the Persian Palace, one of the offending venues, to be shut down as a lesson to other dancing shows. The Palace later gained an injunction against the closing. After leaving the fair, Comstock authored a negative piece on the Chicago exposition for the *St. Louis Post Dispatch*. St. Louis of course was a previous rival for the world's fair and its paper served as a willing accomplice in the maligning of Chicago.[82]

Upon the close of the fair, tales of the exotic dancing of the fair grew in their retelling until they exceeded reality. Stories began to circulate about the enticing dances of a shadowy figure known as Little Egypt. This figure came to embody the supposed scandal of the Midway, and to symbolize the fair officials' choice to allow "low-brow" offerings at their world's fair in exchange for profit. Donna Carlton, author of *Looking for Little Egypt*, chronicles the history of belly-dancing at the Columbian Exposition and finds no concrete evidence of an actual Little Egypt. Many women performed *danse du ventre* on the Midway, several of whom continued their acts after the fair and claimed to have danced as "Little Egypt" in 1893. The myth solidified with a variety of popular reminiscences of the Midway, including "Little Egypt of 1933" who performed at the Century of Progress world's fair in Chicago, a 1935 Ziegfeld film depicting Little Egypt at the 1893 fair, a 1951 film entitled "Little Egypt," and a Jerry Lieber and Mike Stoller song of the same name. The Coasters initially released Lieber and Stoller's song and Elvis Presley later covered it.[83] The long life of this vaguely drawn and most likely fictional persona testifies to the popular fascination with Chicago as a place of ambiguous character.

When visitors poured into Chicago during the summer of 1893, they came to see the fair, but also to witness the spectacle of Chicago. Since the fire of 1871, they had read articles chronicling Chicago's rapid growth; now they wanted to judge the feats of the inland metropolis for themselves. Julian Ralph, writing for *Harper's New Monthly Magazine*, correctly intoned, "Chicago will be the main exhibit of the Columbian Exposition of 1893."[84]

Yet Americans were struck not with the cultural sophistication of this largest of western cities, but with its relentless energy and boundless capacity for change. A writer for *Engineering Magazine* commented on this unforgettable city with its "teeming and polyglot population, with its phenomenally rapid commercial growth, with its web of concentrating railways, with all its feverish energy and enterprise." William Dean Howells, in his "Letters of an Alturian Traveler" in *Cosmopolitan*, considered Chicago from the viewpoint of his character A. Homos from fictional Alturia. Calling Chicago "an ultimated Manhattan," Howells labeled the city "the realized ideal of that largeness, loudness and fastness, which New York has persuaded the Americans is metropolitan." [85] With similar incredulity, a Kansas Senator could not believe how the city had metamorphosed since his last visit in 1859:

> 'I was asked yesterday how the Chicago of that time compared with the Chicago of today.
> "Well," I said, "it is about as the man on the moon is to the cart wheel."
> My friend looked puzzled. "I don't see the force of the comparison, "he said.
> "Neither do I," I replied. "There was *none*." [86]

As seen above, most fairgoers enjoyed the World's Columbian Exposition, and a significant number of cultural critics praised aspects of the event. Yet as the fair brought media focus to Chicago, American cultural producers reflected the long-standing republican tradition of anti-urbanism in their responses. The Chicago boosters fought a fearsome public relations battle in order to win the event for their hometown, and had hopes of erasing the scourge of the Great Chicago Fire, their western location, and their materialistic concerns from their reputation. However, as the nation grew more acquainted with its second city through American popular culture, including coverage of the fair, the connection between Chicago and the country's ambivalence towards urban areas only solidified.

With the production of the wealth of materials covering the Columbian Exposition, the concept of Chicago as a society lacking appropriate social graces proliferated. The widespread praise of some of Chicago's aspects, including reflections on the design merit of the main structures of the White City, acclaim for Dankmar Adler and Louis Sullivan's Auditorium Building, the towering Masonic Temple, and the beautiful homes of its moguls, as well as positive remarks on the Evanston-based Northwestern University and the city's new University of Chicago, did not significantly ameliorate the rhetoric of distaste for Chicago's seemingly continual cultural faux-pas.

One aspect of the criticism targeted Chicago women. The *World's Fair Puck*, offspring of the national *Puck* out of New York City, and other nationally distributed magazines, loved to poke fun at Chicago's female population. Producers of popular culture described these women as uncouth and homely, the opposite of worldly Eastern ladies. *Cosmopolitan* magazine discussed the common assumption that Chicago women lacked physical grace and beauty. Their feet were assumed to be disastrously over-sized. Reprinting comments that appeared in *Life* magazine, a *Cosmopolitan* author reported, tongue-in-cheek, that "a Chicago girl while bathing in Atlantic City yesterday suddenly stepped into a shark's nest. Only two of the dreadful monsters escaped." In interviewing a new butler, *World's Fair Puck's* punsters elaborated, one nouveau-riche Chicago hostess queried, "Well, if, as you say, you've lived in all the *fin de siecle* Boston houses, perhaps you may do for me. But I must test you by a few questions first." She asked, "In arranging the table for a ladies' luncheon party, where would you put the tooth-picks?" [87]

Along with Chicago women, the city's supposed penchant for unfettered capitalism drew comments. Chicago's reputation for materialism stuck fast. Writers stunned at the elaborate nature of the plans for the fair and the wide-range of goods to be displayed at the exposition reinforced this representation of Chicago. This assessment proved long-lived. A character from Henry B. Fuller's 1895 novel *With the Procession*, lamented that Chicago "labors under one peculiar disadvantage: it is the only great city in the world to which all its citizens have come for the one common, avowed object of making money." William T. Stead, editor of Britain's *Pall Mall Gazette*, echoed this common sentiment in his scathing 1894 review of the city, *If Christ Came to Chicago!* This exposé, although written by an Englishman, found many readers in the United States. Like a number of other Europeans, Stead found Chicago even more shocking than the city's American critics, and the strength of his language betrays his repugnance: "This vast and heterogeneous community, which has been collected together from all quarters of the known world, knows only one common bond. Its members came here to make money. They are staying here to make money. The quest of the almighty dollar is their Holy Grail."[88]

Chicago's desire to complete the next business deal presumably affected its cultural output in an adverse way. Some pointed out that this obsession with business was due in part to the tenor of the personalities who ran the city. In short, onlookers thought of leading Chicagoans as new to their substantial finances, and without the understanding and time to produce the cultural offerings that other cities could boast of. Lacking the proper leisure provided by a substantially sized population of families with long-standing and monied backgrounds, many believed Chicago could not claim cultural equality with the eastern seaboard. Henry Loomis Nelson mused:

> It is difficult to properly characterize it [Chicago] without seeming to disparage it. Chicago is not only new, but it is busy, it is active, and it lacks the repose of the older civilization. There are not so many people in Chicago who have generations of wealth behind them as there are in New York or Boston or Philadelphia. There is a rush and hurry, an amount of real business to the city square that is not to be found in the older cities—at least not to be found on the surface.[89]

Along with critiques about its overly-acquisitive nature, Chicago suffered a series of snubs regarding its moral character. Writer Julian Ralph found Chicago society "crude" and concluded that even its most prestigious families drank and gambled in excess of any other Americans. Chicago found itself characterized as a hotbed of lascivious living and as a home to a large criminal element. *World's Fair Puck* presented a conversation between a Chicagoan and a visitor that spoke to the nation's low-regard for the city's morality. The paper joked, "'There goes one of our most prominent citizens,' [said the Chicagoan.] 'In what respect is he prominent?' [asks the visitor.] 'He pays more alimony than any other man in Chicago.'"[90]

The last day of the Columbian Exposition proved to be a day of mourning rather than a celebration of a successful fair. Thus this elaborate attempt to rewrite Chicago's image ended on an extremely sour note, a tragedy which cast a pall over the entire event. Sunday, October 29, 1893 was to be the fair's final, shining moment. On the Saturday night before the closing, however, Eugene Patrick Pendergast assassinated Mayor Carter Harrison in his home. Pendergast ostensibly took revenge on Chicago's mayor because he had been denied a political appointment. The matter took on an even sadder tone when the public learned that Mayor Harrison had recently become engaged. The death brought an odd solemnity to the final moments of the fair. It seemed as if Chicago could not run from its history of scandals, even on this special day. One journalist stated, "The flags were at half-mast in Jackson Park on the last day—on the great day of victory. There is always a touch of tragedy in the career of Chicago. It is the pathetic penalty of great achievement." Mournful crowds gathered to hear a short closing ceremony in the White City, and then dispersed. National fair president Thomas Palmer addressed the crowds, along with friends of the mayor, and Harrison received a twenty-one gun salute as the flags were lowered in the setting sun. In the Midway, however, "depravity" reigned as crowds ran about, unleashed in despair at the mayor's murder.[91]

The fair grossed close to $33 million and played host to 27,529,400 visitors, 21,477,212 of them paying guests. The World's Columbian Exposition failed to draw enough profit to pay back its many creditors, but this had been expected. Creditors had regarded their contributions as donations on behalf of the city rather than lucrative investments. Too, many of those who contributed on a large scale undoubtedly reaped financial rewards when Chicago visitors spent money in their hotels, restaurants, stores, and the like. In early January, 1894, much of the White City, at that point the property of Columbian Exposition Salvage, was destroyed by a fire set by workers involved with the Pullman strike. Attacking the physical remains of the exposition could have been a statement against employer George Pullman, who had given liberally to the fair. Further fires in July took remaining fair structures.[92]

The final legacy of the Columbian Exposition lies somewhere between triumph and failure. Americans enjoyed their vacation from the cares of the world in the White City, but secretly treasured the offerings of the "barnumized" Midway above that of the austere Court of Honor. As a device for advertising the achievements of the city of Chicago, the fair stumbled. The tension between national and local authorities, the lack of enthusiasm for the exposition's "high" cultural offerings, and the proliferation of concessions of dubious moral quality weakened the fair's reputation.

Chicago, the nation's second city, had taken root on the vast prairies of the West, the very place that was to save the national character by serving as a breeding ground for independent yeoman farmers. In place of prosperous family farms, the land at the foot of Lake Michigan played host to the intertwining rails of the nation's transportation system, and to business men who made vast fortunes on the commodities and futures exchanges, slaughtering and packaging the animals raised by others, or selling farm equipment for a handsome profit. In 1893, historian Frederick Jackson Turner had proclaimed that the frontier had vanished. Turn-of-the-century Americans mourned the seeming passage of a way of life that they had treasured, although the "myth of the garden" had only really existed in their imaginations. Despite heroic attempts to alter Chicago's image through the staging of the Inter-State Industrial Exposition and the World's Columbian Exposition, Chicagoans could not adequately reverse the powerful course of American contemporary thought.

Chapter Three
"Turbulent Mistress of the West": Popular Images of Chicago in the Progressive Era

In 1894, English journalist and editor of the *Pall Mall Gazette,* William T. Stead published his scathing volume, *If Christ Came to Chicago!: A Plea for the Union of All Who Love in the Service of All Who Suffer.* Stead, on a visit to Chicago to see the Columbian Exposition in 1893 grew more interested in the city itself than in its temporary pleasure park. Back home in Great Britain, Stead had already crafted a newspaper exposé condemning the realities of prostitution in London entitled *Maiden Tribute of Modern Babylon* (1885). Historian Judith Walkowitz points out that in hoping to pen prostitution's version of *Uncle Tom's Cabin,* Stead had instead written a tabloid work that heightened the public's fear of sexual predators in Victorian London. Walkowitz terms Stead's *Maiden Tribute* "one of the most successful pieces of scandal journalism of the nineteenth century." Stead's work helped activists change girls' age of sexual consent from thirteen to sixteen years of age. Stead himself spent three months in prison for the purchase of a young girl (presumably for investigative purposes) in the course of writing *Maiden Tribute. If Christ Came to Chicago* brought out the scandalous underworld of the middle-American metropolis in the way *Maiden Tribute* did for London. Stead's work sold seventy thousand copies before publication and two times as many volumes subsequently. The journalist spread his message of Chicago's struggles further through well-attended speaking engagements.[1]

Stead condemned Chicago as a center of evil, a place in which the population regularly violated the teachings of Christ. Stead chronicled in detail the multitude of Chicago's transgressions, spending particular care on his special interest, prostitution. In keeping with the dramatic tone of many

European observers of Chicago, the level of Stead's criticism exceeded that of most Americans. However, the substance of his comments fit in with American trends. He berated the city, focusing on the Chicago citizens' failure to give proper service to the community because of their constant pursuit of the dollar. Looking on from outside the culture, Stead found Chicago's egregious behavior particularly American. Money, from Stead's perspective, held the polyglot city together. Stead chided:

> This vast and heterogeneous community, which has been collected together from all quarters of the known world, knows only one common bond. Its members come here to make money. They are staying here to make money. The quest of the almighty dollar is their Holy Grail. From afar the name and the fame of Chicago have gone abroad to the poor and the distressed and the adventurous of all nations, and they have flocked and are still flocking to the place where a few men make millions and all men can get food.[2]

Stead's volume repackaged the story of the errant city for his readers and did its share of damage to any lingering positive effects of the Columbian Exposition. The book's widespread appeal sparked a wave of progressive sentiment among Chicagoans, who were concerned about the reputation of their city and the real problems which Stead's work uncovered. Prompted by Stead's suggestion for the formation of a civic action group in his speech at a mass meeting in November 1893, prominent residents joined together to form the Civic Federation in 1894.[3]

Incorporated by Illinois Secretary of State William Hinrichsen on February 3, 1894, the Civic Federation set itself forth as a non-sectarian, general-approach, progressive organization. The group's aims were broad: "to advance the municipal, philanthropic, industrial and moral interests of Chicago, and to use and aid such forces in promoting honesty, efficiency and economy of its municipal government and the highest welfare of its citizens." Involved in the group during its initial stages were such prominent Chicago personages as Lyman Gage of the First National Bank, Jane Addams of Hull House fame, society leader Bertha Palmer, and Rabbi Emil G. Hirsch.[4]

During November 1893, a group of Chicagoans met to draw up the earliest plans for the civic organization. Forty prominent citizens from the city were extended invitations to join the group. "Especially do we believe it appropriate," the initial founders urged, "that such a movement should begin while our people are yet filled with new ideas, new ambitions and inspirations drawn from the great Exposition." The contemporary condition of destitution in Chicago was considered an emergency requiring immediate action.[5]

The Civic Federation's founding heralded the beginning of a widespread and quite effective progressive effort in the city of Chicago. Chicago became a breeding ground for social action, with the formation of a myriad of clubs. Organized in such groups as the Civic Federation, the Commercial Club, and the Association of Commerce, the Chicago leaders responsible for the headstrong boosterism of the Columbian Exposition began a journey of re-flection on and correction of the woes of their city. Inspired in part by pro-ducers of popular culture like Stead who chose to shine light on Chicago's blemishes, and also caught up in the progressive attitude of the times, these self-appointed leaders turned inward to address the actual difficulties of their metropolis. Having been so engrossed with elevating the reputation of their city during the planning of the 1893 World's Fair, the city leaders now turned their full energies to philanthropic work, including ridding Chicago of vice, regulating the sale of alcohol, cleaning the streets, and eliminating gambling.

The work accomplished by these civic-minded personages did much to improve life in Chicago and contributed to the evolution of the philanthrop-ic philosophy which still guides work in caring for urban communities to-day. Unfortunately the leaders turned their attention towards reform and away from the modeling of their city's reputation at just the moment when the forces of mainstream popular culture had considerably strengthened the mechanisms by which they spoke to the American public. City boosters dropped the fight of words and images for the fight to ease hunger and eco-nomic suffering just as popular national magazines proliferated and massive printings of fictional stories reached many eager readers. The inattention of the boosters allowed popular culture to continue to cast Chicago in a dark light. The urban landscape proved to be the often-chosen fodder for both popular magazines and mainstream fiction in this period. A few contempo-rary writers noticed the change of focus for the erstwhile Chicago boosters. Journalist James Weber Linn, writing in the *New Republic* in 1919, reflected on the sentiment of his period. Linn believed that a significant change in be-havior was manifest in Chicago's leaders. "The old sense of individual re-sponsibility for the city's reputation is gone, " Linn mused, "There are scores of thousands of citizens who are filled with a sense of social responsibility; but their chief interest is no longer in having Chicago appear well before the world."[6]

This chapter chronicles the period in which the Chicago elite's preoccu-pation with progressive reform took precedence over concerns for the city's reputation. At this same time, the negative responses to Chicago grew in American popular culture. While the former boosters found matters like urban poverty engrossing, the myth of Chicago as a dark city found greater currency with Americans. During the period between the Columbian Exposition and the 1930s, Chicago would experience perhaps the greatest number of challenges to her national reputation, including the publication of Upton Sinclair's *The Jungle* in 1906, the race riots of 1919, and the activities of Chicago's infamous gangsters—Big Joe Colosimo, Al Capone, and the rest. Indeed even the city's impressive array of philanthropic activities, heralded in the popular press, only served to announce the existence of Chicago's troubles to a wide audience.

Interestingly, a good many of those people molding popular works on American urban centers in the early part of the twentieth century were reformers themselves. Writing for the mainstream media, these commentators reinforced the negative image of Chicago. Hoping their writings would influence a nationwide movement in civic reform, the writers broadcast stories of Chicago that presented the city as an icon of urban trouble. This brash urban upstart, without the assumed long-lived and solid cultural footing of the Eastern Seaboard cities, had little to recommend it. Swarming with immigrants, Chicago, according to this group of writers, came to most clearly represent the dangers of urbanism. In trying to reconfigure American society, then, many turned to Chicago as a representative American place, but one representative of unwanted change. The reformers looked at Chicago's urban nature as a threat, conceiving of the city as symbolic of what was wrong with the nation. Chicago became the nation's super-typical trouble spot.

Chicago-based reformers failed to organize a coherent response to this attack on their city's image. Instead of replying directly to the increasingly weighty rhetoric of Chicago-aimed anti-urbanism with rhetoric of their own, the Chicago elite decided to confront the actual problems of their city. This high-level of commitment to reform left the city leaders little time for boosterism.

In some ways, too, the progressive efforts put forth by Chicago leaders damaged the city's reputation. In doing so much for their city, and in fighting such a vast array of unwanted elements, Chicago's local philanthropists and social scientists provided role models of civic responsibility and formulated the intellectual groundwork for the academic disciplines of sociology and social work. But in their passion for their work, they also contributed considerably to Chicago's reputation as a home to social disorder. While their work was well-received, many Americans came to see Chicago as the place most in need of such intense philanthropic activity. By the 1940s and 1950s, as we shall see in Chapter Five, the fate of Chicago's reputation lay squarely in the hands of the producers of popular culture—journalists, novelists, movie producers, and, by that time, television programmers. The former boosters had given up the podiums from which they had waxed on about the positive attributes of their city at precisely the time when the flood of media began to sweep through the nation and took strong hold of American public opinion. The boosters could not have known that this budding media was the nascent form of the twenty-four hour, nearly instantaneous onslaught we know as the national media today. Yet the city leaders had stepped away from the world of rhetoric at just the moment that rhetoric began to define Americans interactions with the world to a greater extent.

Attention placed on Chicago as a result of the 1893 World's Fair sparked embarrassment and a reformatory zeal among Chicago's city leaders. As novelist Henry Fuller, himself a source for popular anti-Chicago sentiment with his less than flattering Chicago-based novels *The Cliff-Dwellers* and *With the Procession*, described in the pages of *Atlantic Monthly* in 1897:

> The Fair was a kind of post-graduate course for the men at the heart of Chicago's commercial and mercantile interests; it was the city's intellectual and social annexation to the world at large. The sense of shame and of peril aroused by the comments of outside censors helped to lead at once to a practical associated effort for betterment, and scarcely had the Columbian Exposition drawn to a close when many of the names that had figured so long and familiarly in its directorate began to appear with equal prominence in the councils of the Civic Federation.[7]

Thus, in the post-fair years, the view of Chicago most often taken in by the world was skewed. The city could claim to be a world leader in organizational bodies, a laboratory for urban aid, a hotbed of trendy progressivism. Yet most Americans believed Chicagoans displayed such talent for urban reform because the city needed reform so badly. Even the occasionally positive press Chicago earned often came coupled with sharp barbs. Investigative reporter Lincoln Steffens, writing in *McClure's Magazine* in 1903, found Chicago's reformatory efforts had raised its municipal government beyond the likes of Philadelphia and St. Louis. Chicago could not claim good government, Steffens cautioned, only better. Steffens had written about bad city governments in a series of articles; he then offered up Chicago as a picture of relative governmental health. Steffens knew that his readers would have a hard time accepting Chicago as a governmental model, given the general tenor of the rhetoric surrounding the city. "Yes, Chicago,"

Steffens explained gently to his doubtful readers, was a site of reform. "First in violence, deepest in dirt; loud, lawless, unlovely, ill-smelling, irreverent, new; an overgrown gawk of a village, the 'tough' among cities, a spectacle for the nations—I give Chicago no quarter and Chicago asks for none," Steffens wrote. However, Chicago honestly assessed its own faults and wanted to know when others observed troubles in the prairie capital. Here, Steffens subscribes to the popular view—Chicago could claim a startlingly broad array of problems—yet he does give the city leaders credit for trying to fix them. Steffens' "left-handed" compliment ranked among the most favorable proclamations on Chicago of the time.

In 1895, Steffens related, the Civic Federation, "a respectable but inefficient universal reforming organization," had met to "do something" about the quality of their government bureaucracy. City officials had entered into a series of under-the-table deals with the notorious financier, Charles Yerkes. Yerkes secured rights to control private streetcar systems with well-placed bribes to government officials. Chicagoans in the Civic Federation finally fought back against their city becoming riddled with graft (referred to by many at the time as "boodle"). The Federation spun off an organization called the Municipal Voters' League, placing George E. Cole, a stationer, at its head. By publishing the voting records of Chicago alderman, the League steadily influenced voters to remove corrupt officials from their posts. Steffens reported that after Chicago grew relatively clean, Yerkes fled to London. Some other less-than-reputable businessmen also left the city, speaking ill of Chicago in their new places of residence, and unjustly tarnishing Chicago's name.[8]

A second progressive group, the Commercial Club of Chicago, also figured prominently in the contagious introspection of the period. Founded in 1878, well before the Civic Federation, the Commercial Club had actually offered its facilities as the site of the first annual meeting of the Civic Federation in February 1894.[9] The Commercial Club united for the "purpose of advancing by social intercourse, and by a friendly exchange of views, the commercial prosperity and growth of the city of Chicago." In later years, members added the aim of caring for Chicago's public welfare to their club's constitution. Although coming out of the tradition of run-of-the-mill business clubs, the Commercial Club members grew to have broad, often progressive-minded goals for their organization. Group leaders explained at one meeting that Chicago's role as a business center made it the perfect site for experimentation in social reform. "It is therefore here in our very midst," intoned one group official, "that in all probability will be worked out the future of our democracy, all those social and economic problems which rightly or wrongly solved will influence for better or worse the life and happiness of the people." Early members included such notable Chicago businessmen as retailers L.Z. Leiter and Marshall Field, hotelier John B. Drake, International Harvester chairman John J. Glessner, and sleeping-car mogul George Pullman.[10]

The Commercial Club owed its founding to a quirky, boosterish bit of activity designed to show off Chicago's business prowess to visitors from the more culturally established East. During the fall of 1877, Chicago shoe wholesaler Henry J. Macfarland met with Boston friends Jerome Jones and John W. Candler at the Boston League Club on Beacon Hill. The Boston League Club members planned a trip to Chicago, and Macfarland quickly determined that he wished to introduce the men to Chicago in a grand way. Macfarland and other Chicago businessmen gathered the incredible sum of three thousand dollars for the Bostonians' entertainment fund. Upon arrival in Chicago, Chicago hosts treated their visitors to a train trip to Milwaukee for a luncheon, and showed them Chicago's Stock Yards, Board of Trade, grain elevators, and business houses. After the Easterners' visit, the Chicagoans used the surplus monies to form a permanent business club.[11]

The club that evolved in 1877 came to be much more than a simple businessman's social outlet. The Commercial Club's most enduring historical legacies include their involvement in the formation of the Chicago Manual Training School in 1882, the establishment of Fort Sheridan on a site north of the city in 1887, and the publication of the Plan of Chicago in 1909. Fort Sheridan's construction showcases the conservative bent of the club members. Responding to what they considered the threatening social confusion embodied by the Haymarket Riot of 1886, the Commercial Club had lobbied the federal government for the establishment of a local military post. The erection of the army base Fort Sheridan, ultimately located on six hundred acres of land provided for its use by the Commercial Club, would be the outcome of their efforts.

On a less reactionary note, members of the Commercial Club endorsed and financed the July 1909 publication of Daniel Burnham's sweeping *Plan of Chicago*. Club members discussed the issue "What can be done to make Chicago more attractive?" at their one hundred and thirty-sixth regular meeting on March 27, 1897. Among the speakers addressing the fifty-five members and guests in attendance at the Metropole Hotel was the now famous lead architect of the World's Columbian Exposition, Daniel Burnham. According to club minutes, "Mr. Burnham's address was illustrated by views of proposed improvements of [the] Lake Front and was listened to with utmost attention."[12] The speech became the spark which launched the

Commercial Club's support of Burnham's creative plans for the physical re-fashioning of the city. Burnham was of course the plan's visionary, having been the influence behind the stately white architecture of the 1893 fair. Burnham had also carefully gauged the public's reaction to his fanciful "White City." Visitors had found Chicago wanting and "gray" compared with the perfect white expanses of the fantasy landscape of the exposition. Now Burnham hoped to launch a "City Beautiful" movement, with Chicago as a prime symbol, to strengthen the weight of the governing powers of American cities and to make them more pleasurable places to dwell in and to visit.

The impetus for the plan also came from a similar commercial men's club, the Merchant's Club, which merged with the Commercial Club in 1907 and was subsumed under its name. Drawing from his work for the Columbian Exposition, Burnham spent thirty-nine months working on an updated Chicago. The architect donated his skills to the project, but the Commercial Club spent at least $80,000 on publication of the plan. Due to the plan's elaborate format (complete with reproductions of Jules Guerin's watercolor sketches of the fairground, the club could issue only 1,650 initial copies of the plan.

Burnham's plan involved key changes to the physical infrastructure of the city, including the establishment of concentric traffic routes through greater Chicago for maximum ease of movement. Chicago's already impressive park system was to be considerably enhanced, based on predictions that Chicago's rate of population growth would soon make the city the largest in the world. (This of course proved incorrect.) In his designs, Burnham used trash from the city to build land out into Lake Michigan, land that was to be set aside for park use.[13] Although all elements of the plan did not come to pass, Burnham's vision did provide many of Chicago's more aesthetic elements. Burnham's suggestion of a towering city government building reminiscent of the nation's capital building in Washington, D.C. was never realized. Yet many important elements of Chicago's appeal today, including the city's lake front park, the widened thoroughfare Michigan Avenue, and the functional Wacker Drive, originated from the *Plan of Chicago*.

Although sheer desire to enhance the quality of life and beauty of their city numbered among the club member's motivations for supporting the *Plan of Chicago*, these merchants understood the way in which such civic improvements would benefit them in a pecuniary way. Charles H. Wacker, a former director of the 1893 exposition and the chairman of the Chicago Plan Commission (the body appointed by Mayor Fred Busse to investigate the implementation of the plan), outwardly admitted to the financial returns expected from the physical changes. Writing in his book, *American City*, Wacker spoke of the number of American visitors to Paris each year and the dollars spent abroad. With aesthetic changes, Wacker surmised, Chicago could capture some of the American capital usually diverted to other nations. While on the whole the design project echoed the tendency to turn inward towards real change rather than outwards towards national image-making, at some level the members of the Commercial Club understood that concentrating on the myriad of street by street enhancements suggested by Burnham would better Chicago's reputation. Burnham himself captured this sentiment most memorably with his often quoted words, "make no *little* plans, they have no magic to stir man's blood; make *big* plans, aim high in hope and work." According to Burnham, no commodity paid better than beauty.

Wealthy former brewer Charles Wacker also believed that alterations in the infrastructure could ultimately heighten the quality of feeling Chicagoans expressed for their hometown. "Will not this example of civic unity and civic enterprise," Wacker mused, "foster in Chicagoans a love for their birthplace, and a confidence in their own power of achievement which could be aroused in no other way?" Clearly, Wacker judged the civic commitment of the majority of Chicagoans as lacking.[14] Through a campaign to influence local public opinion, including the use of newspaper articles, a pamphlet, a school textbook, stereopticon lectures, and a film, voters gave their support for the project, even agreeing to tax increases on behalf of the work.[15]

Of the major Chicago voluntary organizations, The Association of Commerce would best maintain efforts to improve the city's national image over the years. The Association of Commerce originated as the Merchants and Travelers Association about the time of the 1893 World's Fair, and later merged with the Chicago Commercial Association. In 1908 members adopted the name The Association of Commerce to avoid confusion with the Commercial Club. The Association of Commerce believed that uplifting Chicago's image led to increased business for their city. They referred to their hometown as "Chicago the Great Central Market."[16]

The Association of Commerce advertised Chicago to the merchants of the greater United States through periodic good-will trips. On one such trip in 1909, Association members covered the Mississippi Valley down to New Orleans, stopping at such points as Memphis, Tennessee, Birmingham, Alabama, and Hot Springs, Arkansas. The Chicagoans visited towns that New York and St. Louis business people believed they controlled. No one sold any goods on the journey, but rather hawked Chicago itself. (Salesmen were probably not far behind, however.) A University of Chicago professor accompanying the group spoke on education, and a banker fielded questions on finance. The host cities responded enthusiastically to the forays, and most likely took Chicago up on its offers of hospitality in the Association of Commerce rooms when it sent business delegates into the field. Most of all, the receiving cities expressed surprise that the Chicagoans talked about *buying* goods from the southern cities, rather than speaking only of selling their own wares. Given Chicago's reputation for greed, such camaraderie was unexpected. The Montgomery *Advertiser* even remarked, not bothering to hide incredulity, "It seems the people of Chicago speak English."[17]

The Association of Commerce was organized into a series of committees. Several committees like those of general publicity and of conventions, reached out to the world beyond Chicago and sought to mold the public's opinion of the city. Others, like those on traffic, postal service, roads, and civic affairs, concentrated on more localized concerns. Yet one group ultimately overshadowed the rest, and although motivated by the best of intentions, probably nullified some of the positive publicity generated by other committees. The branch of the group best known at the national level, the crime fighting businessmen led by Col. Robert Isham Randolph, were the "Secret Six." While seeking to lower Chicago's crime rates, this group raised national awareness of Chicago's criminal element. Like other progressive organizations, then, the Association of Commerce damaged Chicago's reputation with the vigor of its methods. Perhaps paradoxically, as we will see in Chapter Four, the Association would, of all the city's volunteer groups, best understand the public relations potential of 1933–1934 World's Fair.

At the turn-of-the-century, Chicago received some recognition in national periodicals for the growth of its blossoming cultural institutions. In a relatively thorough manner, albeit for just a brief time, the city captured attention for its cultural offerings in the more high-brow of the national periodicals. This brief challenge to the surrounding years of scandal coverage on the city would be the most sustained positive press the city received before the years of Mayor Richard J. Daley (the second mayor, and the more benign, from this legendary family of Chicago and national Democratic leaders). In article after article in the very late 1800s and very early 1900s, journalists rehearsed the litany of improvements made to the new Chicago. The various men's and women's clubs gathered praise, as did the Chicago based literary magazine *The Dial*, the local newspapers, the city's growing group of resident novelists, Jane Addams' Hull House, good public and parochial schools, the symphony orchestra, the Art Institute, and Chicago's libraries, including the Newberry Library (a private research institution), the Chicago Historical Society, the Chicago Public Library, and the Crerar

Library (devoted to the sciences). The well-known Chicago-area writers of the time included Henry B. Fuller, Robert Garland, Robert Herrick, Will Payne, Harriet Monroe, Finley Peter Dunne, George Ade, Emerson Hough, Elia W. Peattie, and Henry K. Webster. It was clear that Chicago was nurturing the fine arts in ways that it had never done before. Yet the small renaissance owed its funding to the crass business leaders, never hidden far below the veneer of artistic achievement. The commercial kings, it seems, had spent at least some of their funds on projects which raised Chicago's cultural capital. Chicago-based writer Elia W. Peattie spoke of Chicago's artistic side in *Atlantic Monthly*. According to Peattie, a past president of the Chicago Art Institute had once remarked, "We have made our money in pigs, but is there any reason we should not spend it in pictures?"[18]

Perhaps most impressive to onlookers was The University of Chicago, located in the city's South Side neighborhood of Hyde Park. Founded in 1892, the university had achieved high status within the academic world by the early twentieth century. Having created one of the largest libraries in the United States literally overnight with an enormous purchase of books from a German book dealer, the university made itself known. The University's extension course offerings at sites around the country also added to national knowledge of the institution. In *New England Magazine*, an editor paid Chicago and its university this left-handed compliment: "Think as we may of the pedigree of the money built into its foundations [monopolistic Standard Oil's John D. Rockefeller enabled the establishment of the university]—and we could all wish it were different—the University of Chicago is one of the wonders of America." The writer believed the university's presence lifted the whole tone of the city.[19] In *Ladies' Home Journal*, George Fitch simultaneously mocked and celebrated the university's success by speaking of its meteoric rise with the same hyperbolic tone often used in descriptions of the city. Fitch wrote, "This university is growing so fast that within ten years the supply of human knowledge will have to be doubled in order to provide work for all its professors."[20]

Although the growth of Chicago's cultural institutions was deemed noteworthy by the press, its overall effect on the actual character of the city's people was found to be minimal. One author concluded, "No city of similar age has done so much for the higher life of its citizens. Yet the effect of this leaven is so far seen only in the suggestions in the faces of the people or refining powers at work under the imperious sway of commercialism."[21]

Surprisingly, the city's contemporary architecture, which we think well of today, mostly gathered criticism from its contemporary assessors. Although architects of the day must have been at least energized by the great design drive that gathered in Chicago at the turn of the century, lay observers and commentators in the mainstream press predominantly expressed displeasure with Chicago's buildings. While a few native Chicagoans defended the city's structures, most saw Chicago's style as an expression of much of what they deemed wrong with the city—including its cultural youth (the city had existed too short a time for any pretensions of architectural mastery, critics propounded) and its seeming devotion to greed.

Today we consider Chicago the birthplace of many of architecture's important forms, and appreciate the way in which the city's commitment to business helped spawn the now familiar skyscrapers. Beginning with William Le Baron Jenney's Home Insurance Building, completed in 1885, Chicago launched a new type of capitalistic design, frugal on the space consumed at ground level but daring in its insistent push towards the sky. Chicago's streets can now be considered among the best the United States has to offer in terms of modern, urban architecture. Although many fine buildings have been lost over the years, one can still find such gems as William Holabird and Martin Roche's Marquette Building, Daniel H. Burnham and John Wellborn Root's Monadnock Building, and the Rookery, designed by Burnham and Root and "updated" by Frank Lloyd Wright.

Challenges to Chicago's architectural design reached mainstream popular culture as early as 1893, with the publication of Chicagoan Henry B. Fuller's *The Cliff Dwellers*. Fuller introduced many Americans to the series of man-made canyons—the brown-hued buildings of Chicago business—through which, "during the course of the last fifty years, the rushing streams of commerce have worn a deep and rugged chasm." The city's large buildings lorded over the streets below like "towering cliffs, and these soaring walls of brick and limestone and granite rise higher and higher with each succeeding year."[22] Other cities had also adopted the skyscraper form, but to Fuller, Chicago's buildings loomed with a particular ominous quality over the commercial center's crowded streets.

In Frank Norris' 1903 bestseller, *The Pit: A Story of Chicago*, the city's commercial architecture foreshadowed danger. In the novel, part of Norris' three-part exploration on the power of wheat, Laura Dearborn arrives in Chicago as a parentless, independently wealthy young woman, looking for a new place to call home. Although Laura finds the city agreeable during her initial interactions with it, Norris' bleak portrayals of her surroundings spoke of the trouble she would later experience. After an evening of opera at which she meets her future husband, speculator Curtis Jadwin, Laura returns home through the darkened Chicago streets. The city around her was threatening, especially the aspects devoted to the doomed Jadwin's chosen trade, finance. Norris described the "Board of Trade Building, black, grave, monolithic, crouching on its foundations, like a monstrous sphinx with blind eyes, silent, grave [sic],—crouching there without a sound, without sign of life under the night and the drifting veil of rain." Although Laura at first appears happy, the reader is led to believe that Chicago ultimately will bring trouble for the young woman. Indeed, Laura gambles her future on Jadwin, a driven Chicago businessman whose greed brings him to ruin. In an attempt to corner the market on wheat, Jadwin loses his entire fortune and his health. In the face of such a downfall, Laura and her husband leave Chicago forever. This derisive view of Chicago proved extremely successful. Serialized in the *Saturday Evening Post* in 1902 and early 1903, the work had to be reprinted even before its initial release due to the numbers of pre-publication orders. The popular work led to a play (1904), a Parker Brother's Board game, "Pit: Exciting Fun for Everyone" (1904), and a silent film (1917).[23]

For many contemporary observers, the type of architecture found so frequently in Chicago signified Chicagoans' lack of refinement. The new style of these buildings, so often supportive of Louis Sullivan's idea that form ought to follow function, did not have the profusion of added decorative adornment characteristic of the primary urban buildings of an earlier age. The change startled some onlookers. In *Atlantic Monthly*, Loren H.B. Knox complained that the city's "buildings reflect the mentality of the people, being purely utilitarian, imitative in design, dull brown, dull gray, and dull red in color, to match the sooty air. Its famous skyscrapers, quickly growing, vast and box-like, in scarcely a single instance are distinguished for architectural grace or adornment." Knox interestingly found the same buildings we today find precedent-setting to be "imitative." Although acknowledging the fame of the city's tall altars of business, Knox considered them stylistically commonplace.[24] Another journalist chose to attack the style of Chicago's architectural offerings in a humorous way, saying:

> As you gaze about you in this section of the city you will see plainly that there is no truth in the charge that Chicago architecture consists of four brick walls and a ninety-nine year lease. Chicago often has more varieties of architecture on one building than can be found in a whole European city. This fine flat building on our left was modeled after an Italian hotel, a Russian church, a Japanese tea-garden and a South Chicago ice-house—which is four times as many styles as most European buildings have.[25]

Seemingly, Chicago had no real style of its own. Writer Franklin Head concluded that the buildings, rather than having derivative design features, carried no aesthetic characteristics at all. In streamlining the buildings in order to provide the largest possible internal areas, Head found that "many of the lofty buildings are as unpicturesque as a dry goods box pierced with holes for windows."[26]

Architectural writers today do find Chicago offers interesting examples of practical-minded structural design. In Chicago the grain elevator and the factory have had a noticeable impact on design, and the everyday workings of commerce are more often heralded than shunned. Picking up on this Chicago tendency for common sense and fearless embrace of capitalistic trappings, the contemporary architectural critics balked. Too, their apparent disregard for buildings which appear so stunning to many today may have stemmed from an unwillingness to attribute the establishment of any significant cultural standards to this Midwestern city.

Besides its apparent lack of architectural appeal for many observers during the first part of the twentieth century, commentators also found Chicago repugnant because of its dirty streets. Authors speaking to wide national audiences repeated this criticism of the city over and over again throughout the years. Julian Ralph, writing for *Harper's Weekly* in 1895, commented that, "the filth in the streets, the bustle and clatter and worry and strain, are still so dreadful as to suggest the citadel of hades [*sic*]." In *Living Age*, a commentator wrote in 1907 that, "After ugliness, the worst foe of Chicago is dirt." George Fitch's article on Chicago in the same year includes a cartoon depicting a plaque placed on Chicago's main shopping thoroughfare, State Street; this fictional plaque proclaimed the date of the last street cleaning to be 1893. And in addition to Chicago's streets, its lake front, actually expanded out into the lake with debris landfill, was scattered with trash. Fitch continued, "This, ladies and gentlemen, is Chicago's celebrated Lake Front. Notice the artistic way in which the tin cans in the background blend with the old barrel hoops." Decades later, Lewis Mumford reached a similar conclusion. He wrote, "That Chicago is dirty is indisputable."[27]

A series of unfortunate events also compounded Chicago's reputation as a troubled urban center. On December 30, 1903, fire once again plagued Chicago. At a matinee show of "Mr. Bluebird" at the Iroquois Theater, the red velvet curtains lining the stage caught on fire, and the fire moved surprisingly quickly through the theater. The Iroquois Theater was located in a bustling location in the city's downtown business and theater district, on Randolph Street between State Street and Dearborn. The $500,000 theater had only just opened on November 23, 1903, complete with claims that it was one of the safest theaters in the world. On the terrible day, patrons fled, only to find all but one of the thirty exits locked and the stairways between floors and seating areas gated. The tragic fire left 596 dead—far more than the Great Fire of 1871. The city observed a day of mourning on New Years Eve. Mayor Carter Harrison Jr. ordered all Chicago theaters investigated.

The Iroquois fire rekindled the memory of the 1871 disaster and reinforced Chicago's image as a chaotic urban center. *Harper's Weekly* issued a supplement which featured large pictures of the charred remains of the theater's interior; photographs showed theater seats burned beyond repair, and aisles filled with debris, presumably some of it the remains of human bodies. A morbid commemorative work on the fire once again claimed the burden of ultimate hardship for the unlucky Midwestern city. Marshall Everett, author of *The Great Theater Disaster*, wrote mournfully, "Chicago, with aching heart and head bowed in grief o'er the graves of its martyred dead, calls forth the pity of the whole world in this, her hour of greatest sorrow—sorrow brought on by a holocaust that has no parallel in the world's history—a calamity which in less time than it takes to tell bereft hundred of homes of their loved ones and made Chicago the most unhappy city on the face of the earth."[28]

Unfortunately, the scandal did not end with the deaths. Inquiries into the disaster later showed that theater inspectors had looked the other way when theater owners violated building codes; bribes had been given. Franklin Matthews, in an article entitled "Chicago as a Storm Centre" in *Critic*, wrote about the Iroquois atrocities. Matthews expounded hopefully on the curative effect of the fire: "Her citizens are organizing to drive out the thugs and purify the laws, her labor pest is being stamped out, her mayor is finally awake, her people are aroused. Chicago has been purified by fire."[29] Here Matthews liberally borrows language from two important sources of American anti-urban rhetoric. His use of "purified" harkens back to similar statements made in the instant-histories which established the Chicago Fire as one of the most well-known urban disasters. His title too, recalls Reverend Josiah Strong's 1885 well-known condemnation of American cities as storm centers.

While Chicago officials and governments around the world established laws regulating theater management after the event, the Iroquois fire hardly marked the end of Chicago's troubles. In 1906, the city garnered additional national notoriety with the publication of Upton Sinclair's indictment of Chicago's meat-packing industry, *The Jungle*. Sinclair first grew interested in the city because of the strike at the Chicago Union Stockyards during the summer of 1904, and the editor of the socialist journal *Appeal to Reason*, Fred D. Warren, encouraged Sinclair to consider writing about Chicago for the alternative periodical. Sinclair visited Chicago's Packingtown for seven weeks in order to gain perspective on the challenges faced by workers there for an upcoming serialized story and novel. Installments of Sinclair's work, *The Jungle*, began running in *Appeal to Reason* at the end of February 1905. Some chapters also found their way into the quarterly, *One Hoss Philosophy*. Although the *Appeal's* subscription rates barely budged upon publication of Sinclair's muckraking socialist novel (optimistic, its publishers had hoped to sell a run of a million copies), the Doubleday, Page book version of the story quickly became an international best-seller.

The *Jungle* spawned news stories focusing in on the less-than-sanitary conditions of the meat plants, which supplied food to markets all over the world. Sinclair became a well-known personality. President Theodore Roosevelt, the most famous reader of the book, berated Sinclair's support for socialism but worked to push through the legislation which became the Pure Food and Drug Act and the Meat Inspection Act in mid-1906. Sinclair was heartened by the numbers of people reading his work, but was afraid that they had missed the point. What Sinclair had designed as a tract to show the inevitable fall of his worker-hero, Jurgis Rudkis, and inspire a move towards socialist tenets, became a work that inspired criticism of the cleanliness of the meat industry. As Sinclair relates in his autobiography, "I aimed at the public's heart, but by accident I hit it in the stomach."[30]

Sinclair's work established a link between the nation's overall conception of Chicago and the teeming, turbulent stockyards that still resonates nearly a century later. Visitors who ventured to Chicago before the stockyards completely closed in the early 1970s wanted to see the fabled sites. Although Chicagoans without specific business in Packingtown themselves rarely thought of the yards (unless a wind blew the foul smell towards the city), outsiders could think of little else. Even in Sinclair's own work, the Rudkis family assumes that the word "Chicago" is synonymous with the packing plants; they do not understand the confusion caused when, having finally exited the train in the large city, they ask for directions to "Chicago" and get only confused stares. After a day of utter confusion, and spending the night in the police station, the family learns a new word, "stockyards."[31]

Growing racial tensions in Illinois' largest city also brought unwanted publicity. July 27, 1919 marked the beginning of a brutal race riot in Chicago. John Harris, brothers Charles and Lawrence Williams, and unrelated friends Paul and Eugene Williams tried to cool off at their private beach spot between the 25th Street beach designated for black Chicagoans and the 29th Street beach frequented by whites. While the boys were swimming, several African-Americans had tried to enter the 29th Street beach area. Tensions mounted, during which a white beach patron threw a rock at Eugene

Williams, who instantly sank into Lake Michigan and drowned. A white officer, Daniel Callahan, refused to arrest the white man who had thrown the rock, and also prevented a black officer from arresting the suspect. Callahan did, however, arrest a black at the scene at the request of a white.

Stories surrounding the actual occurrence grew dim as the news traveled around the South Side. Crowds grew, and James Crawford, an African-American, fired his gun into a group of policemen, wounding one. Crawford was subsequently shot and killed by a black officer, and other bullets followed. For five days following this event, whites and blacks fought throughout the city.[32] Chicago was not the only city in recent memory to experience racial strife, but in Chicago's case the tragic conflict further battered the city's overly weakened reputation.

Chicago's vice districts also darkened its name. Since the Civil War era, Chicago had served as a popular travel destination for men interested in visiting prostitution resorts. Perhaps two hundred to two hundred and fifty brothels were in operation in Chicago by the 1860s. By 1910, extremely conservative estimates placed the number of prostitution houses at one thousand and twenty. Of course, brothels only accounted for part of the prostitution industry. Streetwalkers, or prostitutes without connection to an established house, also plied their wares in the city streets, completing their business in whatever spaces were available to them, whether it was in a private apartment, stairwell, or the street itself. Brothels were scattered about the city in vice districts bearing such names as the Levee, Cheyenne, and Hell's Half-Acre. The Levee grew to be Chicago's central red-light district. Stead's *If Christ Came to Chicago* advertised the offerings of Chicago's sex workers to an eager audience in 1893. In Chicago, warned Stead, one could find "unnatural crimes" that one "fondly imagined existed only in the corruption of the later Roman Empire." Historian Lloyd Lewis comments that visitors to the Columbian Exposition "who wanted a 'hot time' were not disappointed."[33] Neither were later travelers.

Although a good many Chicago bordellos experienced moments of relative fame, the club with the most sustained and hard-hitting impact on Chicago's reputation as a vice center was the Everleigh Club, located on one of the city's central business streets, Dearborn. Two sisters, known as Ada and Minna Everleigh (pronounced Ever-lay), left their husbands, claiming abuse, and opened a brothel to service visitors to the Trans-Mississippi Exposition in Omaha, Nebraska in 1898. The entrepreneurial sisters were in their twenties at the time, as Ada had been born in 1876 and Minna in 1878. When the fair ended, the sisters looked for another location. By February 1900 they had opened the Everleigh Club in Chicago, renting two buildings formerly used for the same purpose. Although claiming their adopted last name and the name for the club derived from their grandmother's habit of signing notes "Everly yours," the double entendre was intended.

The Everleigh Club gained prominence through its lavish decorations. The brothel boasted of themed rooms—Moorish, Gold, Silver, Copper, Red, Rose, Green, Blue, Oriental, Japanese, Egyptian, Chinese, Music, and Ballroom—along with a gold-plated piano, gold spittoons, perfumed fountains, and two four-piece orchestras. The Everleighs told an interviewer that men who did not spend at least fifty dollars for an evening were requested not to return. The Everleighs also insisted their club was the site of the world's first instance of a man drinking wine from a woman's slipper—a trend which oddly enough gained popularity in the period.[34]

Local criticism of the club grew upon the 1911 publication of an elaborate brochure advertising the Everleigh to out-of-town visitors. According to Herbert Asbury's *Gem of the Prairie* (the 1940 study of the Chicago underworld that itself substantially furthered the distribution of details regarding Chicago's seamier side), the brochure was "a nifty pamphlet that rubes in neighboring cities were saying made Chicago a modern Babylon." Mayor Carter Harrison Jr., believing the pamphlet heightened Chicago's reputation as a place where vice ran rampant, ordered the Everleigh Club closed on Tuesday, October 24, 1911. Speaking to the *Chicago Record-Herald*, the Mayor expressed more aggravation over the tenor of the city's reputation than the existence of prostitution. He said, "Vice in Chicago can exist only under the most stringent regulations. The Everleigh Club has been advertised far and wide. I am against this advertisement of Chicago's dives and intend to close up all such places."[35]

Although the 1911 raid on the Everleigh Club led to an energized effort to shut down the concentrated vice areas of the city, Harrison's administration could not claim to have made the only attempt to cut down on prostitution in Chicago. Progressives considered vice one of the main concerns of civic reform, and urban activists had objected to the obvious presence of prostitution in Chicago since the city had gained prominence for its vice districts during the Civil War. In 1896, the Civic Federation had asked Mayor George B. Swift to control houses of prostitution. Brothel windows (where women often displayed themselves to passersby) were ordered to be painted over and kept closed. In 1909 evangelist Gipsy Smith led twelve thousand Christians through the city's 22nd Street red light district to protest the area's existence.[36] One should note that Chicago folklore claims that brothels were so intricately linked with the city that even the expression "red-light" district stemmed from the existence of red glass over the transoms of brothels in Chicago's Levee. In 1910, the most informed move against vice came with the publication of the Chicago Vice Commission's report, *The Social Evil in Chicago*.

The Vice Commission grew out of a January 31, 1910 meeting of members of the Chicago Church Federation of Clergy, representing six hundred congregations from the city. The theme of that meeting at the Central Y.M.C.A. was the "Social Evil Problem in Chicago," and Dean Walter T. Sumner of the Episcopal Cathedral of SS. Peter and Paul on the city's West Side gave the paper. After Sumner's presentation, the body unanimously resolved to ask the mayor to appoint a vice commission. On March 5, 1910, Mayor Frank Busse appointed Sumner the temporary chairman of the committee, consisting of thirty mayoral appointees. The list of members included Sears and Roebuck's Julius Rosenwald, Association of Commerce activist Edward M. Skinner, and Northwestern University president Abram W. Harris. Their aim was to "inquire into conditions existing within the limits of the city with reference to vice of various forms including all practices which are physically and morally debasing and degrading, and which affect the moral and physical welfare of the inhabitants of the city."[37]

On April 5, 1911 the Vice Commission presented its report to the Mayor and the City Council. The Commission recommended the appointment of a Morals Commission and a Morals Court, to specially deal with the legal cases against vice which came up in Chicago. The nearly four hundred page report (the aforementioned work, *The Social Evil in Chicago*) and the press that followed added another scandalous section to Chicago's history, but the language of the report claimed confidence in Chicago's ability to face the findings and benefit from them. "We believe that Chicago has a public conscience," wrote the commissioners, "which, when aroused, cannot be easily stilled—a conscience built upon moral and ethical teachings of the purest American type—a conscience which when aroused to the truth will instantly rebel against the Social Evil in all its phases."[38] Interestingly, Chicago's Mayor Frank Busse understood that the appointment of the Vice Commission would lead to the perception that Chicago suffered from an unusually high level of prostitution. Busse displayed an insight, relatively rare for the period, of the possible damage that would be caused by the aggressive fight against prostitution and the publication of study findings. In a statement to the press, Busse expressed:

> I think we can fairly assume that our vice problem is exactly like that of any American city. To exploit publicly the details of it, can serve no useful end and such exploitation is not the purpose of this commission proposition. On the other hand exploitation may do much more harm

by leading the uninformed to believe that conditions exist here which are
of recent origin or which are worse than exist in other American cities.[39]

Despite the detailed report's exposure of the extensive level of prostitution in Chicago, Chicago officials failed to attempt to close down Chicago's
segregated vice district in its entirety until 1912. Prostitution, which had
never been legalized in Chicago, had been permitted to exist for decades.
Through the years, public opinion had wavered over whether to attempt to
eliminate vice altogether, regulate it through a variety rules, or confine it
physically in one area, as was ultimately done in the Levee. The 1912 push
to close the Levee was a substantive change in the city's attitude towards the
problem, but it did not mark the end of prostitution in Chicago by any
means. In a 1914 edition of *Collier's*, reporter Julian Street interviewed Alderman Michael Kenna, one half of the notorious Chicago political two-
some of the city's First Ward known to many as Hinky Dink Kenna and
Bathhouse John Coughlin. Hinky Dink told Street that vice in Chicago
would not disappear; segregated vice districts (good centers of bribes for political leaders like himself) were the best solution. The city continued to battle prostitution, as all American cities must, up to the present day. As
technology blossomed, access to prostitution proliferated and became harder to censure. In an age of telephones, those interested in procuring sex did
not have to venture out to a concentrated red light area. The later introduction of the internet, as observers in the early twenty-first century understand
all too well, adds an additionally complicated dimension to the sex industry.[40]

Chicago's crusade against vice became nationally known through a variety of magazine and newspaper stories.[41] Even Chicago journalist Finley
Peter Dunne's fictional alter-ego character, Mr. Dooley, took to musing
about the control of vice. Dunne, who wrote for both the *Chicago Post* and
the *Chicago Times-Herald*, spoke through the colloquialisms of Mr. Dooley
in a series of columns that ran between 1893 and 1898. Reprinted in papers
across the country, and eventually published in several book length collections, Mr. Dooley's Irish brogue and irreverent insights became for many the
voice of Chicago, if not of all ethnic urban dwellers. As literary historian
Barbara Schaaf explains, Dunne/Dooley "was among the first and best
transmitters of American urban culture."[42]

In one column, Mr. Dooley poked fun of the devotion of those who
fought prostitution. According to Dooley, the progressives said, "This here
city is a verytable Sodom an' it must be cleaned out', an' iverybody takes a
broom at it. Th' churches appints comities an' so does th' Stock Exchange
an' th' Brewers' Society an' afther awhile other organizations jumps into th'

fray." The crusades would go as far as having men wear marriage certifi-
cates outside of their coats, if they had their way, Dooley believed. The boss
of the progressives, Dooley mocked, thought that "When I get through they
won't be enough crime left in this city to amuse a sthranger fr'm Hannybal
Missoury f'r twinty minyits." Dooley expressed no surprise at Chicago politicians' habitual quiescence on the existence of brothels. "I don't expict to
gather calla lillies in Hogan's turnip patch. Why shud I expict to pick bunch-
es iv spotless statesmen fr'm th' gradooation class iv th' house iv correction?
[where, presumably, Dooley believed Chicago politicians came from]"[43]

The most concentrated hit Chicago took to its reputation came in the
form of reams of expository writing on the city's crime problems. The images of the crazed, tipsy men who were mentioned in so many articles on the
Great Chicago Fire of 1871 had evolved over time into stories of organized
criminals who sold alcohol and other sinful goods and opportunities (including prostitutes and gambling) to the public. These men, visualized as immigrants, and "their" women, usually imagined as negative stereotypes such
as over-protective immigrant mamas and flagrantly sexual young women,
threatened any remaining decorum in the city with their previously unfamiliar religions, ethnicities, and moral codes. Organized criminals had taken
the American ethic of hard-work but applied their labors and business acu-
men to underground economies, thus threatening, according to the world
view of many Americans, much of what the nation stood for. Chicago, cast
as the particularly troubled American city since 1871, reached the nadir of
its reputation in the 1920s and 1930s with the wide circulation of stories on
its criminals.

William L. Chenery, editor of *Collier's*, penned an editorial on Chicago
entitled "Turbulent Mistress of the West," in March 1930. Chenery wrote,
"You have to see Chicago to believe it. There's nothing quite like it in all the
world. Nowhere else, surely, is magnificent achievement so strangely overshadowed by blatant politics and violent crime." These sentiments had been
in the air for some time. In 1904, a journalist writing for *Critic* had said of
Chicago, "And black—yes, blacker than the pall of smoke which envelopes
her—has been her record of crime." Writers were so sure of the extent of
Chicago's infamous reputation that they could produce blithe pronouncements as to the relative weight of the anti-Chicago rhetoric in comparison
with that of other cities without long explanatory statements. Their readers
understood. Chicago had a reputation like no other place; a reputation
which long preceded it and was well known by the American public. In
1907, George Kibbe Turner could state simply in *McClure's*, "The

reputation of Chicago for crime has fastened upon the imagination of the United States as that of no other city has done."[44]

In 1929, John Landesco, a graduate student at the University of Chicago, published *Organized Crime in Chicago*, the third volume of the Illinois Crime Survey. The work, relying on recently evolving theories of crime from the University of Chicago sociology department, was the most far-reaching study on crime in its day. The crime survey was not in print for long and cannot be said to have significantly stimulated Chicago's reputation as a particularly crime-ridden city. Still, the book does testify to the depth of contemporary thought linking cities and crime. According to the University of Chicago sociology school, crime occurred naturally from certain neighborhoods; the culture and social structure of neighborhoods, *the city itself*, stimulated lawlessness. Landesco found that Chicago crime stemmed from the city's inherent deficiencies. He blamed both the city's role as a pleasure center for the surrounding countryside and its huge concentration of capital. In addition, as a very young city in the throws of rapid growth, the city bred crime. As Andrew Bruce, author of Landesco's original introduction, explained:

> Every student of public affairs must realize that the prevalence of crime in Chicago and in America is in large measure *due to our very newness and to our very democracy*. To a certain extent it is due to our very altruism. Crime is the problem of adolescent/youth and the failure to properly deal with crime is nearly always a weakness of an adolescent city and of an adolescent nation. *There has always been crime upon the frontier.* The main trouble with Chicago is that it is too young and has grown too fast.[45]

In part, Chicago's reputation as a crime center stemmed from fact. Organized crime had taken root in Chicago; no one could deny that. Other, less "organized" criminal activities also took place. As Herbert Asbury explains, "In one period of six months in 1906 there was a burglary every three hours, a holdup every six hours, and a murder every day." Chicago gained notoriety through the presence of such criminals as Mickey Finn, the bartender who medicated patrons' drinks so that he could rob them, Henry H. Holmes, who killed visitors to the Columbian Exposition so that he could sell their bodies to medical schools, and Herman Billik, a fortune-teller who murdered members of the Vzral family in order to attempt to claim the insurance.[46] Organized crime bosses, Big Jim Colosimo, Johnny Torrio, and Al Capone of the West Side syndicate, and rival North Side leaders Dion O'Banion, Hymie Weiss, and George "Bugs" Moran, elevated the urgency of Chicago crime coverage even further.

Big Jim Colosimo, Chicago's first notorious crime boss, earned fifty thousand dollars a month through his underworld dealings, according to some estimates. Yet when Colosimo fell in love with actress and singer Dale Winter, who became his second wife, he lost interest in the day-to-day dealings of racketeering and handed over control to his underling, Johnny Torrio. And it was through Torrio that Al Capone, who would so capture the American imagination, came to Chicago from New York, where he had been a member of the Five Points Gang. Capone ran Torrio's Chicago club, Four Deuces, and the Maple Inn brothel in the suburban community of Forest View. In 1920, Colosimo was murdered, perhaps at the behest of Torrio; Brooklyn racketeer Frankie Yale and Al Capone have both been considered as the possible trigger-man, although no clear determination was ever made.

On November 10, 1924, rival gang leader Dion O'Banion was murdered in the flower shop of which he was co-owner, presumably in an attack ordered by Torrio and Capone. After O'Banion's death, second-generation Polish immigrant Hymie Weiss took up the leadership of the North Side gang. In January of 1925, Torrio himself was attacked, although not killed. After this brush with death, Torrio passed on leadership responsibilities to Capone and left Chicago. Although Capone would only serve as an underworld boss for three to four years, his personality captured attention. Visitors to Chicago in the 1920s thought no trip complete without a glimpse of the mob leader. By 1930, the Chicago Crime Commission (a division of the Association of Commerce), organized in the height of progressive spirit in 1919, placed Alphonse Capone at the top of their list of the twenty-eight leading criminals. In this move, Capone became forever known as "Public Enemy Number One." The crime leader became a symbol of Chicago's unruliness, one that needed to be confronted when civic-minded Chicagoans again turned their attentions to the production of Chicago's reputation in the late 1920s. Capone's popular image connects in several ways with the aims of this study, so he will be discussed at several points in the text. Awareness of Capone's activities is a key element in comprehending the failures of the 1933–1934 World's Fair, which we explore in Chapter Four. And in Chapter Five, which explores the reign of Chicago's scandalous reputation in the 1930s, 1940s, and 1950s through an onslaught of negative books, films, and other media, we will further take up the way in which the producers of popular culture gravitated towards Capone's image.

The incident that most invoked Capone's name and most soiled Chicago's popular image in the 1920s was the Valentine's Day Massacre. On Valentine's Day in 1929, seven members and friends of the Moran gang were murdered by gangsters dressed as police while waiting for a shipment of liquor from Detroit. Chicago law enforcement immediately thought that Capone and his men were to blame, but this could not be proven. Capone had an airtight alibi for the day of the crime (he was in Miami), but the order for the deaths probably came from him. Some believe the actual murderers to have been members of the Capone-connected Jewish mob organization, the Purple Gang, out of Detroit. Detroit, with its easy access to Canada and Canadian liquor, served as a convenient point of entry for those importing illegal alcohol. Organized crime in Detroit, while less well known than Chicago's version, flourished in the Prohibition years.

Despite his years of terrorizing Chicago, Capone went to jail only twice. In 1929, Capone and bodyguard Frankie Rio served one year on concealed weapons charges. On October 17, 1931, Capone was convicted of five counts of tax evasion, for which the court sentenced him to eleven years in prison. In 1934 Capone was transferred from an Atlanta penitentiary to Alcatraz. Released early for his sentence on account of illness in 1939, Capone died of syphilis in Florida on January 25, 1947.[47]

With the influence of the many less than flattering stories that circulated about Chicago in the forty years after the Columbian Exposition, Chicago reached the low point of its reputation. Arriving in Chicago for the 1893 fair, visitors hoped to enjoy the spectacle of the event and its host city, and perhaps secretly wanted their misgivings about the upstart Illinois city proven true. English visitor William Stead and others found the seamy underbelly of the city they had searched for and then broadcast these assertions to a national and even an international audience. Just at the turn of the century, Chicago had enjoyed a brief respite from the very dim pictures of its urban character; some journalists and critics of the time realized that the city had built up many laudable cultural institutions. But the publication of these flatteries was short-lived. Soon the derisive comments regarding Chicago deepened in the darkness of their language and grew more plentiful. The proliferation of major national periodicals in the twentieth century did little or nothing to expand the breadth of opinion on the city's personality; indeed, the multiplication of coverage only appears to have narrowed the possible rhetorical choices.

It remains fascinating that Chicago's character so often was the subject of journalistic musing. What was it about the city that so captured writers from inside and outside its boundaries and inspired them to set pen to paper? Many writers even chose to comment on the way in which the subject of the city's reputation had grown scandalous, and so fascinated national and international audiences. In 1929, Samuel Merwin, who spent his youth in Chicago and still thought the city magnificent himself, wrote about the widely held negative perceptions of the city in the *Saturday Evening Post*:

> The spread of the Chicago legend is a strange phenomenon of our modern life. It is, I believe, universally accepted from Maine to California. It is taken as a matter of course in England. It is widely known on the continent of Europe. It carries with it a picture of complete breakdown of law, of corruption unequaled in any other American city.

When Merwin spoke to friends of visiting the city, "not one of them failed either to warn me or at least joke about the need of a bulletproof vest. Not one." And Merwin topped off his coloration of the city with his evaluation, "Chicago has today, it is probably fair to say, the worst publicity—if I may use the term—of any city since Sodom and Gomorrah."[48] In a similar vein, the article "Why is Chicago," in the magazine, *World Tomorrow*, even-handedly considered the case of the city's reputation and still found the criticisms fundamentally true:

> The very word Chicago has a world-wide connotation which suggests robbery, crime, and sudden death. And while loyal Chicagoans may wince under this odium and eagerly urge that there is also a Chicago which possessed Hull House and Jane Addams, a great progressive university, an art institute and a symphony orchestra, they are driven in their hearts to admit that while the evil reputation of the city is exaggerated, it is nevertheless a substantially accurate characterization of a devastatingly large sector of the city's life.[49]

Lewis Mumford, writing for the *New Republic* in 1929, expressed his own distasteful impressions of Chicago. He compared Chicago unfavorably to both Boston and New York and said, in short, that Chicago was "a synopsis of twentieth century hell." Mumford painted a forlorn picture of the Midwestern city in what had become a classic view of Chicago—as seen from the train. Chicago served as the train hub of the nation, and passengers had prolonged contact with the city because of the stipulation that all train routes utilizing the city's facilities begin or end in Chicago. This practice required many travelers to spend the night in the city, and at least forced them to endure a slow ride through the city as the train began or ended its journey and ran at reduced speeds. The lumbering exiting or entering train afforded a good, long look at Chicago. According to Mumford, one could get a very good sense of Chicago's lack of East Coast culture by its very approach:

> My repeated impressions of Chicago are, apparently, doomed to be un-
> favorable: one wakes up on a dreary winter morning to find oneself
> passing through a slatternly Indiana town, and then, as on an endless
> repetitious reel, come low-lying wooden boxes, their roofs scarcely lifted
> above the stagnant blackness of the prairie, and abandoned factories
> with their windows full of jagged glass, and grain elevators, standing in
> lofty dejection amid the merest defecation of landscape and more
> cramped boxes and freight-yards and factories and elevators, with now
> and again the sudden snout of a lake steamer, unloading her ores, until
> finally, when one is almost convinced that the tedium and horror will
> not cease, unless by dint of vast muscular effort one can wake up, one is
> turned into the blare of the Chicago Union Station.[50]

Of course, part of the blame for the maligning of Chicago can be placed
on the individual journalist's desire to get published, and for their editors'
desire to sell the product to the broadest possible audience. Publishers had
fully understood the draw of "yellow journalism" since the Spanish-Ameri-
can War of 1898, and this book's examination of the reporting of the Great
Chicago Fire demonstrates an even earlier comprehension of the salability
of scandal. In part, Chicago's brazen image was conceived out of the efforts
of its own local newspapers. Efforts to curb undue muckraking by local
newspapers had had various periods of success over the years. Yet many na-
tionally-run articles critical of the city were reprints or rehashings of information which originated in Chicago papers. In 1926, concerned citizen
Henry Stone wrote Mayor William E. Dever to express concern over the
matter. Stone said, "Having just returned from a six months trip [sic] which
has taken me from Chicago to the Atlantic coast, to Florida and the South,
the Pacific coast, and back here and in my mind there is no question but that
newspapers of this city are unintentionally injuring Chicago by featuring
crime news in glaring headlines."[51]

Commentators believed Chicago's troubles stemmed from inherent
character flaws, including undue love of money and irrepressible youth. Onlookers judged the city as they would a person, anthropomorphism being
hard to avoid when addressing the question of urban "personality." In a
sense, popular images of cities are just the combination of the impressions
of many individuals regarding that place, writ large. Chicago's many persistent, even pushy, new-style business people proved to have considerable effect on Chicago's characterization. Jack Lait, in an apparent attempt to
soothe over this sore point, explained in *American Magazine* that "any man
who has money in abundance is regarded as coarse. If that man made his
wad quickly instead of taking eighty generations to get it—to get it with
germs of scandal or blotches of questionable antecedents—he is regarded as

especially venal and rude. A city is judged the same way, only a city, being a collection of millions of got-rich-quick men, gets its verdict millions-fold."[52]

Interestingly, at the same time that Chicago's deficiencies were pointed out, many found the city intrinsically American in nature. Indeed, its very deficiencies were American in type. Like the nation, Chicago was young, earnest, hard-working, bold, and individualistic, as well as boastful, ill-mannered, and committed to capitalism to an embarrassing degree. Chicago's representativeness, then, disheartened many. Yet this anti-urbanism was at times softened by a hope for the future; the city had problems but might someday see its way out. Journalist Franklin Matthews openly conceded that Chicago had her burdens to bear, but he found a good heart deep inside. Matthews wrote:

> Unfeeling critics of Chicago have referred to it as the 'tough' of American cities, and unfortunately there is some justification for the designation, but that isn't the whole story. The truth is that in many things she is typically American, not an entirely pleasant thing to say. She may be loud and awkward yes, even a little vulgar—but she has a good heart, although she is constantly getting up capers, ever since Mrs. O'Leary's cow kicked over that lamp, and when she stirs herself in the path of virtue look out for a mighty wrath. Spread this broadcast to her everlasting credit: She has put down anarchists and she has put down boodlers. She may be a good deal of a smudge, not nice to look at, but inside she's white.[53]

Chicago's Americanness was paradoxical; the city contained the good and the bad of the nation, and Americans loved and hated the Illinois city for this. Frank Norris described the city's situation in *The Pit* with a deft hand:

> Here, midmost in the land, beat the Heart of the Nation, whence inevitably must come its immeasurable power, its infinite, infinite, inexhaustible vitality. Here, of all cities, throbbed true life—the true power and spirit of America; gigantic, crude with the crudity of youth, disdaining rivalry; sane and healthy and vigorous; brutal in its ambition, arrogant in the new-found knowledge of its giant strength, prodigal of its wealth, infinite in its desires. In its capacity boundless, in its courage indomitable; subduing the wilderness in a single generation, defying calamity, and through the flame and the debris of a commonwealth in ashes, rising suddenly renewed, formidable, and Titanic.[54]

And at some level, the series of misfortunes in Chicago's history endeared Americans to the city and made them hopeful regarding its future. In a sense rooting for the underdog, Americans wanted to see if the city could succeed and grow into its own. Given this attitude, a significant number of commentators described Chicago's plethora of troubles with an empathetic hand. Chicago was wicked, even hellish, but hope remained. Chicago writer Elia Peattie explained, "Chicago has a passionate zest for life; it is arrogant, swaggering, half-drunken [*sic*] with pride, puffed up at its benevolence, its largemindedness, and its ingenuity; and it conceals, as a blustering young man will conceal a virtue or a tenderness, the nostalgia for beauty which yearns in its heart."[55]

Figure 1 Area of Chicago after Great Chicago Fire. Courtesy of the *Chicago Daily News* Collection, Chicago Historical Society.

Figure 2 North Side of Chicago, after the Great Chicago Fire. Library of Congress, American Memory Collection.

Figure 3 The Interstate Exposition building, designed by W.W. Boyington, on South Michigan and East Adams streets in Chicago. Courtesy of the *Chicago Daily News* Collection, Chicago Historical Society.

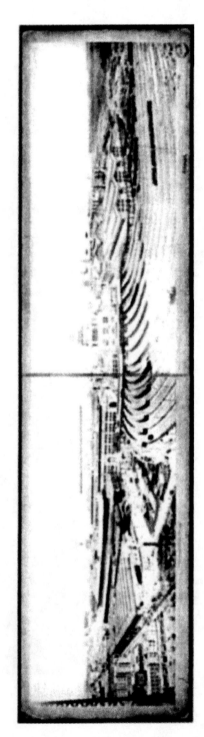

Figure 4 Birdseye view of the Columbian Exposition, 1893. Library of Congress, American Memory Collection.

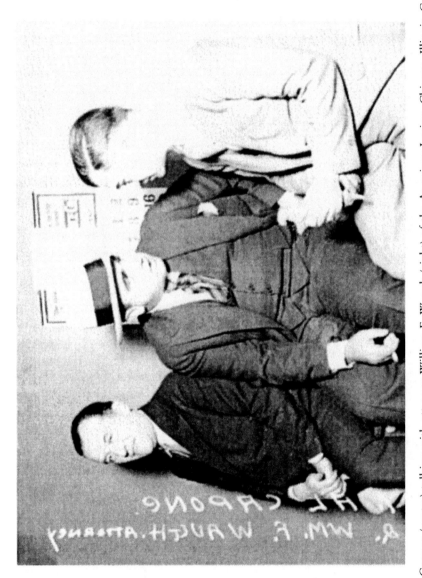

Figure 5 Al Capone (center) talking with attorney William F. Waugh (right) of the American Legion, Chicago, Illinois. Courtesy of the Chicago Daily News Collection, Chicago Historical Society.

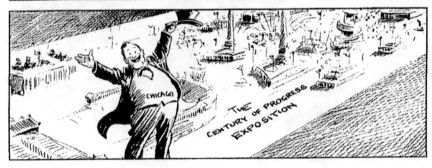

Figure 6 Cartoon by John T. McCutcheon depicting hoped for changes to Chicago's national reputation as a result of A Century of Progress. Courtesy of the Chicago Historical Society.

Figure 7 Fair general manager Lenox Lohr, fair president Rufus Dawes, and Vice President of the United States Charles Gates Dawes. Courtesy of the *Chicago Daily News* Collection, Chicago Historical Society.

Figure 8 Travel and Transport building, A Century of Progress. Courtesy of the Chicago Historical Society.

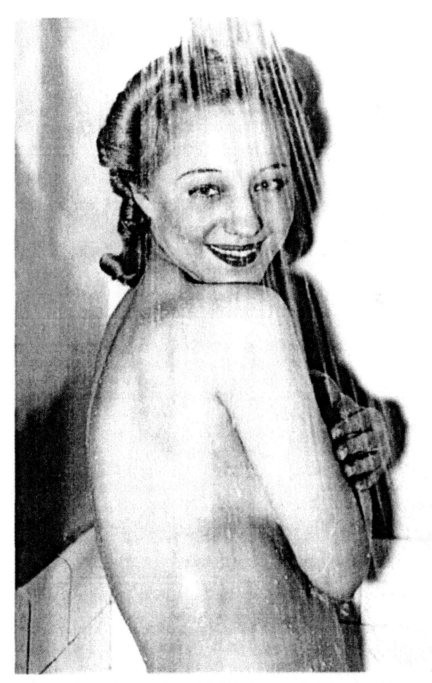

Figure 9 Sally Rand, whose fan and bubble dances took A Century of Progress, and the nation, by storm. Courtesy of the Chicago Historical Society.

Chapter Four

"All the World is Waiting for the Sunrise": A Century of Progress and the National Image of Chicago

In the Progressive era, the national cultural producers wielded the most concentrated power over Chicago's image. Image-making had been momentarily abandoned by metropolitan leaders during the inward turn discussed earlier. These leaders not only devoted themselves to civic reform but did so in such a thorough-going fashion that they felt compelled to broadcast their new-found institutional capabilities on the national level as models for other urban centers. Chicagoans accomplished valiant and necessary work on urban issues like the reduction of crime and poverty. Leading Chicagoans assisted the city's booming immigrant population with the assimilation process. City leaders chose to spend their volunteer hours on the most deserving causes in their city. Yet the timing of their move away from boosterism and towards serious service to their communities proved unfortunate. When viewing the mounting power of popular culture during this same period with the lens of hindsight, we can gauge the trouble a later set of boosters would have in regaining some control over the city's national reputation.

It is a difficult challenge for those people located in the day-to-day reality of a place to consider the issue of that place's representation. In Chicago's case, it was the city's business leaders, predominantly engaged in the pursuit of hard dollars, who most passionately tried their skills at shaping popular understanding. Why do people try to succeed in realms so foreign to their own professional knowledge? Certainly, the business people felt an improved reputation for Chicago helped their own monetary interests, especially if they had investments related to tourism or real estate in the city. Some of the interest in the city's image also no doubt sprung from personal pride; Chicago represented the "home team" in the game of urban booster-ism, and urban activists did not want to give up on their side.

Perhaps too, the line between those involved with crafting the reality of place and those involved with image-making is a boundary that proves quite tempting for those on either side to step tentatively across. The desire on the part of civic leaders to shape their city's reputation as well as lead its social campaigns may be in part related to a very modern impetus—that of the nation's image makers in the late twentieth and early twenty-first century to attempt to build their own actual spaces. Aida Hozic investigates the line between reality and imagination in *Hollyworld: Space, Power, and Fantasy in the American Economy*. In 1993, Hozic explains, Universal Studios, already having established its company town, Universal City, in 1915, again tried its hand at constructing an actual place with its Universal CityWalk. The venue is a strange combination of theme park and mall. Universal has tried to introduce elements of urban culture—like make-believe graffiti and street performers—into private space in order to recreate city life for a generation of people who perhaps have grown to fear adventures in the public urban environment. In 1994, the creators of The Magic Kingdom began the physical work of building a real-life community in Osceola County, Florida. Disney built "Celebration" on land purchased by the company in 1965. Celebration owed its philosophical origins in part to the back-to-basics thinking of the New Urbanism movement, Walt Disney's original plans for his EPCOT center (Experimental Prototype Community of Tomorrow—first conceived as a real town), and in a convoluted sort of way, even to the white plaster Beaux Arts architecture of Chicago's World's Columbian Exposition, for which Elias Disney, Walt's father, had worked construction.[1]

The flurry of press, far from all positive, on the Celebration project, interestingly shows that even a modern master of popular culture like the Disney corporation cannot adequately control image making when it comes to the image of an actual, living place, inhabited by regular Americans. How then could those quite distant from the image-making apparatus ever have succeeded in an earlier age? In the second Chicago World's Fair, we find a courageous, yet flawed, attempt on the part of urban leaders to reassert some representational power at the dawn of a highly public age. This somewhat outmoded event ultimately could not function as the means to combat Chicago's infamous image at the national level. A new period had begun, partly foreshadowed by the unveiling of the medium of television at this world's fair. Popular culture had grown too unpredictable for even an expensive event like this to affect wide-reaching change.

Opened in late May 1933 and reopened for a second season in the summer of 1934, Chicago's second World's Fair, named by its trustees "A Century of Progress," celebrated the city's 100th birthday and heralded the achievements of science and its gifts to industry since Chicago's incorporation as a town in 1833. Elite Chicagoans had turned inward for over thirty years in the spirit of progressivism that had swept the country. Now these leaders had come to understand that control over their city's image had passed into the hands of media producers. The former progressives wished to swiftly dominate the creation of Chicago's popular representation. Although they knew of the troubles of the Columbian Exposition, Chicago boosters began to consider the possibility of mounting another world's fair in the early 1920s. Chicagoans were experienced fair connoisseurs, and had been left a rich legacy of documents from the organizers of the city's first world's fair. In addition, a world's fair was simply the weightiest tool in the booster's bag of tricks, the only thing that could possibly wield the degree of influence over American popular culture now needed. Supporters of A Century of Progress desperately hoped to combat some of the negative images spread by media coverage of the city's problems and to bring increased business to their hometown. As Chicago poet Harriet Monroe explained, fair planners hoped to "adorn Chicago's reputation with something more decorative than grafting politicians and murdering racketeers."[2]

Great changes took place in America's cities in the decade between the early 1920s and the early 1930s. The financial tightening caused by the Great Depression affected the mindset of the fair planners. Although the fair was conceived in the height of the 1920s financial boom, the bulk of the fair planning took place in Depression-era Chicago, when the city's business sector felt hard-pressed to draw traveler's dollars and favorable publicity to the city. They hoped to reinvigorate Chicago's economy through this influx of visitors and to instill hope in the city's financial future by the presentation of the lavish fair. But the period of the Great Depression also proved in some ways to be a difficult time to launch a spectacle honoring the potentials of capitalism.

City elite also strove to challenge Chicago's unruly, adolescent image by staging a sophisticated cultural event of the kind only well-established cities could mount. Chicago leaders needed to confront the East Coast bias as they had in the planning stages of the World's Columbian Exposition. Forty years later, many across the nation still doubted that Chicago could produce an event of the highest cultural caliber. In order to stabilize the fair's claims of cultural leadership, the fair leaders borrowed cultural capital from wherever they could. Organizers first appealed to the National Research Council in

1928. The NRC agreed to provide assistance with the exposition's wide-ranging scientific theme and the presentation of exhibits, which the Chicagoans of course appreciated.[3] City leaders calculated that A Century of Progress would be the epitome of successful boosterism, casting the turbulent metropolis in the most favorable possible light.

Despite the care bestowed on the creation of the second Chicago World's Fair, popular images of the event ultimately deviated sharply from those hoped for by its planners. The fair became known for far more than its exhibits of Lincoln's birthplace, electric animated dinosaurs, and "The Transparent Man." Although organizers had attempted to present a carefully culled image to its various publics, A Century of Progress would be known more for the curious architectural styles of its exhibit buildings and the fair's various adult entertainment offerings. No doubt the most remembered image of the fair was Sally Rand's risqué fan dance. While A Century of Progress was an economic boon for the city, the exposition's effect on Chicago's reputation could only garner mixed reviews. As a device designed to urge Americans to see Chicago as a modern, culturally rich, and sophisticated urban center, the event was a failure. Despite the undeniable zeal of the boosters, the American desire to see Chicago as a troubled city proved too strong. In the midst of the Great Depression, the fair officials' intended message about the cultural attainments of their city rang false. The images of the city that had persisted since the Great Fire could not be erased by a single display, despite careful planning and high investment costs.

Throughout the history of the United States, discussion surrounding the nature of the country's cities has substantially contributed to the project of defining what it means to be American. And during the chaotic 1930s, Americans needed to define themselves more than ever. The uncertainty caused by the financial devastation of the Great Depression led citizens to question what held the nation together. Americans needed solutions for their monetary crisis, and they needed scapegoats on which to pin the blame for the upheaval. Chicago, with its newness, its large and misunderstood immigrant populations, and its seeming tendency to be wicked, appeared to provide at least a partial scapegoat. The rocky financial situation faced by the nation made the multifaceted goals of the fair tricky for fair planners to negotiate. Perhaps no fair could ever have substantially changed the reputation of a city, even under the best circumstances, but this one did not function as planned. A Century of Progress failed to erase previous damage to Chicago's name and even succeeded in adding some new smudges.

Although this has been heretofore little understood, the main motivation behind A Century of Progress was to do battle with the perpetrators of the city's negative image. In this spirit, city leaders struggled against actual crime and to quell the rumors that exaggerated Chicago's dangers. Particularly disordered areas within the city had to be cleaned up or at least hidden from high-level media scrutiny before a successful fair could be opened. Century of Progress trustee and president of the Association of Commerce Robert I. Randolph, who had organized a secret committee of millionaire businessmen to investigate Chicago's crime, announced that "our committee has been assured of financial and moral support from 'big business' in its campaign to clean up Chicago before the 1933 world's fair. Everyone working together will be able to do it. The situation is serious, but it isn't critical." Speaking with a reporter from the *Saturday Evening Post*, Randolph provided his reasoning for why Chicago's reputation had gotten out of control. "Millions of people living in cities having a higher homicidal [sic] rate than ours regard Chicago with holy terror," Randolph explained, "because the editors of their papers bury their own crime news in their back pages while giving the latest reports from Chicago gangland front-page position." Observers of Chicago supported the assumptions of the fair planners. One Chicago visitor expounded in 1931, "Unless gang rule is wiped out in Chicago before the Century of Progress exposition [sic], there will be no visitors here in 1933, for the simple reason that people will be too scared to come."[4]

A Century of Progress' primary direction came from the exposition's general manager, Major Lenox Lohr. Lohr had worked as an engineer for the army, had taught at West Point, and had served as editor of *Military Engineer*. His talent for language and the organizational skills instilled by his military background served Lohr well in his new position. Under his guidance, *Military Engineer* had become a leading periodical in the engineering field and drew corporate leaders to subscribe. The magazine touted the corporation as a model organizational form. Thus, his work of selling Chicago and its businesses through the exposition fit in with Lohr's previous career. And through his work with the fair, Lohr evolved into an ace at conceptualizing grand public entertainment/education events. Lohr immersed himself in the exposition, even living in special quarters off the operations office located on the fair grounds. Lohr's devotion brought him recognition and increased connections. Tellingly, Lohr later served as president of both the National Broadcasting Company and the Museum of Science and Industry in Chicago.[5]

Speaking on a WGN radio broadcast on July 10, 1929, Major Lenox Lohr provided a thorough exploration of his understanding of Chicago's reputation (an understanding which echoed that of many prominent Chicagoans), which is worth quoting at length:

There are many people in the outside world who give us the atmosphere of a wicked city. Chicago, I believe, is forty-ninth in the list of American cities in the matter of homicides on the basis of population.

Then why this reputation? It is one of the invariable penalties of greatness. That which the little man does may be of small consequence. But if the big man, let us say, wears even a gay necktie, it is a matter of comment just because he is outstanding.

It is certain that our second world's fair will be a most powerful influence in overcoming the unfavorable impression the people living beyond our city boundaries have gained.

In 1933 the world will talk about our exposition and not our crime. Visitors will see our culture, our beautiful buildings and parks, our giant industries, and will carry away a different conception of Chicago.[6]

This type of rhetoric continued through the actual opening of the fair in May. Those trying to reinvent the city's image placed blame for Chicago's well-known wayward reputation squarely on the city's tendency to arouse imaginations. Literature speaking against the city's connection with crime was handed out to fair goers in 1933. In a tract entitled "Chicago: Greatest Advertised City in the World, Not the Wickedest," Lee Alexander Stone put forth a familiar defense against Chicago-directed anti-urbanism:

Chicagoans always deal with superlatives. They hear them from birth and come to look upon them as the normal level of thought and expression. Only Chicago could produce that consistent set of expansive phrases which has grown to form a typical part of the city's folklore. Heralded by these phrases, Chicago appears before the outside world; and it is only natural that outsiders tend to adopt some of its own superlatives when considering it. Unfortunately enough, this habit of strong emphasis reaches to undesirables as well as to the desirable side of our civic life; so that in the present age of general restlessness Chicago's share of the turbulence has received an abnormal degree of advertising and prominence.

Stone was not alone in his assertion that what crime did exist in Chicago could be attributed to Italian-Americans. According to Stone, people of foreign extraction committed ninety percent of Chicago's crimes. Stone saw the remedy in immigration law, inter-marriage, and a heavy hand. He wrote, "This situation will never be overcome until we develop a determination to handle the Mafia and other outlaw organizations in the same ironhanded manner with which Mussolini has recently handled them."[7]

Chicago elites also had a sense that the fair would inspire leagues of everyday Chicagoans with renewed public spirit. At some level, the Chicagoans who had devoted themselves to a progressive clean-up of their city over the years may have felt they were working at cross-purposes with the general populace. Perhaps the failure to quell all of Chicago's problems came from the insufficient number of those involved in the work. At a February 1931 luncheon of Loop business owners, fair president and Association of Commerce leader Rufus Dawes proclaimed that the fair should provoke more Chicagoans to "correct the city's evils."[8]

With the onset of the financial hardships of the Great Depression, Chicago civic leaders also openly hoped that the exposition would prove financially fruitful. In a speech to area business leaders, one fair official assuaged his listeners with his comments, "You probably have heard over the radio that 'all the world is waiting for the sunrise.' A Century of Progress may be the business sunrise that the world is waiting for, and it will be a demonstration of the splendid strength and vitality of the city of Chicago on which you gentlemen can cash in not only from June 1 to November 1, but for many years to come." Here, the official was most likely referring to the popular song, "The World is Waiting for the Sunrise," by Canadians Ernest Seitz and Gene Lockhart, first introduced in 1920 and of a nature to inspire radio listeners in the dark days of the Depression.[9]

That the fair stimulated Chicago's economy and proved to be financially sound in-and-of itself is not in doubt. Thirty-nine million visitors toured the fairs in its two seasons, enabling the fair board to repay all its debts, give bondholders a 6 percent return on investments, and end up in the black. In an assessment after the event, the Century of Progress administration asserted that the fair employed many out-of-work Chicagoans, and brought many out-of-town dollars to the city. Fair general manager Lenox Lohr announced that the fair had employed 25,000 people, 20,000 of which had been out of work before being hired, and that the financial run-off from the exposition had created jobs for over 200,000 people around the city. Lohr also concluded that the fair had brought two hundred million dollars of new capital into the city.[10] Yet in considering carefully what the original visionaries of the fair had hoped the fair would achieve, and in thinking beyond finances to the fair as a cultural event, one encounters some less-successful elements of the celebration.

The first important attempt to organize the fair can be traced to the minister Myron E. Adams, a member of the Chicago Plan Commission, who wrote Mayor William E. Dever in 1923 to suggest a fair in honor of Chicago's centennial. Adams contended that a World's Exposition would stimulate the completion of public projects and that "the challenge of world attention will increase the sense of responsibility among Chicago citizens." Between September of 1923 and December 1925, Adams polled "leading" citizens, civic organizations, and newspapers to get a better idea of elite Chicago's acceptance of the idea. Adams found the fair agreeable to the city's boosters. The enormous undertaking appeared to be in keeping with the elite citizenry's continual and strong commitment to their home. Adams wrote:

> Chicago has never lost the spirit of those who generation after generation have built up and rebuilt this city ever aspiring for something finer and better, realizing defects by never developing an inferior [sic] complex. It has gone on pushing into the Lake [sic], turning rivers backwards, tearing away streets to rebuild broad avenues, developing its marvelous boulevard and forest systems, increasing the number of its educational institutions and, perhaps greatest of all, building up in this city not one great business community but hundreds of minor ones, each growing into a center of importance by itself.[11]

Organizers had the plans for the civic celebration well underway when those in the financial circles voiced some opposition. Some businesspeople feared that a recession would follow the 1933 fair as it had with the Columbian Exposition—although the 1893 downturn had, in truth, been felt nationally and the fair most likely delayed the onset of financial problems in Chicago. Heeding the criticism, then Mayor William Thompson declared the plan dead. When a public outcry answered "Big Bill" Thompson's proclamation, he relented, and asked city treasurer Charles S. Peterson to look into public support for the event. Finally, the fair organizing resumed speed and in January 1928, the state of Illinois granted the enterprise a charter, in the name of the "Chicago Second World's Fair Centennial Celebration." The event's official name was later changed to "A Century of Progress."[12]

When well into planning in 1928, the fair's board sought out the National Research Council, asking for the organization's input on a suitable scientific theme for the new endeavor. The event would be a celebration of Chicago's establishment, but its leaders also wanted it to appeal to a broad audience. As Lenox Lohr, the General Manager of A Century of Progress said to the advertising council of the Chicago Association of Commerce, "We have a glorious opportunity here to put over something not only for Chicago, but for the world."[13] A tribute to scientific achievement was deemed an appropriate theme for the World's Fair, as Chicago had always been intimately linked with technology, and the theme did serve to incite interest. Dr. Henry Crew of Northwestern University, responsible for oversight of all basic science presentations commented that "A Century of

Progress from the start, took as its goal not the celebration of a particular event but the demonstration of a great theorem. This theorem is that industry, manufacture and commerce depend almost immediately upon the pure sciences." A group of scientific advisors worked hard to produce exhibits that were informative as well as entertaining. The advisors urged that the exhibits be as animated as possible, the better to catch the public's eye.[14]

As a front-page cartoon in the *Chicago Daily Tribune* announced, A Century of Progress was "The Bargain of the Century." "A good college education costs anywhere from $1,200 to $10,000 according to the size of Dad's bankroll," it explained. But "Chicago offers a liberal education for 50 cents." The fair could claim a myriad of carefully crafted scientific exhibits on its official grounds, as well as formal relationships with a number of science-themed resources at its disposal in the city. Once completed, the exposition had separate buildings dedicated to transportation, electricity, and horticulture, as well as a massive "Hall of Science." Exhibits were dedicated to dairy production and agriculture; A Century of Progress also relied on the preexisting Adler Planetarium, located right on the fair grounds, as well as the Shedd Aquarium and the Field Museum of Natural History, situated nearby.[15] Corporations built their own structures for exhibiting their products, or rented space in fair-owned buildings. In addition to the scientific theme, the fair also housed the sprawling Hall of Religion, the Illinois Host House, the Federal Building, the States Building, the foreign exhibitions, and the American-run international theme villages, like the popular Streets of Paris.

As during the Columbian Exposition, an extensive promotion department and subsidiary groups of interested Chicagoans produced thousands and thousands of pages of publicity materials in support of the world's fair. In addition to the prolific official Promotion Department of A Century of Progress, the Association of Commerce assisted efforts through their central publicity committee, their convention bureau (which promoted Chicago as the ideal 1933 convention city), and their fair booster publications *Commerce* and *Progress*. Openly conceiving of the onslaught of materials as "selling" Chicago to America, fair organizers were zealous in their efforts. In one three week period, the Promotion Department answered seventy-seven thousand inquiries for written material on the fair.[16] In 1928, an early version of the Promotion Department, the Committee on Public Information, had decided not pay for formal advertisements, which would run into the millions of dollars, but to rely on an extensive series of press releases and public awareness activities. This cost-cutting decision, interestingly, took place even before the onset of the Depression and no doubt helped the fair keep its finances in order. Chicagoans had learned difficult lessons about the power of the media, and now planned to use it for their own ends.

The World's Fair Legion organization sparked interest in A Century of Progress by selling five dollar memberships. Commemorative travel guides were authorized, as well as license plates reading "Chicago World's Fair 1933." American celebrities like Bette Davis and Gracie Allen visited the yet unopened fairgrounds in order to generate publicity. As the first world's fair catering to motorists, planners paid careful attention to producing maps of the Chicago region, marked fair routes with special road signs from seventy-five miles outside the city, and located information booths twenty miles from Chicago in several directions. Regular promotional radio broadcasts were made on the far-reaching WGN radio network and representatives of the press, including newsreel producers, were given extensive access the fair facilities.[17]

The people of Chicago were inspired by fair publicists and city officials to do their part for A Century of Progress. On May 18, Mayor Edward Kelly declared a seven day "prosperity drive," called "Let's Go Chicago!" week, as a way "for Chicagoans to get ready to show to the millions of visitors expected during the fair that Chicago is still the wonder city of the world." Citizens were encouraged to buy before prices rose with the incoming tourists. City leaders hoped that this sudden increased spending would herald the beginning to a sustained upturn in the economy. Chicagoans in business were urged to hire new employees, and everyone was asked to clean up the city. The shot of a cannon officially opened the festivities of the "Let's Go Chicago!" week (between May 22 and May 28), and at noon factory whistles, church bells, and car horns chimed in. The telephone company answered all calls with a greeting referring to "Let's Go Chicago Week" and special commemorative milk bottles were distributed. Stores in the Chicago metropolitan region hung special decorations and hundreds of billboards advertised the celebration to residents. In addition, stickers reading "Come to the Fair" were distributed for placement in car windows; taxi cabs as far away as New York City sported them.[18]

As its underlying goal, the fair's public relations effort sought financial growth in the city's depression-era economy and a positive spin on Chicago's image. This vigorous pro-urban, pro-capitalism campaign reflected the personal concerns of the city's current set of boosters. Deeply devoted to Chicago, in no small part because the city was home to their own business ventures, the planners conceptualized that a more vital and well-respected city would be beneficial to their personal interests and a great help to their neighbors. While they had become more concerned with fighting the city's problems during the heart of the progressive era, Chicago leaders now exhibited an interest in image-making. They hoped that the representation they planned to sell to the nation (and even, at some level, the world) would stand in sharp distinction to the rampant anti-urban and anti-capitalistic pictures of the city hawked by those writing for the popular media.

But, as the old saying goes, even "the best laid plans" do not always turn out as intended. Chicago's second world's fair did bring increased income to the city, in the form of higher retail sales, full-to-bursting hotels, and even a lowering of the percentage of Chicago families on public relief. Yet the event did not bring to Chicago the ultra-sophisticated public image that the city boosters had envisioned.

Fair organizers understandably most often reflected favorably upon the fair. In his speech to mark the closing of the exposition, fair president Rufus Dawes, brother of Herbert Hoover's Vice President Charles Dawes, waxed nostalgic over the fair's accomplishments. "This Exposition spoke to a world in distress," he explained, "and it spoke with the authentic voice of Chicago, asserting pride and announcing faith."[19]

Certainly, visitors to the fair had a good time on the grounds; such a source of joy was appreciated—by those who could afford the entrance fee—as an escape from the hardships of the Great Depression. As Lohr announced, the "Fair was a bright spot in a world of gloom." However, the national media critiquing the fair found the event far from a cultural coup. The event hardly erased the city's darker connections from the public's memories. Jack Dearborn of *Real America* concluded, "Over all hovers the aroma of the days of Bath House John and Hinky Dink, while Al Capone must be grinding his teeth in Atlanta at the opportunities for loot that are being deliberately overlooked."[20]

The outside commentators who positively assessed the fair celebrated its "lowbrow" amusements rather than the "highbrow" offerings the boosters had worked so hard to procure. In some respects, the viewer's attitude toward the fair could be reduced to his or her preset bias for or against the open commercialization. Looking to register itself as a cultural Mecca, this association with American business was a connection Chicago boosters did not wish to place in the foreground of their image-making efforts. One of the fair planners' goals surely was to reinvigorate the city's sluggish economy, and, as business leaders, to restore their personal financial health. Yet somehow they believed these practical goals could be accomplished surreptitiously.

Reporter Jerome Beatty openly enjoyed demonstrations for commercial products by "the prettiest girls you ever saw," and laughed sympathetically at the husbands racing for the exotic dancing shows. Beatty found the fair's unabashed displays of the female body and thoroughly commercial appeal refreshing. Beatty wrote, "Everything American that is likely to interest you is there. If you look at the fair slowly and thoughtfully there will [be] times when you gasp in awe, when instinctively you take off your hat, when your heart beats a little faster and you say softly to yourself, 'What a great country this is, after all!'" Articles in *Christian Century*, however, criticized fair organizers for making "a fair which the multitude would enjoy" rather than a place of idealized beauty. Writers for the magazine noted the way in which the amusement concessions for the fair were placed inside the fair grounds, mixed in with more "cultural" offerings. Unlike the 1893 fair, no decidedly separate Midway existed at A Century of Progress. *Christian Century* complained, "It was a commercial fair, predominantly. That is to say, its exhibits were drawn chiefly from commercial and industrial enterprise. Advertising of wares was its conspicuous note, and the actual selling of wares so pervaded the entire exposition as to make it seem like a vast oriental market." Such commercial notes even penetrated the Hall of Religion, according to the magazine.[21]

The quality of the fair's architecture was a frequent subject of criticism. This fair did not offer the classically inspired, heavily decorated pure white buildings of the Columbian Exposition, the buildings that had moved many visitors to push for architectural changes in the downtown areas of their hometowns. Rather the 1933 fair featured modern and functional designs. The architectural innovations of the 1933 fair—flat expanses of wall without windows and the newly-conceived temporary building methods the designers deemed appropriate for a rapidly changing world—cultivated attention, but not of the intended nature. While pre-fair magazine articles eagerly anticipated the fair's modern architecture, it did not receive high marks in later reviews. Many visitors liked the contemporary model homes on display, like Chicago architect George Fred Keck's "House of Tomorrow,"—a twelve-sided home made of glass and steel—yet the designs of the major exposition structures were widely demeaned. As a writer for the *Saturday Evening Post* remarked, "The peculiar architecture of the Century of Progress Exposition has been the target for as many shafts of criticism as prohibition, the Farm Board, or the League of Nations." The fair was, he added, the "hottest controversial art topic of the hour."[22]

Journalist Bruce Bliven found that the buildings were "dumpy" compared to the city's skyscrapers, and were not even modernist designs, as claimed. Calling them modernist, he declared, "will give a black eye to the functional movement in architecture for years to come." Press releases written by A Century of Progress' promotion department boasted that the much anticipated Travel and Transport building contained the largest unobstructed area beneath one roof—the perfect space for exhibition. The roof hung from steel cables, and its steel panels slid over one another as weather changes caused them to expand and contract. Yet this supposed architectural wonder became known in the general public as the "glorified gas tank."[23]

In a special edition of *Architectural Forum*, noted architects of the day weighed in on the subject of the fair's design. At the center of the considerable criticism given by America's leading architects lay the fair's unembarrassed embrace of its money-making functions. A Century of Progress flaunted the "fair" aspect of its offerings with its blowsy overall style; the refined finish of the World's Columbian Exposition style was nowhere to be seen. Ely Jacques Kahn felt first impressions of the fair troublesome, saying, "One stumbles over information booths, hot dog stands, souvenir rubbish, ad nauseum." Detroit architect Albert Kahn liked the joy in designer Joseph Urban's twenty-three tone color scheme. Fair buildings were painted a myriad of intense colors, each building done in a combination of hues so as to produce a carnivalesque atmosphere. However Kahn surmised that the incredible range of colors and the windowless buildings had little application in actual modern architecture; in fact, he felt even referring to the designs as "architecture" was misleading. Buckminster Fuller condemned the 1933 buildings, referring to them as marred by "desperate yet futile plagiarisms, pseudo-scientific wonders, and garish advertising-mania."[24]

Most of the general public visiting the fair expressed similar discomfort with the exposition style. The style proved unpopular with the general public as well as those schooled in architectural theory—the attempt at unfettered, accessible forms was not appreciated. Although Joel Newston, an advertiser from Chicago, said self-deprecatingly, "It's all quite elaborate and very impressive, even to the advanced mind, much less the feeble one such as my own," most lay fairgoers could clearly label the sights as disappointing. Dr. Frederick Foley of St. Paul Minnesota admitted, "If you ask me what I think of the architectural scheme, I'll be frank and tell you I think it's crazy." Fairgoers found the stark lines of the 1933–1934 structures unsettling, far from the fairyland architecture of the 1893 fair. Many had enjoyed the Columbian Exposition firsthand and considered it a cultural triumph for Chicago. A woman from Grand Rapids, Michigan expressed, "When I came in on the train yesterday morning and saw all this from the car window I was just sick, and I said, 'Well, for land's sakes! Is *that* thing there the Century of Progress!' I never was so disappointed in all my life, and I said to myself, 'If *that* is Progress you can just give me the old times.'"[25]

One of the scandals of the 1893 Columbian Exposition had surrounded the trustees' failure to rely on Chicago-based architectural talent; this blunder replayed itself in the 1930s when fair organizers omitted the great Chicago designer Frank Lloyd Wright from their roster. The fair's architectural committee was slow in including *any* Chicago-based talent, due both to fair planners' desire to inspire national involvement in their world's fair and because of lingering doubts about Chicago's homegrown cultural achievements. Initially, Rufus Dawes had asked architects Raymond Hood of New York and Paul Phillippe Cret of Philadelphia to consider building a design team for the fair. Hood and Cret chose to work with Harvey Wiley Corbett of New York, Arthur Brown Jr. of San Francisco, and Ralph T. Walker of New York. This group then chose three Chicago architects, Edward H. Bennett, John A. Holabird, and Hubert Burnham, to join them. Later on, the committee asked Joseph Urban, a Broadway set designer, Ferrucio Vitale, an accomplished landscape designer, and architect Daniel H. Burnham, Jr., a second Burnham son, to join their ranks.[26]

Urban scholar Lewis Mumford complained that the 1933 event could have had a "beneficial influence upon the development of all the Arts in America during the next generation," if Wright had not been excluded. Wright himself thought that the architecture of the fair could not be justly called modern. A fair more fittingly in the Chicago style, he suggested, would be one in which all of the exhibits were housed in one "huge skyscraper a mile high." Wright called the fair an "economic crime," but he appealed to the American Union of Decorative Artists and Draftsmen not to take official note of the absence of his name from the fair's architectural committee as they had planned.[27]

Biting criticisms of Chicago littered the commentary on the fair in the popular media, obscuring more favorable remarks. Journalist Llewellyn Jones complained of the discriminatory treatment of African-Americans, both patrons and employees, by fair authorities. African-Americans who had been denied service at exposition restaurants filed suit against the organization. A businessman claimed to have been told outright that no contracts for concessions would be signed with African-Americans. Jones also expressed dismay at the "temporary magnificence" of the fair in contrast with the surrounding city slums. He recalled the destruction of Hoovervilles—squatter settlements of homeless Chicagoans—previously located on the fair site. He wrote that "the spirit which is abroad in the whole undertaking, which indeed made such a vast display possible in times like these, is one of naked exploitation." A Century of Progress did not inspire all who beheld it to raise their estimation of the cultural status of the region. The vision of Midwesterners as a people lacking in the cultural savvy of their eastern cousins remained. One journalist mocked, "This Fair, then, has been of, by, and for the Middle West; the territory which hardly knows, even yet, that Europe exists; the territory of short, friendly, round-headed people who serve the salad at the beginning of the meal and drink their coffee from gigantic cups one-third full of cream."[28]

Additionally, attitudes towards the fair and the city were rocked by the fair's seemingly endless reliance on female sexuality as entertainment. Exotic dancers, most notably Sally Rand and her fan dance, evolved into one of the main symbols of the Chicago Century of Progress. Rather than recalling displays of molecular structures or the towering "Sky Ride," as promoters had hoped, fair patrons went home dreaming of the risqué "Streets of Paris." Fair intern Julian Jackson later recalled, "Little did I care if General Motors was turning out Chevrolets as fast as Fords, Firestone was fabricating tires that were [not] puncture prone, or RCA was televising its nascent corporate image to a million gapers...God was in her heaven to supervise the nightly fireworks and Satan was superintendent along the Midway, and that's exactly where the action was and I, too." Jess Kreuger, reporter for the *Chicago American* and author of a pamphlet entitled "Fair Nights," similarly attested to the influence of exotic dancing at the fair. Kreuger queried, "Wonder which will be remembered most forty years from now, Sally Rand or the sky ride. (As if there was any doubt!)" [29]

Fair officials were aware of the presence of stripping, dancing, and nude or semi-nude posing on the Century of Progress grounds, and even advertised the existence of these concessions in order to draw crowds to the fair. They were particularly concerned with soliciting a late-night, adult crowd in order to make a larger financial return. But they had not counted on these attractions defining the fair overall. Allowing concessions of dubious moral value at first appeared a relatively small faux-pas in such an uncomfortable economy, and certainly the organizers could not have anticipated the degree of interest the offerings would encourage. They could not have known of the savvy marketing skills of one particular dancer, Sally Rand, who shrewdly used the fair to rocket to national fame. They had simply made a mistake, but this mistake lost them much of the control over the fair's image.

Early fair coverage intimated that the 1933 event would not stoop to the tactics of the organizers of Columbian Exposition, where exotic dancers on the Midway simultaneously dazzled and disgusted Gilded Age fair goers. 1930s audiences were assumed to be simply too sophisticated for this type of entertainment. Forrest Crissey wrote that "American bathing and chorus beauties...have educated the American male beyond interest in the amateurish antics of the imported Turkish maidens who made whoopee for the World's Columbian celebration. The Century of Progress will not bother much about sex appeal; it isn't going to be that kind of show, even on the sidelines. Its first duty, as it seems, is to be novel."[30]

Yet it turned out to be precisely "that kind of show." As a racy pamphlet entitled "A Century of Nudity" carefully described to its readers in text and pictures, the fair had plenty to offer in terms of female entertainment. The pamphlet, marked "This Book Not To Be Sent Through the Mail," explained, "Nudity has burst upon Chicago during the summer of 1933 with all the suddenness of a traffic policeman popping [out] from a dark side street. The result has been profitable to enterprising entrepreneurs at the World's Fair, diverting to a large number of citizens, and bewildering to those gentlemen who are entrusted with keeping the community in a tolerable state of decorum." The fair offered rather innocuous presentations of the female body in a wide range of beauty contests, dancing shows, and modeling throughout the fair grounds. Snapshots of women from the fair graced nearly every issue of the sanctioned publication, *World Fair News*, and seemingly every picture of record-setting fair goers—the millionth, the four millionth, the five millionth—were of attractive young white women. *World Fair News* also regularly advertised more off-color entertainments, boasting of the nudist colony, the artist's studio with live undressed models, "Little Egypt of 1933," and exotic dancing performed by Sally Rand and others. As Rand's fame grew, the concessions offering fan dancing and other elaborate exotic dancing attractions multiplied. Rosalie Davis, part of the Old Mexico concession, danced with small red fans to Spanish airs. Princess Aki, billed as a Chinese dancer, performed in the Streets of Paris. Dancer Jeanne Wood wore only a pair of long sleeves during her shows at the Hollywood concession. Rand, however, as explained in one issue of *World Fair News*, could be considered the "Talk of [the] Fair." Underneath a picture of the platinum blond woman in a white sheer dress, the article continued, "Sally Rand is a name on the lips of thousands of visitors to the Chicago World's Fair—A Century of Progress—these days. Clothed in nothing by a pair of fans and a smile, Sally dances nightly for the revelers in the Cafe de la Paix of the Streets of Paris."[31]

No one seemed able to forget her. A business man, John Van Gilder, provided his employees with an "Outline for A Quick Two or Three Day Visit to the Cream of A Century of Progress Exposition" and suggested that no one leave out Sally Rand's "bubble dance," a performance style Rand introduced in 1934. He went as far as to tell the story of his meeting with Rand; he bought her flowers and earned a kiss in return. He nostalgically recalled for his readers the beauty of Rand's body and how "one felt as though secretly watching some little woodland creature at play in the moonlight," as she danced with her specially-made, giant iridescent balloon under a blue spotlight. And Van Gilder was not alone in his passion for Rand; the number of husbands who claimed they had gotten "lost" for substantial periods of time at the fair became a running joke during the period. Audiences for Rand's shows included more types of fair goers than wayward husbands, however. Men, women, and even children viewed Rand's performances. According to a critical article in *Christian Century*, the Streets of Paris lured "college presidents, Sunday school teachers, clergymen, editors of religious journals, church deacons, women's club presidents, mothers and fathers (frequently accompanied by their children) mixing with the mine run of humanity in unfeigned and unapologetic titillation at the tawdry, infantile, vulgar...and inane amusements which the place affords."[32]

Born Helen Gould Beck, Sally Rand, the daughter of Missouri Quakers, had talents for both dancing and self-promotion. Chicago legend has it that the out-of-work silent film actress and dancer first appeared at A Century of Progress "dressed" as Lady Godiva in a unauthorized stunt designed to land her a job at the fair. Her horseback ride through opening day festivities must have quickly spread through the city, as newspaper coverage of the day hinted at the event as though its readership were already informed. On the society page of the *Chicago Daily Tribune*, a young male Chicagoan, holding the reins of a horse, posed with his wife. The paper reported that "Mr. Barnes was determined to take the place of the lovely young model who impersonated Lady Godiva and he went so far as to mount her white horse, but his pretty young wife, the former Helen Howell, persuaded him to dismount." Rand later joined the staff of The Streets of Paris as a fan dancer, making a living by performing daily shows at A Century of Progress, as well as the downtown venues of the Chicago Theater and the Paramount Club.[33] Rand incorrectly claimed to have been the first to invent the fan dance, and unconvincingly insisted that she first danced nude by accident, having been called on stage unexpectedly. In 1934, Rand added another talent, the bubble dance, to her repertoire, to encourage repeat customers. In both the fan dance and the bubble dance, Rand usually performed covered head to toe with a thick, white body paint and powder. The makeup application caused many to debate whether or not Rand was indeed nude when she danced. The swiftness with which she would reveal portions of her body also made this a difficult call. Onlookers were also confused about whether or not the dancing could be considered acceptable entertainment. Banned at the outset of the 1934 fair, Rand eventually worked her way into the Italian Village concession.

Although female fair organizer Martha McGrew (who served as Lenox Lohr's special assistant) was even rumored to disapprove of the allowance of taxi dancers—dancers who were paid to dance with patrons and considered akin to exotic dancers—at A Century of Progress, many of the male fair officials initially believed the strip shows and other such fare to be innocuous. A group consisting of General Manager Lenox Lohr, Assistant Director of Operations Col. James Bell, Director of Operations Robert Isham Randolph, and Randolph's wife, all attended "girl shows" throughout Chicago in order to gauge the appropriateness of the medium to the fair crowds. All of them agreed publicly that such entertainment was in good taste. Lohr commented that "In this day, nude women mean but little, and morals depend on no standard point of view."[34] Later, upon assessing the fair's own shows, Lohr announced, "I don't think any of the shows should be closed, nor do I believe policemen should be stationed in these places to interfere with the performances."[35]

Fair organizers understood, however, that the concessions should be carefully monitored from within. Lohr did insist that night club concessions close at 1:30 A.M., although concessionaires regularly flouted the rules. Fair managers hoped to allow for fun, but also to keep all evening entertainment within containable limits. Fair president Rufus Dawes, speaking to the *Chicago Tribune*, admitted, "The night life men are good men, but some of them get too much drink in them. An orgy or a tragedy would take away the fair name of the city. There are many questions involved and we have to be careful. The Fair is a reflection of the times and some of the shows must be closed early."[36]

The performances of scantily clothed women proved acceptable to fair organizers because of these concessions' financial contribution to the fair. Although all such displays were managed by outside business interests, fair management drew a percentage of all concession profits. Increased attendance at the fair due to the shows also increased overall ticket sales and other purchases made on the grounds. Activities that specifically drew adults kept crowds at the fair during its evening hours. In addition, well-placed Chicagoans had made large investments in fair concessions, and fair managers could hardly object too strenuously to their colleagues' attempts to make money. Included in the backers of the Streets of Paris were meat packers Laurence H. Armour and E.A. Cudahy, Jr. and department store magnate Leon Mandel. Reflecting on the fair's financial success, journalist T.R. Carsakadon laid the responsibility for the coup on Sally Rand. Carsakadon wrote, "The Adler Planetarium is playing to poor business; the wonders of the Travel and Transport Building are drawing but fair to average crowds; forty men could toss a medicine ball around in the Hall of Science and never bother the customers; the panorama of the Fort Dearborn massacre has had to close for lack of business ... But Sally Rand, dancing nude on the Streets of Paris, has been jamming the place nightly." He said, "For Sally Rand is neither an accident nor a person; she is a symbol, an industry, a state of mind."[37]

Although the savvy business people directing the fair honestly assessed the potential draw of the fair's adult entertainments, they could not predict the way in which the overall image of the exposition in national popular culture would ultimately be linked to the fan dance. The news of the fair's delights spread through scandal; following the tradition in Chicago history, the more people who joined the chorus of voices against what they judged to be indecent, the greater the power of the rumors which circulated about Chicago's big show. Public interest in Rand's dancing increased after her initial arrest for indecency. When she appeared in Judge Joseph B. David's courtroom in the summer of 1933, and David supposedly dismissed the charges against her with the now legendary comment that "some people would like to put pants on horses." Mayor Edward Kelly then visited A Century of Progress and found the shows there "filthy." He ordered Lohr and Superintendent George T. Donoghue of the South Park Board, under whose jurisdiction the fair lay, to stop the indecent performances. Mary Belle Spencer, an attorney who had attempted to have the Streets of Paris closed, praised the Mayor. "He should be commended heartily," she exclaimed, "Now many people who plan to leave Chicago because they have been shocked at the fair may stay on and enjoy the exposition." Previously, Spencer had referred to the fan dance as "a national shame of humiliation—nay, an ulcer upon Chicago and a cancer upon the state of Illinois."[38]

But despite the turmoil, the dancing went on, and the visitors kept coming. Although Rand herself was arrested as often as four times a day while performing at the Chicago Theater, the legal wrangling only strengthened her resolve to keep up the act. On September 23, 1933, Rand received the most serious threat to her career; the dancer was again brought into court for indecency but this arrest and trial by jury resulted in a $200 fine and a one year jail sentence. Luckily for the fair's finances, Rand won an appeal. In later years, Rand remembered "I was so humiliated and embarrassed. I thought, 'if I'm going to lose everything—my dancing—then I may as well die.' I fought these courts with a passion." She utilized the scandals that followed her to build a life-long career in exotic dancing, and A Century of

Progress garnered heightened attendance. The fair reported twenty-two million paid admissions in 1933, and two million visitors to the Streets of Paris. When the fair was reopened in the summer of 1934 (as an ultimately successful measure to generate enough profit to pay back all of its debts), the fair took in another sixteen million paid admissions.

Rand put forth a provocative but less-than-believable theory that all the attention placed on her was actually a ruse to lead the public culture away from other stains on Chicago's image. In 1973, she reflected, "It was so obvious. I was the red herring. This was back when Machine Gun So and So was roaming the streets and couldn't be found. The political machines were vast and the courts were backlogged with citizen's needs. And yet they took time and money to pursue something like me!"[39]

Sally Rand and her white feather fans were ultimately remembered as symbolic of the 1933 fair. As Robert Rydell relates in his book *World of Fairs*, a large ostrich fan used in an exhibit in the New York World's Fair of 1939–1940 was declared "THE SYMBOL OF THE CHICAGO FAIR." Director of the American Social Hygiene Association, Bascom Johnson, complained about how this demonstrated the extent to which "Sally Rand and her nude Fan Dance has permeated the warp and woof of the Nation." And while few remember A Century of Progress today, the image of the fan dancer still remains. With her success at the fair (she at times grossed in the neighborhood of $5,000 a week), Rand launched a dancing career, making appearances at fairs and theaters throughout the United States and in such films as the 1934 *Bolero*, for which she earned $20,000. Rand went on to perform her fan dance into her mid-seventies, repeating the act forty weeks a year, for a total of approximately fifty thousand shows by 1973. She danced for last time in Chicago in November of 1978, just a year before she died. Some attended her shows out of nostalgia, others because they had heard of Rand all their lives but had never expected to see her. Despite her age, spectators of Rand's later shows commented on her body. The *Chicago Tribune* reported:

> Her figure is attractive too. Her waist is slim, her bosom full. Sally explains that easily: "Those fans weigh seven and a half pounds apiece. You wave them around for 42 years and you're going to develop pectoral muscles that will hold your boobs up very effectively." Rand said that she had "new fans, but the same fanny," and added, "God knows, I like doing this. It's better than doing needle-point on the patio."[40]

The act that shocked many viewers in the 1930s apparently read as rather tame in 1970s Chicago. Rand explained that she could be considered "an exercise in achieving respectability thru [sic] tenure. My fan dance is so demure by comparison with what we see today that it's almost quaint." The older Rand too, had become religious, claiming to have found God in a mathematics college textbook when she went to back to college at fifty-two. Struck by the concept of infinity, Rand committed herself to Christianity. In 1973, Rand returned to Chicago as a guest speaker during a weekly service at the Central Church of Chicago. Her old reputation, however, still lingered; some elderly women left the church as Rand read "An Actor's Prayer" to the assembly. Rand's college education also provided her with the training she used to become a children's speech therapist in Pomona, California.[41]

Chicago boosters initially considered A Century of Progress as a promotion tool of enormous magnitude. Tired of the repeated barbs aimed at their city by a belligerent press, fair officials hoped to refashion the national understanding of Chicago by linking it with science and sophistication, rather than gangsters, gunfire, racial conflict, and suspiciously-processed meat. Through hard effort and heavy investment, elite Chicagoans wanted to bring a new "sunrise" to their city's reputation and make up for their decades of relative inattention to Chicago's image. And millions did see the fair's carefully constructed scientific exhibits. But this extravagant attempt to rewrite the city's reputation ultimately failed; in the popular discourse, Chicago's wicked image lived on. Far from the high cultural event its planners had intended, the fair became, out of financial necessity and simply through the accident of Rand's fame, a symbol of the troubled realities of capitalism. Capitalism spurred on some types of progress, yet set a place at the table for decadence as well. In attempting to allow both an elaborate and costly presentation of high culture and unfettered investment opportunities for concessionaires, the fair directors had lost control.

As Americans searched for a conception of themselves and their country during the stormy 1930s, they chose not to glorify this Midwestern metropolis. Instead of celebrating Chicago's one hundred years of meteoric development, instead of seeing A Century of Progress as a display of all that Chicagoans had achieved, most saw the fair at best as a good time, and at worst, as somehow indicative of the financial and moral ruin of the nation. Chicago's second World's Fair was not a college, but a circus, not a testament to the high-brow culture of this city, but a demonstration of the popularity of its more low-brow amusements. Despite ten years of fair planning, Chicago was still looked to as a momentary imaginative escape rather than as a force for leading the nation out of the Depression.

Chapter Five

Infamous City: Chicago and the Reworking of Reality in American Popular Culture

A close look at a variety of popular media produced between the 1930s and the 1960s demonstrates that during this period Chicago sustained the negative national image established at the turn of the century. Much of the force behind the city's image in this period came from the retelling of stories familiar to the American public. Unlike other historical benchmarks—for example the Columbian Exposition, of which memories persisted, yet diminished, with time, some of the historical events of the 1930s–1960s period actually grew in their ability to capture the American imagination years after they had occurred. The remembrance of these events outweighed or at least rivaled their actuality in the resonance of their cultural power. Perhaps most representative of this trend is the tales of Al Capone's gangster hierarchy. American culture of the 1930s and of the Cold War period reworked these historical tales to perpetuate Chicago's role as an infamous city. Chicago continued to serve as an image of anti-urbanism. The infamous city can at times function as shorthand in American culture, instantly evoking many of the aspects of the rapidly changing society that most instill fear, simply by mentioning its name. In the mid-twentieth century, the infamous city called to mind crime, sexual danger, political corruption, and racial antagonism, among other malevolent characteristics.

Thus, the primary damage to Chicago's name in the mid-twentieth century stemmed from investigations of Chicago's history rather than the distribution of current news stories about the city. Chicago's own struggles of the era, such as the troubles surrounding attempts to racially integrate its public housing and its suburbs, while covered locally, surprisingly received only a moderate level of attention in the national media, and usually in periodicals aimed at a niche, liberal audience rather than mainstream America. As usual, the difficulties stemming from Chicago's particularly vivacious political machine (Democratic) did spark their share of headlines, but these stories had less effect on the nation than the lingering tales of Chicago's yesterdays.

By the 1940s, Chicago boosters had completely lost control of the city's national image. With *The Untouchables* book and spin-off television shows, the book and movie versions of *Scarface*, and a variety of other popular investigations of the underworld, Chicago found its 1920s and 1930s gangster heyday re-explored and publicized. Although the federal government had already forcibly removed Al Capone from Chicago and safely resettled him on Alcatraz Island, Americans well remembered his connection with the city.

The majority of the powerful popular images of Chicago centered on reworkings of historical events. Yet an additional, relatively small, group of representations based on current reflections of the city also significantly molded public opinion and are worthy of mention here. Hugh Hefner's *Playboy Magazine*, established in 1953, and his subsequent television shows, compounded Chicago's unflattering reputation. Writers like Nelson Algren, Richard Wright, and Saul Bellow added their dark illustrations to the mix. Together, the historically-based and new visions of the city had quite an affect on Chicago's reputation. Between the 1930s and 1960s, Chicago remained one of the most visible symbols of urban strife. Like its famous criminal, Chicago became for many "Public Enemy Number One."

The Great Chicago fire re-entered the forefront of the national imagination in this period with a major Hollywood film. In 1938, producer Darryl Zanuck's popular and Academy Award winning "In Old Chicago" reworked images of Chicago's corrupt political past and the Great Chicago Fire. The motion picture modified the family history of the famous O'Leary family, recasting them not as the social downtrodden, but as central players in the city's political life. Zanuck's O'Leary family boasts both Dion O'Leary, the saloon owner and political henchman played by Tyrone Power, and Jack O'Leary, the ethical attorney turned reform mayor, played by Don Ameche. Patrick O'Leary, the men's father, brings the family to Illinois in a covered wagon, and then dies just as the sojourners reach the edge of the state's great metropolis. Fittingly, old-fashioned Patrick dies as a result of his racing his cumbersome buggy against a train heading into the city; his horses disconnect from the wagon's frame and O'Leary is dragged on by his team. Old O'Leary, we learn, literally cannot exist in the face of Chicago's modern technology. Only the fit and the young can face the city's many challenges.

The film first brings us to Chicago in 1854, and a shot of the muddy, overly crowded downtown features the caption: "A city of easy money, easy ways, ugly, dirty, open night and day to newcomers from all parts of the world...a fighting, laughing, aggressive American city." Indeed, the movie's characters later discuss the moral challenges of Chicago, and Jack O'Leary deems it "the worst city in the world." Seemingly the highest culture in this representation of Chicago revolves around alluring saloons and scanti- ly-dressed female dancers. The only hope for this immoral place apparently lies in the possibility that it could begin again. Mayor Jack O'Leary alludes to this when he confides in his brother, "I see Chicago as a great city. A place people can be proud of. I'd wipe out all this mushroom growth. Start all over on a sound basis. With steel and stone." After Jack dies in an attempt to stop the blaze, the burden of reestablishing the city must be shouldered by Dion, now newly wed to a burlesque star. Watching the fire destroy Chicago, Di- on, his wife Belle, and his mother Molly take refuge from the heat on top of a wagon that is partially submerged in Lake Michigan. The fire provides the backdrop for one of the more didactic speeches in Hollywood history. While the camera takes in their silhouettes against the blazing horizon, Molly rises and prophesies in halting language:

> It's gone, and my boy's gone with it. But what he stood for will never die. It was a city of wood and now it's ashes. But out of the fire will come the steel. You didn't get to see it my lad, no more than your father did before you. God rest the two of you. But there's Dion left, and his chil- dren to come after.

Apparently, all hope for the flawed urban center lays in the morally suspect Dion and his offspring. The future seems impossible, but the audience roots for Molly O'Leary as she concludes, "We O'Leary's are a strange tribe. There's strength in us. And what we set out to do we finish."[1]

As in Twentieth Century Fox' portrayal of Chicago's disastrous fire, popular images of Chicago's gangster history sensationalized historical real- ity. Although Alphonse Capone had only ruled the city's rackets between roughly 1925 and 1931, Capone's story served as ample fodder for a seem- ingly unending flow of books, magazine articles, comic strips, films, and television programs. Capone became a favorite fictionalized character in the Cold War era, drawn as a grasping immigrant and a dandy at a time in which foreigners were suspect and the definitions of "true" manhood rigidly defined. Capone and his henchmen epitomized the threat of the city; in ur- ban space men could become completely unglued from the traditional Amer- ican way, for instead of hard-working farmers, men became mobsters and ruthless capitalists. Gangsters provided lessons about what was wrong with the city's culture of consumerism and the unfettered search for wealth. If Americans were headed towards a completely urban existence, the self-centered mobster would be our destiny. These immigrants, misunderstanding the unstated limits of Anglo-American capitalism, took economic individualism to the extreme, violating the law to sell alcohol, marketing prostitutes and gambling to the urban male, and killing business competitors. The presence of these criminals in urban areas, according to many public commentators, threatened the democratic standards of the nation. Alson J. Smith, in the 1954 *Syndicate City: The Chicago Crime Cartel and What to Do About It* warned:

> until the crime syndicate is routed not only in Chicago but in New York, New Jersey, Florida, Louisiana, Missouri and other places where it is firmly established—American democracy will be in as much danger from criminal subversion as from Communist subversion. Indeed, a nation whose moral fiber and ethical standards are eaten away by termite-criminals in its great cities will be an easy prey to any dynamic barbarism that appears to challenge it.[2]

The 1930 pulp-fiction novel by Armitrage Trail entitled *Scarface* served as a major contributing element in the maintenance of the public's fascination with Al Capone. Trail, whose real name was Maurice Coons, wrote for detective magazines. Fascinated by the gangsters, Trail went to Chicago in 1925 to learn more about the underworld of the city first-hand. This apparent research, however, had little effect on the veracity of the book; the novel remained mostly imaginative. Dead at twenty-eight from a heart attack brought on by obesity, Trail did not live to see his book remade into the popular film, *Scarface*, in 1932.

Scarface's book jacket taunted, "The Bloody, Bullet-Spattered Novel based on Al Capone—America's Most Notorious Public Enemy." Trail's fictionalized Capone, known first as Tony Guarino and later as Tony Camonte (after he changed his name to avoid prosecution for a crime), was drawn somewhat sympathetically. Though written in matter-of-fact prose, the novel presents Camonte as a man who acts upon reasonable assumptions. Love, not simply a brutish character, pushed Tony to commit his first murder; he killed Al Spingola to clearly stake his right to date Spingola's former "moll" Vyvyan Lovejoy. Trail's central gang leader resembled a businessman more than a thug. With time, Trail tells his readers, Camonte "became a real modern gangster, a member of a big, powerful wealthy organization that collected more than a third of all profits that came from liquor, gambling and vice in America's second largest city and a considerable territory around it." Camonte eventually considered leaving the illegal business he had created for the field of real estate, only to realize that his formerly sworn commitment to his underlings would make such a move impossible. Apparently, he was stuck inside the criminal world. In building up his organization, he had created a "Frankenstein, a monster that, acting upon the principles he had instilled into it, would feel justified in destroying him should he attempt to desert now." Trail also attempted to win the reader's understanding of his protagonist with his portrayal of Camonte's final moments; in the end, Camonte proved unable to pull his gun against the police officer, his brother, Ben Guarino, who ultimately killed Camonte unaware of the family connection. Camonte remained committed to family even though he had to sacrifice his own life. Trail invites the readers to respect Camonte's loyalty.

According to Trail, Camonte and his associates killed only when necessary and killed only those who would kill them if given a chance. The business of the underworld, Trail claimed, did not compromise the safety of the general citizen. Apologists of the gangsters often employed this explanation for violence in the media of the day. Outwardly, no one would know that Camonte and his girlfriend Jane were killers. Nobody could dream that the pair:

> had killed, not in the heat of passion, but coolly and deliberately—for money; and that they would kill again, whenever the occasion seemed to demand. And yet they were not murderers, except legally. In their own minds they felt completely justified for everything they had done. And their operation never had been and never would be the slightest menace to the general public. When they stalked with murderous intent, they invariably were after some certain person who had it coming to him and who would have done the same to them without any more compunction than they showed. And they always took care not to harm innocent bystanders.

Trail juxtaposed the supposedly "businesslike" Camonte with the "'strong-arm' type" of Steve Libati, a member of Camonte's own organization who Tony disliked from the start and who eventually double-crossed him. Libati, Trail imagined, was a "gangster of the old school, the type that wore sweaters and shapeless checked caps and lounged in front of frowsy corner saloons with a cigarette dangling from one corner of their ugly mouths while they talked hoarsely from the other. He had hard gray eyes and a nose bent slightly to one side and a mean mouth that sneered easily and nastily."

Even one of the characters in the *Scarface* story realized that the presence of the gangsters in the city damaged the city's national image. A police officer warns Camonte's erstwhile boss, Johnny Lovo, "'It isn't your business that I am objecting to; it's this damned shooting that's going on among you. It's getting the city a bad name, and what's more important, the newspapers are beginning to ride me and my administration.'" This of course is ironic—a warning about possible damage to the city's reputation inside a novel which itself played a significant part in lowering this reputation. Interestingly, Trail did not clearly identify the site of his drama by name. Not referring directly to "Chicago," he only hinted broadly at the location by mentioning such well-known locales as Lake Shore Drive and Cicero.[3]

The 1932 film based quite loosely on Trail's book featured Jewish Chicagoan Paul Muni as the Capone-equivalent character, Tony Camonte. The work established the careers of Muni and actor George Raft, and also featured actress Ann Dvorak as Camonte's sister, and a young Boris Karloff. As would become common to the various media reflecting Chicago's underworld life, the film began by denying the prurient interest inherent in watching the stories of gangsters, and claimed only to show the sordid stories as a moral lesson. "This film is an indictment of gang rule in America," claimed the opening credits, "and of the callous indifference of the government to this constantly increasing menace to our safety and our liberty." The film insisted that all of the incidents it portrayed were based on real events, and asked its viewers, "What are you going to do about it?"

The film *Scarface* begins with the death of Louie Costillo, a thinly veiled code-name for Chicago mob boss Jim Colosimo. Tony Camonte (Capone), complete with deeply scarred cheek, had served as Costillo's body guard and now turned to new leader Johnny Lovo (Johnny Torrio). Camonte's motivating motto, "Do it first. Do it yourself. And keep on doing it," smacked of the rank urban individualism and the suspect, yet driven, type of "work" ethic so feared by urban detractors, as did Lovo's insistence that he and Camonte get the underworld "organized" and run it like a business. Lovo seems to have understood that big crime, like big business, best functioned through consolidation and monopolistic practices, because sole suppliers could control pricing of their products.

Brought to life in the cinematic version of this story, Muni played Tony Camonte as a stereotypical, threatening Italian mobster, complete with thick accent, hulking physical presence, and a willingness to transgress sexual mores himself but a belief that his sister should remain a virgin until marriage. Although the book and the movie vary greatly in their storylines, both relate an episode in which Tony kills his sister's boyfriend believing he had tempted her into sex. After the murder, Camonte learns that his sister had recently married the gangster.[4]

The Warner Brothers' film *Public Enemy* also brought a Capone-like tale to a large, national audience. The 1931 movie cast James Cagney as the criminal Tom Powers. *Public Enemy* chronicles Tom's evolution from a beer-drinking adolescent who enjoys tripping his best friend's sister to a full-fledged member of the Chicago underworld. Predictably, the film's producers insisted upon the high-minded intentions of their project: "It is the ambition of the authors of 'The Public Enemy' to honestly depict an environment that exists today in a certain strata of American life, rather than glorify the hoodlum or the criminal." Supposedly the film is intended to spark disgust in its audience members as they watch Tom progress from attempting to steal furs, to distributing stolen cigars, to stealing alcohol, to helping out with an illegal brewery. Even though Tom recanted his way of life upon being shot, his apology apparently comes too late in this morality play. Tom had transgressed too many societal mores to be allowed a chance at rehabilitation. Members of a rival mob kidnap Powers from the hospital and return him, dead, to his mother's doorstep. The film warns, "The end of Tom Powers is the end of every hoodlum…"[5]

A bevy of popular short books and pamphlets similarly sold Capone and his city as the pinnacle symbols of urban confusion. These works feigned a call to action against the growing urban menace, but they in fact celebrated the exploits of the Chicago rackets. *Does Crime Pay? No! Life Story of Al Capone in Pictures, as Shown by the Uncensored Photos in this Book*, proclaimed that its publishers did not seek to fulfill the public's morbid curiosity, but to show brutal murder scene pictures as crime deterrents. Rather than replacing the victim's face with the letter X as was popularly done, the work published uncensored pictures, and included morgue shots of most of the leading crime personalities. Yet this slim volume assumed a complementary tone when exploring the life of Capone. The work referred to the Capone gang's impressive set of connections in major U.S. cities, mentioned Capone's generosity, and complementarily labeled a picture of a smiling, benign-looking boss as "Al Capone—the master mind."[6] A similar work, *Life of Al Capone in Pictures! and Chicago's Gang Wars*, featured a lurid red cover highlighted by a smiling, colorized, Capone likeness. This book also entreated Americans to shun the lures of crime, but its authors could not refrain from selling the gruesome tales as alluring entertainment. The inside cover chided, "A graphic warning to Americans of the peril that lies in organized crime through the rise of the great gangs! That is the purpose of this book which turns the spotlight on the horrors of gang warfare and reveals the life of Al Capone, ruler of rackets. The editors hope this piti-less publicity, by word and picture, will serve to awaken the law-abiding to [a] renewed fight against forces of crime that defy government." Yet the blurb went on to sell its fare as a tantalizing read. "The complete story of the murder-warfare that cost 500 lives in Chicago is told in the LANGUAGE OF THE GANGSTER! [capitalization in original]," crowed the book, "Gross brutality, [and] contempt for human life is revealed in the colorful, sardonic phrases of the underworld." The book concluded that Capone de-served a place in the annals of history for his achievements as much as the usual cast of characters. "General Grant and George Washington and Rob-ert E. Lee are in the schoolbooks. Why not Al?" the text asked, continuing, "He has ducked more bullets than Grant heard at Vicksburg. They've been shooting at Al for ten years!" [7]

Producers of popular culture wavered over whether they wished to por-tray Capone as an evil master mind or as an animalistic, subhuman charac-ter. John Roeburt, author of *Al Capone, a novel*, (the basis for the motion picture, *Al Capone*) found Capone a brutal personage. Arriving in Chicago in 1919, Capone, in Roeburt's vision, "was stockily-built, with homely fea-tures. He had a spatulate nose and thick, scabrous lips. His clothes were rumpled and looked slept in."[8] Fred Pasley, in the 1930 *Al Capone: The Bi-ography of a Self-Made Man*, spoke of Capone as a skilled businessman who controlled his criminal empire with intellect. To Pasley, Capone could be considered, "the John D. Rockefeller of some twenty thousand anti-Volstead filling stations—controlling the sources of supply from Cana-da and the Florida east coast and the operations of local breweries and distilleries; frequently referred to as the municipal cabinet member without portfolio—commissioner of lawlessness."[9]

In 1957, Eliot Ness and Oscar Fraley's book *The Untouchables* brought Capone's legacy to a broad audience. Ness had worked for the U.S. Depart-ment of Justice, Prohibition Bureau, in Chicago during Capone's heyday and had attempted to control his bootlegging activities. Late in life, Ness worked with journalist Fraley to bring a highly self-congratulatory version of his government work to a mass audience. The popularity of *The Untouchables* would make it one of the most relied upon sources for the Capone myth, de-spite its many historical inaccuracies. In a mode of popular history not known for its attention to searching out trusted sources, Ness and Fraley's apparently complete story easily lent itself to wholesale adoption by ama-teur historians of gangster history. It remains to this day an oft-cited work in shoddily researched books, thus perpetuating its errors. The popularity of the 1987 film *The Untouchables*, starring Kevin Costner as the unstoppable crime-fighter Ness, also gave weight and longevity to this inaccurate story. Ness' telling of the Capone saga cast the story as a morality play, pitting the character of the all-good Ness against the all-evil Capone. The story was the tale of two men, well-matched rivals, who locked horns over the issue of Prohibition. Ness credits Capone with "genius for organization" to elevate his own ability to bring down the criminal boss.[10]

In *The Untouchables*, the authors represent Chicago as a city in dire need of a knight in shining armor like Ness. According to Ness and Fraley, Chicago in 1929 could be characterized as "a city ruled by the knife, pistol, shotgun, tommygun and 'pineapple' of the underworld, a jungle of steel and concrete clutched fast in the fat, diamond-studded hand of a scar-faced killer named Al Capone." While Ness lived quietly at home with his parents, Capone had a fortune of fifty million dollars. According to the legend set out by Ness, Capone owned a thirty thousand dollar car complete with steel plating and bullet proof windows, a Florida estate worth five hundred thousand dollars, and an eleven carat diamond ring. Ness wrote that Capone always carried at least fifty thousand dollars in cash on his person.[11]

But Ness claimed to be up for the challenge that this powerful criminal presented. Although Capone's men made several attempts on his life, Ness would not give up his fight. Daringly, Ness even arranged to parade the forty-five trucks he had confiscated from Capone's ring past the leader's offices in the Lexington Hotel. Ness and his hand-picked, unbribable assistants (hence the moniker "the untouchables") made their strength and gall clear. Ness bragged, "What we had done this day was certain to enrage the bloodiest mob in criminal history. But it would do much more than that, I thought. We had hurled the deviance of 'The Untouchables' into their teeth; they surely knew by now that we were prepared for a fight to the finish." Capone, enraged by this display, then supposedly threatened to kill Ness with his own hands. Indeed, Ness gives himself credit for Capone's eventual demise, although the arrest really came through the efforts of the Internal Revenue Service. When Capone addresses the press upon news of his conviction, saying, "Well, I'm on my way to do eleven years. I've got to do it, that's all. I'm not sore at anybody," Ness felt the words were directed right to him.[12]

The Desilu Playhouse began its very popular television series *The Untouchables* in 1959. The opening credits of the show appeared over a darkened, forbidding Chicago skyline, highlighted with the catchy musical theme by Nelson Riddle. Robert Stack played Eliot Ness, and the serious voice of Walter Winchell narrated the program. *The Untouchables* sought to contrast a svelte, dignified, Anglicized Ness (Ness was actually of Norwegian

background) with the exaggerated foreignness of Capone and his co-con-
spirators. Although the non-fictional Capone was born in the United States,
his television persona struggled with English in a manner that would suggest
to the viewing audience that he was a newly arrived immigrant. During the
first episode of the program, an angry Capone smashed a glass decanter and
threatened, "Thatsa whatsa gonna happen to Ness." Ness apparently also
trumped Capone in the area of morality. In the program's second install-
ment, Capone appeared in public escorting two women, while the conservative Ness married his fiancée Betty Anderson.[13] Here, television kept to its
pat distinctions between acceptable and non-acceptable behavior despite the
realities. During Ness' pursuit of Capone, Ness had in fact been unmarried,
while Capone was married, and, according to common understanding, happily so.

Although Capone remained central in America's ongoing fascination
with gangsters, the nation remained interested in stories about the current
underworld problems of the 1940s and 1950s. Capone's passing in 1947
hardly meant the end of organized crime, even though Prohibition had been
rescinded in 1933. *Life* magazine consoled its ever curious readers in 1948
that "Chicago is still one of the crookedest cities in the world." *Collier's*
Lester Velie informed in 1950, "Al Capone's venereal disease rotted body
took its last ride three years ago. But the evil that men do lives after them.
Sometimes it grows. Today, 'The Big Fellow's' influence on Chicago is greater than ever." In this period, Chicago's criminals made the lion's share of
their living from gambling; the underworld processed and then took a sizable cut from about five hundred million in bets placed on horses and some
two hundred million bets on policy wheels each year. Other businesses controlled by organized crime in Chicago included prostitution, night clubs,
vending machines, slot machines, bottled water, brewing, and such services
as towel rental for hotels and cleaning and dyeing. Organized crime had lucrative connections with labor unions. Gangsters earned money by harness-
ing themselves to the strong political machines. Members of criminal
organizations made their way onto city payrolls as ghost employees (never
actually seen at work!). The *Chicago Sun-Times* reflected in 1952 that
"gangland is openly campaigning for political power with bullets instead of
ballots."[14]

Virgil Peterson of the Chicago Crime Commission testified in front of
the U.S. Senate Crime Investigating Committee of 1951, informing the officials and the American public that members of Capone's gang still involved
themselves actively in crime in his city. Peterson's fact gathering led to the
1952 publication of the book, *Barbarians in Our Midst*, a scholarly work

on Chicago crime that, like the progressive tracts of the early part of the century, heightened interest in Chicago's underworld culture. In 1954, author Alson Smith reflected on the slew of such works and on how Peterson's work fit into a pattern of writing on Chicago:

> By now there is a sizable literature on Chicago crime, running from Lincoln Steffen's *Shame of the Cities* through the works of Herbert Asbury, Herman Kogan and Lloyd Wendt, Lloyd Lewis and Henry Justin Smith, Fred Pasley, John Bartlow Martin, and others down through the sensational (but largely true) disclosers of Jack Lait and Lee Mortimer to the sober and factual documentation of the Kefauver Committee and Virgil Peterson. The latter's *Barbarians in Our Midst*, published by Little, Brown, and Co., in 1952, is the most serious and valuable contribution to this literature since the publication of the mammoth *Illinois Crime Survey* by the Association for Criminal Justice in 1930.[15]

Reflecting on the event of Peterson's 1951 testimony in *Holiday*, reporter Robert J. Casey asserted that the "pleasing folklore" produced by uninformed onlookers (not experts like Peterson,) that cast Chicago criminals as Robin Hood types rather than as ruthless bandits, spurred interest in these characters. Tales of the men spoke of them as good parents and sons, and as brave men, ready to die whenever called upon to defend the honor of their group. With this kind of coverage, Casey believed, it was "no wonder Chicago began to get a reputation."[16]

Popular fiction of the period, tending to feature tales of Chicago's present-day strife, further scarred popular perceptions of Chicago. While reworkings of Chicago history remained popular culture's most frequently chosen view of the Illinois city, representations of Chicago's present also tended to cast it as a challenge to American morality. Nelson Algren's *Never Come Morning* (1942) and *Man with the Golden Arm* (1949) brought biting, unsympathetic visions of a Polish criminal element to millions of readers. Algren, who was of Swedish and German Jewish ancestry himself, drew the ire of the Chicago Polish community for his representations of their neighborhoods.

Southern Review first published a portion of *Never Come Morning*, a short story entitled "A Bottle of Milk for Mother" (1941), and the story found an audience through inclusion in the O. Henry Memorial Volume for 1941 and as a radio drama for the National Broadcasting Company. *Never Come Morning* itself had sold more than a million copies by 1945. In his 1951 poem-like exposition on Chicago, *Chicago: City on the Make*, Algren expresses a kind of mixed-up love for his home city, but in his books *Never Come Morning* and *Man with the Golden Arm* he presents a persistently foul image of Chicago. Algren obviously spent years writing about Chicago because he loved her, but the attraction remains less than obvious in these two novels. Algren's city dehumanized its inhabitants, leading them to crime and even soiling their relations with those that they love. Algren's grim pictures of the city can only captivate those who find this low picture of life interesting—but given the popularity of his books, this number is higher than might be expected. Algren embodies the central challenge of Chicago's long-lived, sullied reputation; Americans must find something they *like* about such an image in order to have spent so much energy over the years producing and consuming such representations. Algren openly explains his version of the feeling, and his ability to speak of these passions so articulately must account for his success. Algren admits, "Yet once you've come to be part of this particular patch, you'll never love another. Like loving a woman with a broken nose, you may find lovelier lovelies. But never a lovely so real." In fact, Algren mistrusts the kind of love that only embraces the finer side of things. He challenges:

> It isn't hard to love a town for its greater and its lesser towers, its pleasant parks or its flashing ballet. Or for its broad and bending boulevards, where continuous headlights follow, one dark driver after the next, one swift car after another, all night, all night and all night. But you never truly love it till you can love its alleys too.[17]

Perhaps Algren's fiction can serve as a test; if the reader makes it through with any positive feeling left for the city than one must have true love for the place. For Algren's sagas take place solely in the city's most appalling areas. In one excruciating moment in *Never Come Morning*, budding criminal Bruno "Lefty" Bicek tried to rationalize his allowance of the gang-rape of his girlfriend, the trusting Steffi Rostenkowski. "Dames got to get experience just like fellas," Bruno thought to himself.[18] Young men got in line to have a chance with Steffi, and Bruno brooded over his mistake, grew angry, and finally fought with a boy in line, probably killing him. The ruined Steffi was given over to the madam Mama Tomek, for whom she must now go to work. Bruno subsequently found himself arrested for another crime—shooting a drunk.

Algren's *The Man with the Golden Arm* uses Chicago as a setting for a critique of American style capitalism. Algren's protagonist, Frankie Machine, watched as lines of disheveled men join him in a city jail. Although he had never met his fellow in-mates, Machine felt he knew them intimately. All shared with him "the great, secret and special American guilt of owning nothing, nothing at all, in the one land where ownership and virtue are one."[19]

Algren presents his Chicago as a place of unrelenting darkness. Algren may be the only twentieth-century writer to successfully sustain a fictional story line of length without giving his characters a glimmer of hope for the future. Even in realist novels like those of Sinclair, Zola, or Dreiser, which also describe the city as a place where unexpected challenges continually confront inhabitants, readers have some cause to hope that the characters can eventually escape their turbulent, urban realities. Algren offers no such hope. Frankie could not flee the lure of morphine, a habit that he picked up in the armed forces during World War II. The rush of the drug could only allow him to slip away temporarily from the grinding problems of the city, and the reader senses the inevitable bad end to come from Frankie's choice of chemical avoidance. People in the neighborhood knew Frankie Machine (born Frankie Majcinek) as the quick-handed card dealer, but this talent failed to free Frankie from his fractured marriage or his inability to pursue his dream of becoming a drummer. Machine's desire for drumming, drugs, and dealing made him the "man with the golden arm," but his everyday reality was far from golden.

Frankie's wife, Sophie (also called "Zosh" or "Zoshka"), spent her days confined to a wheelchair in their apartment, cutting out newspaper stories about accidents and pasting them into a scrapbook. Zoshka, who faked a pregnancy to snare her husband, later pretended to be unable to walk in order to keep him. Zoshka's "injury" followed a car accident Frankie caused after a night of drinking at a seedy pub, Algren's unforgivingly named Tug & Maul. Guilt ate at Frankie day after day. Although he stayed in the marriage, he wished to leave his wife for Molly Novotny, a dark haired woman who worked hustling drinks in the Club Safari. Machine spent the bulk of his time with Solly "Sparrow" Saltskin, a petty thief and repeat dog-napper. Although Sparrow was far from an intellectual, Machine often lamented that he could not keep up with his friend's line of thought. Together, Sparrow and Machine fell into trouble, killing the drug dealer Louie Fomorowski almost by accident, and stealing irons from Nieboldts' department store.

Ultimately, the police trace Fomorowski's murder to Frankie with the help of testimony from Sparrow. Shot while running from the police, Machine checked into a men's hotel and hung himself with newspaper twine. His end was as lowly as the reader expected.

Frank Sinatra's portrayal of the morphine addict Machine in the 1955 film further strengthened the reach of Algren's sordid Chicago. While the film offered audiences a vision of an extremely bleak world, the film version of the story proved more forgiving than the original novel. In this retelling of the story, Machine successfully kicks his morphine habit with girlfriend Molly's assistance. Having endured his withdrawal symptoms, Frankie delights at the bright morning, saying, "It's the most gorgeous day I ever saw. I think it's the first day I ever saw." And in the film, the sham invalid Zosh, rather than Frankie, murders the drug dealer, and although the police originally suspect Frankie of the crime, they ascertain the real killer eventually. Zoshka ultimately throws herself from the balcony of their apartment building, declaring her love for Machine as she falls. Molly and Frankie then walk off down the street together in silence. This cinematic city is filled with pain and suffering, but at least Molly and Frankie have each other to help them through.

Highly regarded and often read authors Saul Bellow and Richard Wright also contributed to the creation of the city's image. These two writers aimed to recreate the inner thoughts of troubled youths in their respective works, *The Adventures of Augie March* (1953) and *Native Son* (1940), and not necessarily to highlight the troubles of a particular urban space. Yet their fiction nonetheless added weight to Chicago's image problems. Bellow's melancholy Augie March encounters a stream of unpleasant Chicago figures, including minor criminals like Augie's boss William Einhorn. Einhorn describes Chicago as the "one place where a person who goes out for a peaceful walk is liable to come home with a shiner and a bloody nose," an injury, according to Einhorn, as likely to be inflicted by the police as an errant youngster.[20]

In Wright's *Native Son*, Chicago became the setting for the violence of Bigger Thomas, a young black man who murders his employer's daughter and his girlfriend, and considers his crimes an almost inevitable part of his troubled, urban life. Thomas thinks to himself, "His crime seemed natural, he felt that all of his life had been leading to something like this." Wright's own memoir, *Black Boy*, one of the best-selling works of 1945, told of his hope for opportunity in Chicago, and his quick disillusionment with the city. Despite the desire for personal advancement in Chicago, and the widespread belief among blacks that Chicago could offer them a life of greater dignity, those who made the Great Migration to the North were cognizant of the city's unflattering reputation. Again, personal, national, and even group conceptions of place can coexist, even if highly divergent. Wright's work broadcast his reiteration of Chicago as a desolate place, even while the success of his autobiography confirmed the city as a site of African-American achievement. Wright reflected, "My first glimpse of the flat black stretches of Chicago depressed and dismayed me, mocked all my fantasies. Chicago seemed an unreal city whose mythical houses were built of slabs of black coal wreathed in palls of gray smoke, houses whose foundations were sinking slowly into the dank prairie."[21]

Further, the newly generated images of a morally untraditional Chicago reached the eager audiences of Hugh Hefner's Chicago-based *Playboy Magazine*, first published in 1953. Hefner left the staff of *Esquire* in 1952 when they refused to offer him a pay raise upon the journal's move from Chicago to New York. He founded his own competitor, a magazine aimed at "the young city-bred male—a sophisticated guy, intelligent if not intellectual, who finds most of his entertainment indoors." Hefner saw his periodical as a rebellion against the proliferation of male "outdoors" magazines and marketed *Playboy* to "the urban male." He described this personage in detail, claiming a high class lifestyle for his readers, saying:

> Lest you assume we mean it is a magazine for wastrels, ne'er do wells and fashionable bums, however, permit us to sketch the kind of man we have in mind when we use the word 'playboy.' He can be a sharp-minded young business executive, a worker in the arts, a university professor, an architect or engineer. He can be many things, providing he possesses a certain point of view. He must see life not as a vale of tears, but as a happy time; he must take joy in his work, without regarding it as the end and all of living; he must be an alert man, an aware man, a man of taste, a man sensitive to pleasure, a man who—without acquiring the stigma of the voluptuary or dilettante—can live life to the hilt.[22]

Hefner's magazine followed a trend of gradual loosening of societal restrictions regarding sexual matters and of course had considerable influence on American mores itself over time. The publication of Indiana University professor Alfred Kinsey's *Sexual Behavior in the Human Male* in 1948 and *Sexual Behavior in the Human Female* in 1953 challenged American preconceptions about homosexuality, adultery, and premarital sex. The great popularity of these volumes attests to the public's great interest in sexuality. Even the exceedingly dry prose of these traditional scientific studies did not slow their distribution. Historians of the 1950s, like Joanne Meyerowitz, editor of *Not June Cleaver: Women and Gender in Postwar America, 1945–1960*, now challenge the prior image of the postwar period as a staid, conventional landscape. Hefner himself speaks of how Kinsey's work altered general perceptions towards sex in the 1950s. Hefner remarks, "He [Kinsey] had confirmed, using values that I had had since childhood, that attitudes towards sex were not only very repressive, they were hurtful and hypocritical." Hefner, who believed himself a liberal leader of the 1950s and

1960s, expressed shock when some feminists denounced *Playboy Magazine* in the 1970s.[23]

By 1955, *Playboy* could claim the highest number of newsstand sales of any periodical priced at fifty cents or more. Readers the world over began to know that Chicago served as the home for this irreverent magazine. Despite the publication's downward tug on Chicago's name, Hefner himself looked kindly on his home town, at least in the earlier days of his business. He asserted that the kind of talent needed to pull *Playboy* together existed only in Chicago. Hefner lamented outsiders' claims that the Midwestern city faltered culturally when compared to coastal cities. He explained, "I've had a real love affair with this city and real resentment against the Second City syndrome and the fact that so many good things started in Chicago, then drained away to New York and Los Angeles. I think it's a pretty special city. I've never really managed to get it on with New York."[24]

Hefner's creation of his own stylized persona was the subject of a great many magazine articles. A 1967 cover story on Hefner in *Time*, along with a rash of other newspaper and magazine articles, encouraged familiarity with the *Playboy* lifestyle. Hefner lived the "indoor" life propagated in his publication, rarely venturing out of doors. The publishing giant transformed the James Gamble Rodgers mansion at 1340 North State Parkway, originally designed for city father Dr. George S. Isham, into the "Playboy Mansion." Hefner set up a windowless apartment for himself within the home, a place in which he could not discern the difference between night and day. Hefner often went to sleep at eight or nine in the morning, and woke at three or four in the afternoon to begin work. Between 1963 and the middle of 1965, Hefner was said to have left his home only nine times.[25]

The presence of the *Playboy* executive office building (the transformed Palmolive Building on which Hefner had a ninety-nine year lease) in Chicago's skyline also linked Chicago and *Playboy* in the public mind. So did the proliferation of Playboy Clubs. The first Playboy Club opened in Chicago in 1960, and the fad of Playboy "key clubs" soon spread across the country. By 1967 the clubs had one million members and branches in such places as New York, Miami, London, New Orleans, and Los Angeles. Hefner aimed to have the clubs reflect the temper of the magazine, claiming that the haunts were:

> dedicated to projecting the plush and romantic mood of the nation's most sophisticated publication plus the fun and excitement that you also expect to find in PLAYBOY'S pages. We've attempted to make every detail of the Club, in every room, suggest to you the warmth, the intimacy and the fun of a private cocktail party, with fine food, drink,

entertainment, and of course, numberless beautiful women—many of them Playmates from past issues of the magazine.[26]

The television series, *Playboy Penthouse* begun in 1960 and *Playboy After Dark,* which began in 1968–1969, both opened with shots of Chicago at night, and painted images of naughty pleasures to be had in the Midwestern city. The shows challenged social norms by featuring African-Americans as well as whites as entertainers. But the programs allowed for only half-hearted integration. For instance in 1969, when Ike and Tina Turner performed on *Playboy After Dark,* the pair did not take part in the games and discussion sequences that preceded their appearance. Strikingly, the black "party guests" who watched the Turners sing "Big Wheels Keep on Turning" and "Rolling Down the River" disappeared during the other portions of the show.[27]

The proliferation of negative portrayals of Chicago between the 1930s and 1960s cannot be disputed. Yet Chicago's claim for a degree of sophistication can be said to have grown during the period, as well. Chicago remained an edgy sort of place, a city Americans might not want to see as an embodiment of America's foundational values, but one that onlookers grudgingly admitted displayed the nation's modern driving capitalism and other similar contemporary attributes. Too, American attitudes towards obvious capitalism were changing; if we all desired financial gain, went the thought, why hide it under an air of aloofness towards money? The image of the city as an uncultured country cousin had begun to wear off, but this stigma could not be said to be completely erased. The October 1951 edition of *Holiday* devoted its pages to a focus on Chicago as a suitable travel destination for the sophisticated American. According to *Holiday,* the city's energy and its pantheon of business leaders had made it one of the great shopping destinations, second only to New York. The magazine chronicled Chicago's society set and its improving restaurants. Yet Chicago's checkered past brought the curious sightseer to the city. Albert Halper explained in *Holiday*:

> Thanks to headlines and certain old movies, people still come to Chicago all primed to see the unexpected. They no longer hope, or fear, to be on the spot while a gunman is being cornered, but they do crave the tingle of recognition. And Chicago grants their wish, because Chicago is what it's cracked up to be. It is never dull, seldom even tranquil. Its tempo, its rawness, its beauty jolt the visitor like a still electrical charge, and he knows he is in the liveliest city on earth.[28]

In 1954, *Holiday* explained that the city's history of extremes gave it plenty of interesting, oversize places to visit. Writer Fanny Butcher wrote that "Chicago boasts the biggest hotel in the world, the biggest commercial building, biggest stockyards, biggest grain market, biggest mail-order house, and assorted other colossi."[29] This type of list of "the biggest" things that Chicago contained commonly found its way into discussions of the city; both its supporters and detractors spoke of Chicago's largesse.

Yet *The New Yorker* magazine did its share to bring down America's second largest city. Journalist Stanley Walker could not go far enough with his attacks on Chicago in 1946. Walker rehearsed for his readers all of his opinions on the city over the years. He held a "faint distaste" for the city in the early twenties, and his dislike deepened with the rise of Capone, the St. Valentine's Day Massacre, the stories of political corruption, and the outspoken, anti-Semitic isolationist movement which centered in Chicago during World War II. And although some claimed Chicago's restaurants had begun to evolve, Walker mocked Chicago as "a great town for cole slaw and Idaho potatoes." Walker summarized, "Life here [Chicago] is not only violent in spots; it is depressingly garish, loud, and almost wholly devoid of either taste or conscience."[30]

The New Yorker also launched Chicago's label "Second City," with a series of articles by A.J. Liebling in 1952. Chicago had become the second city in terms of population in 1890, but Liebling helped the nickname to stick. Liebling, like Walker, had come of age with a feeling that he could do without Chicago. When he visited, he found it shabbier and older-looking than New York. He reported:

> There was an outer-London dinginess to the streets; the low buildings, the industrial plants, and the railroad crossings at grade produced less the feeling of being in a great city than of riding through an endless succession of factory-town main streets. The transition to the Loop and its tall buildings was abrupt, like entering a walled city. I found it beguilingly medieval.[31]

According to Liebling, Chicago's attempt at becoming a grand city had failed. Even native residents conceded their city's lack of cultural status. Chicagoans assumed that their versions of plays were worse than those staged in New York, even if the show's entire cast remained intact. Up-scale Chicagoans would not buy fashions from their own shops, but waited to procure their wardrobes on New York vacations during the afternoons they could not attend theatrical matinees. Liebling laughed at the Chicagoans' assessments of their city, and then concurred. In terms of theatrical attractions, he insisted, Oslo (a city of four hundred thousand) rivaled Chicago. Chicago instead offered a great many strip-tease joints, popular with the city's numerous convention visitors. All in all, Liebling characterized Chicago as a city that, no matter how hard its residents try to change things, would remain number two, or lower, culturally. To Liebling, "the city consequently has the personality of a man brought up in the expectation of a legacy who has learned in middle age that it will never be his."[32]

In the middle of the twentieth century, the rhetoric and popular images which shaped Chicago's dark reputation flowed on. Considering the question in 1933, noted author Edgar Lee Masters admitted, "In all parts of America, in the eastern states and cities in particular, Chicago has an evil or ignominious reputation, depending upon the supposed facts connected with its life and career which may at the moment be under discussion." Masters believed many of the things said about the Midwestern center were untrue, and he spoke of the city's strong inner spirit. But many others had incorporated the decades of unflattering statements about Chicago into their own conceptions of the city, equating these sentiments with the city's reality. A writer for *Life* magazine reflected in 1944, "in vitality and lustiness and sprawling disorder the city has not changed since 1870. It is just bigger and better looking. Its history since then has been splashed with labor riots, gang warfare, municipal graft, evanescent reforms." Alson J. Smith, author of *Syndicate City: The Chicago Crime Cartel and What to do About It* (1954) went further, claiming:

> [The] apathy towards crime in America's second and the world's fourth city is a serious disease which threatens the very life of American democracy. It is in the cities that democracy breaks down, that the American dream becomes a disordered and frightening nightmare. And of all the cities to be afflicted with this disease none is sicker than Chicago. The city has never known a thoroughgoing reform like the one that brought Fusion and La Guardia victory in New York, or the one that crumpled the Vare machine in Philadelphia, or even the mild one that broke the power of old Jim Curley in Boston. To the political boodler and the Syndicate hoodlum, Chicago is still what the Chinese call the Number One city—Kum Shan, the Golden Hill.[33]

Chicago's national image between the 1930s and 1960s resulted primarily from a reworking of historical events like the Great Chicago Fire and the city's gangster past in various popular media. While real troubles, like inter-racial conflict over housing, dominated the city's local headlines and the minds of its leaders, national culture concerned itself with reminding the public about the more unsavory aspects of the city's history. Chicago remained the national symbol for urban disorder in the post-war period, but popular culture found much of the fodder for this image in the city's past rather than its present. Perhaps the public, although outraged by these images, found considering the various lurid tales less unsettling on the surface than the contemporary racial and Cold-War tensions. Yet, surely images of past urban unrest ultimately prompted thoughts of current troubles—the overly-played foreign characteristics of the gangsters evoking the threat of "foreign-born" communism, reconsiderations of the city's great fire leading Americans again to consider that, indeed, the city might be a better place if it all could just be begun anew. In the middle of the twentieth century, Chicago found itself wrapped in layers of dark images regarding its urban personality, a tangle of historical misinterpretations, and a generation of new unflattering documents, all of which portrayed the city as a threatening urban space to a shocked, yet titillated, American public.

Chapter Six

The End of the Myth: Chicago in the Tumultuous 1960s

By the 1960s, Chicago's role as a primary focus for anti-urban sentiment had begun to ebb away. In these years, the myth that had been linked with Chicago's name no longer regenerated itself with every scandal that broke out inside the city limits. The past remained, but it no longer cast its pall over the city's present and future to the degree it once had. The strength of the city's dark reputation did not lessen due to an increasing respect for Chicago as much as through a growth in the competing negative images of other urban spaces. Chicago still felt its share of urban disorder, but now these events were deemed typical. The tumultuous 1960s brought civil disruption to many American cities; Watts erupted in 1965, students took over university buildings on college campuses, such as in the much-watched Columbia University take over in New York City in 1968, and Newark and Detroit faced devastating racial violence in 1967. Chicago itself faced race riots after the assassination of Martin Luther King in the spring of 1968 and the so-called "police riots" during the Democratic National Convention of August 1968. But much of the popular rhetoric explained Chicago's violent moments as part of the general emotional landscape of the 1960s rather than an aberrant form of Chicago-style outburst.

Two key factors moved popular images of Chicago from the consideration of the city as one of the worst examples of American urbanity to the belief that the city was typical. First, Chicago's national image benefited from its failure to erupt during the pressure-filled summer of 1967. While Detroit faced the worst race riots of the century and Newark followed closely behind, Chicago's streets remained relatively calm. If Chicago could withstand such a tense moment without incident, the city deserved a revised standing in popular culture.

Second, Chicago's long-lived mayor, Richard J. Daley, who served Chicago between 1955 and 1976, brought stability and energy to the city. While his administration certainly faced a number of scandals, Daley's stewardship brought grudging praise rather than criticism from most national journalists of his day. In some ways, Daley's style of leadership marked a kind of restoration of the boosters' partial control of Chicago's image. Like earlier urban leaders, Daley did alter popular thought. However he did so in an unusual way. Part of Daley's influence on the city's national reputation stemmed from his giant personality and ability to make "good copy" for news writers rather than simply his own concerted efforts on behalf of the city's image. At times, Daley transformed the image of Chicago *despite* himself. True, his hard-nosed politics led to a local building boom and other positives for the city and certainly helped transform Chicago's image. Yet it was also the "everyman" quality lurking below Daley's repeated public speaking blunders and clear bewilderment at the rapid changes of the 1960s that endeared him to many white middle class Americans. Daley's party politics looked relatively trustworthy given the temper of the times. His seemingly solvent Chicago appeared praiseworthy in the face of New York City's financial demise. And his strong hold on the leadership of the Chicago Democratic Party (Daley was both the mayor and the chairman of the Cook County Democratic Party), while clearly an example of a political "machine," seemed more practical than ominous. Even the notorious "police riots" that occurred when tense Chicago police met with anti-war demonstrators in public areas of the city during the 1968 Democratic National Convention (DNC) failed to permanently recapture Chicago's primacy as an anti-urban symbol. While Daley bungled the proceedings inside and outside of the convention site, Chicago's problems seemed more typical than not in the precarious atmosphere of the late 1960s. And many even applauded Daley for taking a forceful stand against the protest groups. After all, 1968 was the year in which the American public chose as their national leader the man who spoke for "the silent majority"—Republican Richard Nixon.

In the late 1960s, many American cities made headlines when violence erupted in their lower-income neighborhoods. Watts, a low-income section of Los Angeles, California, was the site of rioting in August 1965. Following the arrest of a young African-American man, Marquette Frye, Watts erupted in looting and arson. Police and National Guardsmen met the disruption with force. Thirty-four people died, hundreds were wounded, and four thousand were arrested.[1]

Between July 12 and July 17, 1967, the city of Newark, New Jersey faced unrest triggered by the arrest and police beating of cab driver John

Smith. Stopped for a dubious street violation and detained due to an expired license, Smith became the victim of violence perpetrated by police officers who had lost control. Officers kicked and stomped Smith and struck him on the back of the head with a gun while his head lay in a toilet bowl. Word spread about the injustice, leading to rioting in the streets. Fires broke out, and looting was rampant. Ultimately, about twenty African-Americans died, and about one thousand suffered injuries.[2]

And also during July 1967, the city of Detroit made national news with a riot sparked by tensions between blacks and whites in this heavily divided city. Since at least the 1940s, whites had been deserting the central city for the suburbs, following industrial plants that sought out the lower real estate prices of the outlying areas. As the city's tax base lessened, those who remained made due with dwindling resources, and relations between the mostly white police force and the increasingly black citizenry grew troubled. The 1967 riots reminded Detroiters of past urban violence. Detroit also had faced significant racial unrest back in June 1943, when fighting between whites and blacks on the city's island park, Belle Isle, spilled over into the central city. In 1943, Detroit police, siding with the white rioters in most instances, added to the terror, shooting and killing seventeen blacks, but no whites. Thirty-four people in total died in the unrest.

It is important to explore the July 1967 Detroit events, because the scale of the riots and the considerable governmental confusion—both at the local and the national level—regarding the proper response to the riots, demonstrate in their details how Chicago's role as the leading symbol of urban disorder came to fade away. Even today, Detroit bears the scars—in terms of vacant lots and the financial effects of white flight—of the 1967 clash. In understanding the 1967 Detroit riot, we better comprehend the national context for the troubles Chicago faced during the 1968 Democratic National Convention.

Detroiters felt they had learned a significant lesson from the 1943 incident, and believed that despite the tense mood of the 1960s their city would remain quiet. Forty percent of the city's black families owned homes, a figure that seemed to attest to the black population's general contentment. Detroit's Mayor Jerome Cavanagh spent the considerable War on Poverty funds he acquired open-handedly, trying to quell lingering difficulties. Public figures bragged openly that the unrest that swept the nation would not land in Detroit. A journalist for *Time* magazine remembered, "For the last couple of years, city officials have been saying proudly: 'That sort of thing can't happen here.' It had seemed a reasonable enough prediction." Floyd

McKissick, director of the Congress of Racial Equality, did not place Detroit on his 1966 list of potential American hot spots.

On a Sunday morning, July 23, 1967, a police raid on an illegal (unlicensed) tavern went wrong. A virtual tradition in Detroit since its years as a center of Prohibition bootlegging, illegal bars were quite plentiful in the city. The well-known entities were known locally as "blind pigs." This particular bar, located on 12th Street, pandered its wares in a neighborhood that had evolved from Jewish to African-American. The bar served as a community center of sorts. Referred to as the "United Community League for Civic Action," the establishment was known to promote anti-white invective and to serve drinks to minors. Police had gotten word that the place would soon erupt. Just before four o'clock A.M., police, led by 10th Precinct Sergeant Arthur Howison, entered the bar and arrested approximately eighty-two customers and the bartender. The arrest of the customers broke with usual procedure; most often only the employees of illegal establishments faced arrest. As neighborhood residents began to pick up on the situation, a crowd of approximately two hundred people gathered outside of the tavern and yelled at the police. Someone threw a bottle against a squad car window, and this served as a symbol of sorts, calling forth a riot.

Mobs gathered on the West Side and soon crossed the city's central access road, Woodward Avenue, to move into the East Side of the city. Detroit police decided to remain in the area but not to stop the mob with violence; Police Commissioner Ray Girardin instructed his men not to use their guns unless absolutely necessary. The force's "no-shoot" policy may have encouraged the mob to resort to more lawlessness. Looters rifled through the contents of area stores, and angry residents began fires. Approximately 250 of Detroit's 630 liquor stores faced looting. More than 1,600 blazes broke out over the week of rioting. Fires spread from stores to apartment buildings and houses. Protestors kept the fire department from attempting to put out the fires, even when the city sent all-black fire fighting teams out into the streets. Onlookers reported sniping from area rooftops. Representative John Conyers, one of the two black congressmen from Detroit, pled with rioters, only to be heckled as an "Uncle Tom." Metropolitan residents and travelers avoided the downtown area, reducing the city's highways to ghostly thoroughfares. Residents of the riot zone attempted to leave the area, but many found themselves thwarted by the failure of the city bus system during the conflict.

Finally National Guard troops entered the city to restore the peace. Michigan Governor George Romney informed U.S. Attorney General Ramsey Clark that the Detroit Police and the Michigan National Guard might not prove sufficient to stop the uprising. President Lyndon Johnson sent former Deputy Defense Secretary and friend Cyrus Vance to Detroit to assess the situation. Desperate, Romney and Cavanagh wired the White House, stating that the situation might not be able to be contained. Defense Secretary Robert McNamara ordered paratroopers into the Selfridge Air Force Base outside Detroit, ready at a moment's notice. Johnson spoke on national television of the need to send in the troops, openly criticizing the city's own attempts to quell the violence. Pointedly critical of Romney, Johnson made continued reference to the governor's inability to keep order in his own state. Johnson knew Republican Romney might be his challenger in the 1968 presidential election and the president wanted to appear to be the hero in this situation. The president already faced mounting concerns about the war in Vietnam. The thousands of troops Johnson sent into the fray were able to quiet the city about five days into the rioting.

Approximately forty-four people lost their lives in the melee. The conflict also rendered five thousand people homeless and caused anywhere between fifty and five hundred million dollars in damages. Law enforcement personnel arrested more than seven thousand rioters. The incident inflicted scars on the city that still remain in the form of vacant lots, destroyed buildings, and distrust between the races. [3]

The Detroit riot proved the worst of the rash of outbursts that wracked the country during the summer of 1967. Lyndon Baines Johnson reflected on the tensions of 1967 as "such no nation should live through: a time of violence and tragedy." New York Senator Robert Kennedy referred to the racial discord as "the greatest domestic crisis since the war between the States." Detroit became the city most linked with the summer's violence. Detroit, once considered a symbol of racial achievement because of its high rate of black homeownership and African-American achievement in the auto industry, had acquired a more sobering image. A writer for *Newsweek* was able to look back by August 1967 and proclaim, "And suddenly Harlem 1964 and Watts 1965 and Newark only three weeks ago fell back into the shadows of memory. Detroit was the new benchmark, its rubble a monument to the most devastating race riot in U.S. history—and a symbol of the domestic crisis grown graver than any since the Civil War." [4]

But while Detroit reigned as the primary symbol of urban disorder, a common assessment was made by the national media that, given the tensions in American cities, *any* city could now erupt. *Newsweek* continued, "No city was safely beyond the battlefield: the homefront war seared 30 cities during the week, perhaps 70 this summer, more than 100 since the whole deadly cycle began in Harlem three years ago."[5] In such an atmosphere, Chicago's position as a stand-out of urban disorder could not hold.

Something else had happened in 1967 that contemporaries failed to award much attention, but which is key to the longitudinal understanding of the evolution of Chicago's reputation. Surprisingly, while unrest swept the nation, Chicago remained relatively calm. Chicago could, of course, not be said to have been without racial conflict, but no major riots broke out in Chicago during the summer of 1967. This comparative level of harmony led to the Democratic Party's selection of Chicago as the site for the 1968 DNC.[6]

Much of the perceived stability of the city drew on the character of Mayor Richard J. Daley. Daley was born in 1902 in Bridgeport, a largely Irish neighborhood in Chicago, to the children of Irish immigrants—Lillian (Dunne) Daley and Michael Daley, a sheet metal worker. Daley entered the Hamburg Social Athletic Club as a young man. The members of this neighborhood political society/club probably took part in attacks on African-Americans during the city's 1919 riot. Throughout his career, Daley remained quiet whenever questioned about his possible participation in the disruption. But the Irish-black conflict in 1919 was well known and the Hamburg Club had been a significant force in its South Side neighborhood.[7] Daley climbed his way up the Democratic political machine in Chicago, finally being elected to the chairmanship of the Cook County Democratic Central Committee in 1953, and then as mayor of Chicago in 1955.[8] Once in office as mayor, Daley continued to serve as the chairman of the county's Democratic Central Committee, despite the intermittent criticism of his dual role. His control of the patronage jobs stemming from his control of the Democratic Party proved too important a power to forfeit.

The national discussion on Daley assumed a range of tones; public commentators deemed the mayor both a highly efficient public servant and the last of the old style political machine leaders. He was hailed as one who brought sophistication back to the city with his energetic spending on the city's infrastructure, but some deemed him reactionary for his militaristic plans for security at the 1968 DNC. For all of his own personal foibles, Daley's longevity and steadfast hand improved Chicago's image. Daley's Chicago, while far from perfect, ranked above tumultuous Detroit, Los Angeles, or Newark, and even above John V. Lindsay's financially floundering New York. As Northwestern University professor Louis Masotti expressed in the *Chicago Tribune*, "The people who criticize Daley the most have never had to live in New York or Los Angeles."[9]

Daley had a number of outspoken fans, some of whom bordered on hyperbole when praising the mayor. Richard G. Stern of *Harper's Magazine* felt Daley to be one of the best mayors in the world in 1962. Richard C. Wade, an urban historian from the University of Chicago, complemented in 1968, "Daley is easily the best mayor Chicago ever had and one of the best in the nation since World War II." Others did not feel quite so kindly. After the events of the 1968 Democratic National Convention, which will be explored more below, an editorialist in *Christian Century* concluded, "Daley is, quite simply, a dictator. He would like to be a benevolent dictator, but he will rule regardless of the means to which he must resort."[10]

According to popular reflections on the city, Daley elevated Chicago culturally by investing heavily in the building of new structures. Journalist James Dugan, in his article, "Mayor Daley's Chicago," considered, "Today four million Chicagoans are trying to elevate the human condition and are thereby physically replacing much of their city." The work accomplished in the city between 1955 and 1976 recalled the city's boisterous personality of earlier times, but achieved a whole new level of cosmopolitan flare. *Time* reported that "Under Daley Chicago has a new rhythm as exciting as any in the city's lusty past." The travel magazine, *Holiday*, urged readers to visit Chicago as Daley had built almost a whole new city. A Chicago advertising executive, interviewed for *U.S. News and World Report*, told readers that, "He's [Daley's] made Chicago a modern city. When I came to Chicago in 1943, there hadn't been a building over two stories built since 1929. The city was dirty. It was ugly. It was corrupt. Today it is none of these. Richard Daley has done more than anything else to change it."[11]

During Daley's tenure, the city built numerous highways and encouraged corporate building downtown. Chicago architect Bertrand Goldberg's Marina City, hovering over the Chicago River on its northern bank, became a well-known symbol for a sophisticated Chicago. The twin towers, completed in 1961, resembled corncobs with their circular and variegated concrete forms. While perhaps unabashedly Midwestern in physical form, snobbish critics found the buildings inspiring and luxurious. Marina City housed well-appointed apartments, offices, and shops within its structures. Daley also ruled Chicago during the completion of projects like the John Hancock Center, designed by the Chicago firm Skidmore, Owings and Merrill and completed in 1968, and the Sears Tower, designed by the same firm, and completed in 1974.[12]

The inability of either corporations or the city to finance infrastructure growth during the Great Depression and the World War II era of course set up the possibility for the post-war building boom. Daley's period of leadership happily coincided with a great, nationwide demand for housing and an economic upsurge. But Daley's tastes also ran towards construction projects; bridges and buildings and highways clearly testified to the claim that his Chicago was "the city that works." But such output was not free. Daley paid for parts of the city's refurbishment by raising taxes; Chicago's property tax doubled during the mayor's first two terms in office, and rose more than forty-one percent between 1958 and 1963. These tax hikes exceeded that any other American city in the period.[13]

While Daley was generally considered a leader who got things done, he did face a number of scandals during his administration. Inequality between whites and blacks led to outbreaks of violence in the poorer sections of the city. Martin Luther King's 1966 move to target racism in Chicago, including its lack of open housing, shamed the Daley administration. While demonstrating against housing segregation on the city's southwest side on August 5, 1966, King became injured when a bystander hurled a rock at his head. King spoke out, "I have seen many demonstrations in the South, but I have never seen anything so hostile and hateful as I've seen here today." King's attempt to make the same type of quick progress in fighting for civil rights in the North as he had in the South proved less than successful. Most understood that King and Daley's ultimate agreement to support open housing in Chicago offered little more than a way for both to save face with their supporters. Historian Arnold Hirsch explains that the agreement "was a vaguely-worded statement of principle that promised little action over an indefinite period. Commentator Len O'Connor noted that few could specify the precise terms of the agreement, and a Daley lieutenant, Tom Keane, later denied its existence."[14]

In March 1963, Chicago made national headlines with the murder of Alderman Benjamin Lewis. Re-elected to his post just two days earlier, Lewis had swept away his competition, earning 12,179 votes to his opponent's 888. Benjamin Lewis was the first African-American alderman elected in the West Side's 24th Ward. Lewis' stylish two hundred dollar suits and his wealth in real estate triggered rumors that he had taken pay-offs from organized crime. Lewis' murder, performed in typical gangland style (Lewis' assailant handcuffed him to a chair and shot him in the back of the head) seemed to indicate that Lewis' reported underworld connections had led to his death. The incident partially renewed the connection between Chicago and the mob in the public mind.[15]

On April 4, 1968, the West Side of Chicago experienced an outbreak of rioting in response to the assassination of Martin Luther King, Jr. in Memphis. Rioters smashed windows, set fire to buildings, and looted stores. The aftermath of the event included nine deaths, forty-six civilians shot, ninety policemen injured, over three thousand arrests, and fourteen million dollars in insured losses. The moment garnered national interest not so much for the violence, which had occurred in other communities devastated over the loss of King, but because of Daley's peculiar response. In commenting on the behavior of his police force, Daley spoke out about his wish that the police had applied an even heavier hand during the riots. Daley expressed that his instructions had been to "shoot to kill" any arsonist or to "shoot to maim or cripple" any looters. Unfortunately, continued Daley, Superintendent of Police James Conlisk had only asked the officers to use their own judgment. Not surprisingly, this off-the-cuff remark, typical of Daley's speaking style, brought considerable criticism and was soon recanted. Earl Bush, Daley's press secretary, chided the media, saying, "It was damn bad reporting. They should have printed what he meant, not what he said."[16]

Scandals emanating from the police force also rocked Daley's Chicago. Early in Daley's career, charges of impropriety among Chicago police officers were heard frequently and often sparked national commentary. A 1957 article in *Life* spoke of the Chicago police as "probably" the most corrupt in the nation. Chicago law enforcement had a reputation for taking bribes from organized crime, an image that began with the Capone myth in the late 1920s. In the 1960s, investigators continued to unearth pay-off sheets, implicating police in cover-ups for illegal gambling and prostitution. In 1968, *Life* magazine's Sandy Smith even blamed the violence perpetrated by the police during the DNC as the result of the extensive bribe taking of the force. Smith wrote, "There is a climate around Chicago police in which organized crime thrives like jungle shrubbery. There are good cops in Chicago but not enough of them." Chicago remained a "30-day town," in which the police expected pay-offs every thirty days. Popular folklore also knew Chicago as a town in which citizens stopped for traffic violations regularly avoided ticketing by handing over a twenty-dollar bill along with their driver's licenses to the investigating officer. Still, while Chicago received considerable notoriety for its police, such occurrences failed to shock the public as they had in the past. Again, the city was seen as more of a typical than atypical site of urban trouble. As *Christian Century* admitted in the fall of 1968, "while Chicago may or may not be the worst U.S. city in this respect [(actions of its police)], one thing is certain: it is not an exception."[17]

Daley also presided over the city during the unfolding of a police incident known as the "Summerdale scandal." Convicted thief Richard Morrison, released from prison in the fall of 1957, shortly thereafter became the advance man for a burglary ring organized by the Summerdale district police. Morrison worked with the Chicago police on various heists, and his police connections allowed him to pocket cash stolen from the premises. He once assisted police officers with a burglary in which they stole fourteen thousand dollars worth of shoes from a local shoe store for themselves and their families. However, when Morrison was arrested in August 1959 by officers who were not part of the burglary ring, Morrison implicated his cohorts in blue to avoid a tough sentence. Morrison was thus known as the "Babbling Burglar." Seventeen police officers were arrested after one hundred and thirty took lie-detector tests. Altogether, the ring had pocketed about one hundred thousand dollars.[18]

Plagued by this situation, Mayor Daley acted quickly to remove Police Commissioner Timothy O'Connor from his leadership role. Demoted to captain, O'Connor took the blame for the situation, despite his own sparklingly clean thirty-two year record.[19] Daley's quick move mitigated any accusations concerning his own culpability and actually brought him praise as a quick-thinker. Daley then appointed a group of Chicago "leading citizens" to choose a new commissioner. The mayor included on the committee Frank Kreml of Northwestern University's Transportation Center and the Operating Director of the Chicago Crime Commission, Virgil Peterson. Orlando W. Wilson, Dean of the School of Criminology at the University of California, served as the panel's chairman. The group screened close to one hundred candidates in six weeks, but found few willing to take command of the city's troubled police force. They then believed that Wilson, their own committee leader, would be the best for the position.

Wilson at first felt accepting the job to be illogical from a personal standpoint; he was only several years from retirement with full pension. Ultimately, however, he felt eager to try out his law enforcement theories in a real big-city setting. Before his academic career, Wilson had served as Chief of Police in Wichita, Kansas. Chicago would provide a more challenging proving ground. Wilson found the bigger city intimidating but believed it would serve as an intriguing site to which to apply his talents. Wilson was familiar with Chicago's infamous image. As Wilson himself explained, "But this was Chicago, our second-largest city—and by reports one of the wickedest."

Wilson's oversight of the Chicago police department soon significantly altered its national reputation. Many came to consider the city's police force one of the best, if not the best, in the nation. Wilson remained well regarded through his retirement in 1967. Still, by his own admission, Wilson could not entirely eliminate the connection between the city's police and organized crime. While he believed Chicago's situation to be same as in other large cities, he saw his inability to reverse the trend as a personal failing. He even spoke openly about the problem in the April 1964 *Harper's Magazine*.[20]

Mayor Daley and prominent Chicagoans envisioned the DNC of 1968 as a way to prominently display the achievements of their community to the nation. Daley and other Chicago leaders attempted to take charge of their city's image despite earlier failures. Business owners believed the convention would bring thirty to forty million dollars into the city and demonstrate the city's amenities to future convention planners. Daley believed the convention would solidify his status within the Democratic Party. Deemed the "kingmaker" for his role in bringing in the votes, legally and illegally, for John Kennedy in 1960, Daley sought to use his power within the Democratic Party to help his city in 1968. Investigations showed that voter fraud had occurred in Chicago during the 1960 presidential election. Even without the electoral votes of Illinois, Kennedy would have secured the presidency. Yet Daley was still well rewarded with lavish attention from the White House after Kennedy's inauguration. His continued clout within the party helped the city secure the job of hosting the convention.

The Chicago Citizen's Committee, a lobbying group formed in 1966 and began working to gain the right to hold the convention. Hotel owners and other interested parties provided six hundred and fifty thousand dollars towards the project, and Daley established a two and one half percent convention hotel tax for additional funding. The tax raised another two hundred and fifty thousand dollars and allowed the city to offer a total bid of nine hundred thousand. Chicago outbid Miami, which had pledged eight hundred thousand dollars. At a meeting held in Washington, D.C. on October 8, 1967, Chicago secured the DNC. The convention would take place between August 26 and 29, 1968.[21]

Because of Chicago's failure to ignite during the summer of 1967, Democratic Party leaders felt the city would be a relatively safe place to hold their important national meeting. Daley's strong form of control over his city proved equally reassuring to the party in the early stages. Determined not to have "his" convention threatened, Daley planned to fortify the city with ample security. He would call in the National Guard *before* any unrest occurred in Chicago. He spoke publicly on the subject, saying, "We will permit dissent, petition, and orderly demonstrations. But we won't let anyone come to take over our city, our streets, or our conventions."[22]

Anti-war demonstrators claimed that one hundred thousand people would flood the streets and parks of Chicago during the DNC, acting out as a response to the Johnson administration's policies on Vietnam. To ready the city, Police Superintendent John Conlisk, Wilson's protégé, put the nearly twelve thousand member police force on twelve hour shifts. The riot-trained Illinois National Guard, five thousand strong, also prepared to act. Seventy five hundred army troops in Fort Hood, Texas waited to be airlifted to Chicago on short notice. The Cook County Sheriff purchased two armored trucks fit with weapons, tear gas, and mace, and arranged for one thousand volunteers. At least two thousand police officers and one thousand federal agents planned to be in the area of the Chicago Amphitheater, the convention headquarters, at any one time. Fearing a fire like the one that had destroyed the city's McCormick Place convention center just the year before, two hundred firemen planned to be on call. Shipments into the nearby Union Stockyards would be thoroughly inspected, as would food served to delegates at the local Stock Yard Inn. Security measures transformed the Chicago Amphitheater into an armed camp. A chain link fence topped with three strands of barbed wire surrounded the grounds of the building. Manholes in the area were sealed with tar, and guards took up duty with rifles, binoculars, and walkie-talkies on catwalks ninety-five feet above the convention proceedings inside.[23]

City services faltered during the national convention, adding to the charged atmosphere. Seventy-five percent of the city's cab drivers went on strike. The International Brotherhood of Electrical Workers (IBEW) struck Illinois Bell, initially forcing the office staffs of presidential candidates to make do with existing telephone wiring—no additional lines were installed until a settlement came through.[24] These lapses brought criticism by the national press. Reporters too were personally affected in their ability to communicate with their publications due to the minimal telephone service.

Daley, donning his booster's mantle, worked diligently to present Chicago's best side to the convention goers. Divider rails on the new Daley expressways were painted, as were city lampposts and fire hydrants. Daley had painted redwood fences erected to hide junkyards and abandoned buildings. Yet observers saw through the cover-up. *Time* reported on August 30, 1968 that "no amount of cosmetics camouflaged breakdowns of the city's essential services. Nor could paint and rhetoric mollify the acrid atmosphere of a city mobilized for combat."[25]

City officials feared a level of street demonstration that never materialized. Before the conflict, anti-war groups placed the number of protestors planning to come to Chicago during the convention at about one hundred thousand, but the actual crowds paled in relation to this optimistic estimate. After-the-fact analysis placed the true number at approximately ten thousand. Various anti-Vietnam protestors found Chicago's Democratic National Convention an appropriate time to speak and act publicly because it provided an opportunity to make a statement against Lyndon Johnson. The main groups leading the demonstrations in Chicago were Jerry Rubin and Abbie Hoffman's Yippies (Youth International Party)—a group invented in New York for the purpose of the 1968 convention—and the National Mobilization to End the War in Vietnam, or Mobe, which had first called for the action in Chicago. The prototypical 1960s student action group, Students for a Democratic Society, served as early training for Mobe leaders Tom Hayden and Rennie Davis.[26]

The activists envisioned staging a number of events to capture media interest and bring public attention to their cause. The Yippies announced a Festival of Life, an event of music and love to stand in juxtaposition to the death in Vietnam. They would also declare a large pig, Pigasus, as their presidential candidate. The Yippies urged their members to Chicago with the call, "Bring blankets, tents, draft cards, body paint, Mrs. O'Leary's cow, food to share, music, eager skin and happiness."[27] The Mobe planned rallies and demonstrations in the streets, including a birthday party for President Johnson. Both groups hoped to camp overnight in the city's large parks, but city officials refused to allow any violation of the 11:00 P.M. park closing regulation. Neither were they forthcoming for permits for any of the planned demonstrations except for a rally in Grant Park. Daley and his government considered the movement members "outsiders," and thought that granting the organizers' requests would disgrace the city and its guests. Yet they knew the protests would go on with or without legal sanction. Given the way in which the plans of the anti-war groups clashed with the tight reign the Chicago Democratic Party hoped to have on their city during this very public hour, savvy observers predicted the troubles to come. In May, 1968, *Christian Century* warned, "Chicago is ripe for insurrection, and the Democratic convention will be coming in August."[28]

During April, too, Chicago police had shown themselves to be less than level-headed when dealing with anti-war activists. On April 27, a group of six thousand marching on behalf of peace in Vietnam met with trouble. Police felt the demonstrators should disperse quickly upon reaching the march's endpoint, the city's Civic Center plaza. After intervention by the American Civil Liberties Union, the group acquired permits to demonstrate and specifically won the right to march as a united group around the plaza before dispersing. Yet the police wanted to keep the marchers from making their protest in this central spot, and urged the first marchers reaching the area of the plaza to leave before the whole group had gathered. Although the demonstrators reportedly remained peaceful, police officers began chasing and beating them, and even vented their anger on bystanders. Fifty arrests were reported. A peace parade scheduled for Saturday, May 4 experienced no difficulties. Nevertheless, this entanglement raised fears about what would happen when Chicago police met greater numbers of dissenters at the DNC.[29]

Chicago officials overreacted to the perceived threat of the anti-war activists. Some city leaders made matters worse by predicting terrible troubles for the late August events. Officials enacted elaborate plans to jail and bring to trial the envisioned mobs of protestors. In a pinch, city workers told the press, they could utilize the athletes' dressing rooms at Soldier Field or simply place the throngs in the exercise yard at the county jail. No traffic court dates were set in order to free the courts to process the demonstrators. Threats by the Yippies to dose the entire Chicago water system with LSD were taken very seriously, although experts informed the city that such a feat would require five tons or nine billion tabs of LSD—an item presumably not on the young people's budget. This level of overreaction was noted by journalists providing the recap of the event. *Time* commented that Daley had erred by amassing such considerable security forces in the city; the ten thousand demonstrators who ultimately took part hardly merited such a show of force.[30] Indeed, the way in which Chicago swirled in blue during the convention heightened the worries of the delegates rather than assuaging them.

During the August convention, the tensions that had been building between the police and the protestors finally erupted. Confrontations stemmed from the police's attempt to clear the parks at 11:00 P.M. and to stop the anti-war groups from taking to the streets en masse for various protests. Tensions between the anti-war groups and the predominantly hawkish members of the police and National Guard forces built until the police began physically attacking the demonstrators. Ultimately, approximately one hundred and fifty members of the Chicago security forces and three hundred demonstrators were injured in the unrest. Approximately six hundred protesters were arrested. Of those placed under arrest, more than eighty-six percent were under thirty. Yet contrary to popular perceptions, fewer than forty percent were students.[31] A number of the Chicago police department members who took part received formal censure for their participation. As of December, 1968, fourteen Chicago police officers had received disciplinary action, ten were suspended for not wearing their badges or nameplates during the melee, and four were recommended dismissed due to use of excessive force. Only one death can be even tenuously linked to the convention. On August 22, Dean Johnson, a seventeen year-old member of the Yippies from Sioux Falls, South Dakota, was stopped by police for a curfew violation and drew a gun from his travel bag. Police reported that Johnson fired at them before they returned fire two times, hitting him once in the heart. Although this incident predates the formal convention, the anticipated protests may have drawn Johnson to Chicago. [32]

News of the various disruptions that occurred during the DNC ultimately spilled onto the convention floor, affecting the course of the proceedings. What became known as the "Battle of Michigan Avenue" particularly inspired dissension within the Democratic Party. During this confrontation, ranks of protestors gathered outside the Conrad Hilton Hotel on Michigan Avenue, as the hotel provided housing to many of the convention delegates and served as the presidential candidate headquarters of Herbert Humphrey, Eugene McCarthy, and Georgia's Lester Maddox. Police who attempted to break up the ranks of demonstrators soon turned to violence. Television cameras captured the police rage, and the activists, aware of the eye of the media, chanted, "The whole world is watching" while tensions heightened. Within an hour, when word of the battle reached the convention floor, Connecticut Senator Abraham Ribicoff, standing at the central podium, vented publicly about the chaos. Speaking on behalf of the presidential candidacy of George McGovern, Ribicoff insisted, "And with George McGovern as President of the United States we wouldn't have those Gestapo tactics on the streets of Chicago. With George McGovern we wouldn't have a National Guard." Daley and his contingent grew visibly upset at this criticism. Feeling personally responsible for maintaining order in the streets, Daley felt these jabs strongly. He yelled back at Ribicoff. Although later claims by the Daley administration and his son Richard M. Daley insisted that Daley yelled "faker" (reportedly a favorite term) at Ribicoff, most in the crowd took his enraged cry to be the expletive "f-cker." [33]

Later, Daley tried to defend his police force. Unfortunately, his usual habit of mangling public statements proved particularly troublesome in such a delicate situation. Daley, trying to mend the police's image, told a crowd, "Gentlemen, get this thing straight once and for all. The policeman isn't there to create disorder. The policeman is there to preserve disorder." [34] This malapropism quickly became key Daley folklore.

Much of the coverage of the Chicago convention lambasted the police and the National Guard for the violence inflicted on the protestors. Yet this sentiment on the part of the press did not apparently match that of the American public in general. The increasingly media savvy, and perhaps increasingly media weary American public took in news articles on Chicago in an unexpected way. Violence had occurred, certainly, but could it have been avoided? Chicago law enforcement had taken a stand against an apparent uprising. Many applauded Daley and his officers. As Daley biographer, historian Roger Biles points out, "In a year notable for the Kennedy and King assassinations, student takeovers of college campuses, ghetto riots, and anarchic anti-war protests, Daley stepped forward to restore order." A poll taken immediately after news of the disruptions found that seventy-one percent of the people polled believed the police actions were called for. Reportedly ninety percent of the more than fifty thousand letters sent to Daley's office by early September voiced support for the mayor. Even Herbert Humphrey, the presidential candidate ultimately chosen at the Chicago proceedings, spoke out that the police had been justified and defended the powerful Democratic leader Richard Daley. Humphrey pronounced, "We ought to quit pretending that Mayor Daley did something that was wrong."[35]

The mismatch between published articles on the Chicago clashes and the majority sentiment stems from a number of factors. Certainly, the calls and letters to Chicago on behalf of Daley and the tactics during the convention do not constitute a representative sample; as is often the case today, the more conservative elements of society have greater means and wherewithal than the liberal to write or phone in support of an issue. Yet it is also the case that the media, especially those involved with covering the DNC, chose to speak out against the violence because they themselves experienced the aggression of the police, who were ostensibly employed to keep the peace in the city. Reporters found themselves beaten along with the anti-war protestors, even when they clearly exhibited press credentials to the attacking officers. Such offenses certainly encouraged retribution in print. But the police also justifiably found the media's actions provoking. Some journalists set up shots in order to create a more violent image to broadcast to the world; others took part in taunting the police along with the demonstrators. And the reporters, like the protestors, were mostly considered "outsiders"—uninvited guests who came to make a mockery of Chicago for the world.

Fearing that stories about the incidents would damage the city's future as a frequently-chosen convention site, the Chicago Convention Bureau held a news conference. Chicago usually played host to at least one thousand conventions a year, earning it the moniker "Convention City." The Convention Bureau wanted "to get this message across to our customers. There has been no physical damage to the city or its convention facilities." Not acknowledging the death of Dean Johnson, the Chicago boosters claimed no one had died in the conflicts. The Bureau invited "concerned" groups to Chicago to visit before holding their conventions. All of the Convention Bureau's tactics did not have such a friendly cast; the city officials also threatened to sue groups that cancelled pre-booked conventions after the events of August 1968.

The American Sociological Association and the American Psychological Association did decide to hold their meetings elsewhere. The American Humanities Association announced a five year ban on staging meetings in Chicago. And the American Historical Association and the American Political Science Association also considered holding their upcoming meetings in other cities.[36]

The events of August 1968 remained in the national consciousness for some time. The publication of formal studies of the DNC-linked violence spurred national debate. Most notably, President Johnson's National Commission on the Causes and Prevention of Violence launched an inquiry into the unrest. The team of researchers, headed by Chicago attorney Daniel Walker, questioned thousands of people involved, scrutinized thousands of photographs, and viewed almost two hundred hours of film before issuing their lengthy report on December 1, 1968. The study concluded that while the police had been severely provoked, they had dissolved into gang behavior. The work, entitled *Rights in Conflict*, termed the police action a "police riot." Other interested parties, including the House Committee on Un-American Activities and a federal grand jury, also launched investigations.[37]

The disorder linked with the DNC also lingered in the public memory with the unfolding events of the trial against the supposed protest organizers. Referred to initially as the "Chicago Eight," leftist leaders Abbie Hoffman, Jerry Rubin, David Dellinger, Tom Hayden, Rennie Davis, John Froines, Lee Weiner, and Bobby Seale faced charges of conspiring to incite a riot. Johnson had pushed through legislation as part of the 1968 Civil Rights Act that made crossing state lines to organize a riot a federal offense. (The group was known as the "Chicago Seven" after Black Panther leader Bobby Seale was found guilty of contempt of court and removed from the group trial.) The trial increased national attention on Chicago, especially when the Students for a Democratic Society's belligerent Weathermen faction staged their "days of rage" in the streets of Chicago in protest of the trial. One hundred Weathermen members went so far as to beat passengers dragged from cars and to urinate on public property. When the trial finally ended in early 1970, all seven men were found not guilty of conspiring to start a riot, but the jury did convict Dellinger, Hoffman, Rubin, Davis, and Hayden of crossing state lines to participate in riots as individuals. The five each received a five-year jail sentence and five thousand dollars in fines, as well as additional contempt charges for their boisterous antics in the courtroom during the trial. However, these sentences were reversed on appeal.[38]

Despite the considerable violence witnessed in Chicago during the late August convention, the national conception of Chicago now moved away from earlier categorizations. Although far from a peaceful city in the late 1960s, Chicago's eruptions heralded from far different sources than those that had rocked the city in earlier decades. The violence experienced in Chicago was clearly linked to the anti-Vietnam sentiment building throughout the nation in 1968, and to the complaints of a mostly middle-class, college-educated body of young people, who found public acts the best way to bring energy to their concerns. While Chicago's scenes riveted the nation, they were not substantially different from the political activism displayed during a whole host of events fueled by student radicalism. The violence of Watts, Detroit, and Newark—violence spurred on by America's deep fissures of race and economic disparity—was a more ominous sign of the years to come than the anti-war protests. Here Chicago failed to lead as the shock-point of anti-urbanism, and its sustained image as an American urban nightmare was tempered slightly.

For all the seeming chaos, in many ways the clashes in Chicago in 1968 ultimately belied expectations. Interestingly, the much anticipated race riot failed to erupt in Chicago during the 1968 convention. The far left had hoped to encourage racial unrest in the city, and city officials, learning of these plans, deemed the protestors capable of this upheaval. The Mobe and the Yippies believed that the public confrontations in the city's central sections might ignite blacks in Chicago. Black comedian and activist Dick Gregory also attempted to mobilize African-Americans, threatening to ruin the convention if possible. City officials believed rioting in Chicago's ghettos to be a likely scenario. But such a situation did not occur.[39]

By the late 1960s, Chicago could be concluded to be a city of some sophistication. While not quite on par with the cultural heights of New York, public commentators felt Chicago a praiseworthy urban center. While no one claimed that theater or fashion or dining standards were set in Chicago, public commentators felt the city no longer needed to shoulder all of the connotations of A.J. Liebling's "Second City" label of the 1950s. The arts could not really be deemed robust, but the city's culinary palate had advanced beyond the typical Midwestern fare of steaks and potatoes. Chicago's shopping and sightseeing offerings featured several notable highlights. The city's interest no longer lay solidly in its more scandalous history. Now, Chicago had acquired a significant, modern charm all of its own.

Alfred Bester, in his travel article, "Chicago Sights and Delights," part of the March 1967 *Holiday* edition devoted to Chicago, explained, "Chicago is the ideal town for visitors. To travelers accustomed to the rudeness of New Yorkers, the insolence of Parisians, the *chutzpah* of Romans, the courtesy and friendliness of Chicagoans comes as a delightful surprise."

Journalist Richard Atcheson raved that Chicago's scenic Old Town neighborhood was "probably the most amusing [as in entertaining] neighborhood in the country." He waxed on, "It may be, in fact, depending on one's residential proclivities, the nicest place in the world." Richard Dunlop proclaimed, "Chicago is fun for kids, too, because Chicagoans are family people."[40] Obviously, Chicago had moved a long way from its speakeasy past.

In 1967, writer Arno Karlen concluded that, at last, Chicago had overcome its infamous image. Karlen reminisced, "For more than a century Chicago lived up to its myth." When Karlen visited the Midwestern city, in decades past, he had found it indeed lived up to its sordid reputation. In the late 1960s, however, things had changed. Karlen mused, "Chicago has begun to cross a crucial threshold, ripening out of its prolonged adolescence and re-forming its myth."[41]

From the late 1960s on, Chicago's infamous city myth faded and softened with time. Even during the fateful 1968 disturbances, the rhetoric used to describe the city's troubled streets assumed a more gentle tone than it had in earlier years. Despite the clash, Chicago's name could not be used in popular culture as a shorthand way of evoking America's urban problems. Blood had flowed in downtown Chicago, but troubles in Newark and Detroit and other of the nation's cities had proven considerably worse. At a time when racial intolerance and the failure of the civil rights movement to cure hundreds of years of racial injustice ranked first among American urban concerns, the population of Chicago's blighted areas had remained quiet in the face of a maelstrom in the city's central streets.

Daley's attempt to elevate Chicago's reputation by hosting the Democratic National Convention had ended disastrously. Again, the boosters' efforts to control the national image had proven no match for the weight of popular culture and its tendency to delight in the more wicked side of life. Nevertheless, popular images of Chicago changed due to the troubles faced by other urban areas in the late 1960s—in such a charged atmosphere the public perceived Chicago as relatively mundane. The cultural debate over Chicago's meaning had taken a turn. The contention that Chicago stood for either progress or moral decay muted due to historical circumstances. Americans now viewed Chicago as *both* a progressive and sophisticated spot and as a center of violence and distrust. Americans held an ambiguous picture of the Midwestern city, as they did of all U.S. cities. American anti-urbanism, for a time, summoned no particular symbol. Chicago's enduring legacy as a special sort of trouble spot, an infamous city, had begun to ameliorate at long last.

Afterword

The period in which Chicago served as "infamous city," a focal point for the nation's anti-urban sentiment, has passed. The producers of American popular culture did not so much rework Chicago's image in the 1960s as include many more cities in the national discussion concerning urban crime and chaos, thereby lessening Chicago's symbolic meaning. Ironically, as we have seen, it was in the late 1960s that Chicago faced some of the most violent urban unrest in its history, but at this point violence had become a common occurrence in many American cities. In fact, Detroit's 1967 racial clashes placed that city at the forefront of the nation's consciousness and linked its name with disorder. And the Watts uprising of 1965 launched the negative rhetoric towards Los Angeles that would cast it as the penultimate troubled city in the United States by the late twentieth century. The 1992 riots in response to the verdict in the Rodney King trial firmly secured L.A.'s tortuous meaning in American popular culture. Thus, in the last three decades of the twentieth century, Chicago was only one possible choice out of many for critics looking to blast urban locales for societal instability.

Chicago's present is perceived positively by many onlookers. Investors have transformed Chicago's downtown into a relatively unforbidding urban playground, where five star restaurants and flagship stores for national retail chains compete for the business of tourists and upper class Chicagoans. Chicago's main shopping thoroughfares, such as Michigan Avenue and State Street, and even side streets like Grand and Ohio, have been transformed by real estate investors and a willing political leadership from the home of traditional urban shopping into a Midwestern version of the Disney experience. The Disney corporation has an actual presence in Chicago, as it now does in other major American cities. Disney's reach has extended past California and Florida to northern landmarks like New York City's Times Square and Chicago's famed Michigan Avenue. Like New York, Chicago has played host to Disney's *Lion King* musical. In Chicago, Mickey Mouse,

Minnie Mouse, and other Disney characters march in major parades. Downtown Chicago for a time also had a Disney-themed entertainment venue, Disney Quest. Yet the city's new tourist offerings go beyond its Disney connection. Diners can revel in a seemingly never-ending array of restaurants, like the chain-venue Rock Bottom Brewery. This restaurant is located in a completely reworked building that once housed Chicago's best jazz and blues store, Jazz Record Mart. (Luckily, Jazz Record Mart, the store related to Chicago's great jazz and blues recording label, Delmark, still exists, yet in a jarring, newly-updated and less prime location.) Shoppers can visit forums like the vast Bloomingdale's home accessories store, incongruously located in the former Medinah Temple, an enticing Arabic style building designed for the Shriner's by Huehl and Schmid architects in 1913.[1] Chicago draws travelers hoping to experience an upscale urban adventure, and pulls in transplants hoping to relocate to a city with a cultural sophistication at least equal to that of the nation's coastal cities. I would argue that the shopping and dining opportunities found in Chicago currently exceed that of the East Coast cities, but that the level of conspicuous consumption available to visitors is rarely directly compared to Chicago's eastern sisters. Today's Chicago boosters would shy away from such an evaluation, and tourists might feel uneasy lauding a Midwestern locale over that of the historically much-vaunted East. While Chicago has come into its own as it nears its 200th birthday, striving for bigger and better continues to be its unique style and a necessary component in its tourism appeal. Even newly beribboned and fresh, as if from a week at the spa, Chicago needs to work harder than New York and Boston to earn travelers' dollars.

While the image of Chicago in American popular culture has evolved considerably since its "infamous" days, some would argue that its reality – in such guises as economic powerhouse, education center, and transportation hub—is not overly transformed from earlier times. Mike Davis, in the introduction to Marco D'Eramo's *The Pig and the Sky Scraper—Chicago: A History of Our Future*, points out that the latest glossy patina on Chicago's shoulders may be only a thin disguise for underlying urban problems. In June 1995, Davis points out, Chicago lost approximately 773 of its citizens to a heat-wave that had been clearly forecast by the National Weather Service and blatantly ignored by city officials, who failed to take action to herd elders and others to air-conditioning and safety. For all its fantastic opulence, Chicago still faces an array of ongoing urban problems. Davis declares that this new veneer, "this white-lie Chicago—where dead bluesmen, gangsters and industrial ruins supply romantic tourist ambience—is only the latest of the fantastic facades behind which ancient class and racial politics continue to be carried out with exemplary greed and brutality."[2] Yet, for all Davis' vehemence, would he really characterize Chicago's current problems as distinct from that of other leading American cities?

The bulk of Marco D'Eramo's book, *The Pig and the Skyscraper* finds Chicago a solid case study for his European vision of America and American-style capitalism. D'Eramo finds a particular brand of capitalism in the United States, an openness towards individualized money-making not yet discovered in Europe (although he predicts an American, aggressive capitalism will soon flourish there). I have argued that Chicago served as the focus of a specifically American kind of anti-urbanism, and thus became one of the most important pieces in the American debate over its future and what constitutes "true" American culture. Written initially in Italian (and subsequently republished in German and English). D'Eramo's work concludes that Chicago can still function as an important symbol from the European point of view. In offering an "archaeology of modernity," D'Eramo digs through an eclectic mix of Chicago's historic and present-day attributes to conclude that he found in Chicago "the stink of modernity." In its capitalistic bent, Chicago "is without a doubt the most American of U.S. cities. No other place in the world can boast the kind of fanatical belief that you find in this city in capital's libratory potential and in the religion of capitalism. If the United States is capitalism's land of Canaan, then surely Chicago is its Jerusalem."[3]

From the start of the research for this book, I found European and American attitudes towards Chicago highly divergent. D'Eramo's conclusion about Chicago's deeply American nature is an important one. Although Americans continue to work through historical memories of Chicago, the city no longer captures as large of a space in the national rhetoric about nationhood and the American character as it once did. Like most European analysis of Chicago, D'Eramo's new book demonstrates that European conceptions of the city are a step in time behind the focus of American attitudes. Where D'Eramo sees Chicago, past and present, as a symbol of unfettered capitalism, Americans, while they had qualms about the city in the past, see the current Chicago an inviting family playground. Americans in general think less specifically about Chicago than D'Eramo does; presently, the city fails to have the explanatory power in the United States that it might have in Europe. Yet, the argument here insists that in an earlier time, Chicago's image indeed did make it a representative place in the dominant rhetoric. Chicago was representative as a place of unapologetic pursuit of the dollar, urban dangers, and unwholesome sexuality—but it was representative nonetheless, and nonetheless seen as very American in some regards. Americans were unsure of who they were and who they were going to be; Americans may have known that, at some level they were all Chicagoans, but many were dragged into the modern, urban world as represented by Chicago with considerable protest.

Chicago's history, while not inspiring the visceral reactions it did formerly, remains known to most Americans. Because the past is read as completely behind the city—especially when one is standing on a well-scrubbed central Chicago street, appointed with fantasy shopping opportunities—the historical stories serve to amuse rather than frighten. Even Americans unfamiliar with the actual city of Chicago know something of its newly acquired status as a luxury travel destination. However, vestiges of the city's prior role remain in memory, and producers of popular culture do continue to use the city as the site for stories concerning the dangers of the urban past. For instance, images of dark Chicago found sizable American audiences in the winter of 2002–2003 with the release of the films *Chicago* and *Road to Perdition*. These films read differently in the early twenty-first century than they would have one hundred years earlier. To today's media savvy audiences, lulled to accept violence as part of popular culture by the barrage of images and sounds of the contemporary world, even the most vicious material of the past appears tamer than the horrific crimes of the present day. A fictional representation of a gangland killing, as blood-thirsty as the act may appear, does not challenge an audience braced in their real lives for the actions of modern terrorists who use explosions of all sorts to kill innocent civilians.

In the film *Chicago*, audiences are treated to a camp and sexy re-enactment of the story of two female murderers who fight for release from prison and the threat of the death sentence by manipulating the media. The film, set in Chicago, casts the city as a particularly lawless setting. The 2002 film draws on the 1975 Broadway musical by the renowned choreographer Bob Fosse, revived in 1997. Indeed, an earlier version of the story premiered in New York City in late 1926, and led to 172 performances, a national theatrical tour, and a number of film versions. The 2002 movie and the most recent revival of the musical demonstrate contemporary Chicagoans' ease with their city's historic media troubles; both attracted significant audiences inside the city despite their negative portrayal of Chicago. Back in 1927, when the original play opened in Chicago, Chicagoans had also flocked to the show to demonstrate their ability to enjoy any type of media their trend-setting New York rivals enjoyed—even if it disparaged their city. Chicago Mayor William Hale Thompson even publicly stated that the play's author, newspaper-woman-turned-playwright Maurine Watkins, ought to serve as a publicity agent for the city of Chicago.[4] Any publicity was good publicity for Mayor Thompson, apparently.

Road to Perdition (2002) also finds Chicago to be the center of ruthless behavior; in this film, Midwest gangsters ruled by Chicago bosses enter into a tangle of relationships ruled by family and work bonds. Connor Rooney, son of mob boss John Rooney, loses his temper and takes the life of a man who has spoken ill of his father. This error loses Connor respectability in this highly honor-bound world, so he attempts to murder the crime witnesses, Mike Sullivan and his twelve year old son, Michael Jr. Mike Sr.'s wife and younger child are mistakenly murdered instead, and thus begins the chase—Connor and John Rooney send a hired killer after the remaining Sullivans. The latter father and son pairing begin their ride to nowhere, their "road to Perdition," as they try to evade the Rooneys' revenge. The film, full of darkness, partial shots, and a relentless, driving rain, portrays the bleak Midwestern winter landscape and Chicago itself as the perfect location for this cycle of mindless revenge. The Sullivans' attempt to pressure Capone and henchman Frank Nitti to give up their support of the Rooney men by systematically robbing banks, targeting only the holdings deposited by the Capone ring. Mike Sr. summarizes the underpinnings of this plan and explains to his son, "Now there's one thing Chicago loves more than anything, and that's their money." These words obviously echo earlier summations on the city and the character of its people.

The cultural power of these nostalgic views of Chicago crime weighs considerably less than that of the films popular with American audiences during the heyday of the Midwestern gangsters. Contemporary Americans perhaps most fear the violence that comes into the places we reside in everyday—our homes, our schools, our workplaces—whether they be urban, suburban, or completely rural in setting. Films like the original *Scarface* (1932) shook their audiences to the core, pushing them to think about the direction of the modern city and to contemplate the kinds of truly awful incidents that could be produced by their period's swirl of organized crime. While *Road to Perdition* makes viewers cringe momentarily with its liberal use of violence, it leads one to broader questions of parenthood and father-son relationships rather than the fate of urban settings. The truly disturbing films are no longer necessarily linked to urban landscapes. In 2002, the presumably pastoral setting of a New England liberal arts college provided the backdrop for director/screenwriter Roger Avary's brutal film, *The Rules of Attraction*. Based on Bret Easton Ellis' book by the same name, the film version moves the story to a bit more contemporary period, but remains true to the deeply pitted boredom of Ellis' 1980s characters. *The Rules of Attraction* rocked audiences with its presentations of violence in a way *Scarface* might have done at the time of its original release; one movie-goer reported that he actually lost consciousness while watching the film's detailed and gruesome suicide scene.[5] While not the profound statement the writer/director hoped he had produced, the film does merit attention for attempting to capture the power of violence on the screen. As the world of illegal liquor led to doom in *Scarface*, *The Rules of Attraction* presents us with a world of underground drugs and drug-related violence. In the latter film's case, the characters involved are white, upper class college students rather than the money-hungry immigrants of *Scarface*. The bloodshed of the recent film, while at times originating in the trade of illegal substances like its violent predecessor, occurs behind mundane suburban facades or in the dormitory bathroom. The threats that had once lived only in the dark city, have traversed the city-suburb boundary and appear destined to remain.

Historians have often commented on the barrage of negative words used to describe Chicago during the nearly one hundred year period documented here. While the reputation of Chicago as "infamous city" dominated popular portrayals of the city in the past and curiously still finds considerable currency among Europeans, few in early twenty-first century America would characterize Chicago as an "infamous city." Today, in some minds, the mention of Chicago conjures up the former Chicago Bull's basketball star Michael Jordan, whose likeness was seriously considered as a possibility for the commemorative state of Illinois twenty-five cent piece. For others, Chicago means deep-dish pizza, with the sauce on top of the cheese and plenty of sausage. The Uno's pizza chain, which launched its initial outlet in Boston, brings a watered-down representation of the city's casual ambiance, as well as a weaker version of Chicago's signature food, to a national audience. Today, Chicago is also the Sears Tower, demoted during the 1990s from its status as the tallest building in the world. Or Chicago is O'Hare Airport, one of the busiest passenger airports in the world. For others, Chicago connotes the shopping available in the city's "Miracle Mile," a section of Michigan Avenue with a wide selection of high-end retail vendors. Chicago remains brash, larger than life, and captivating, but its reputation proves infectious in a benign, rather than sinister, manner.

We do remember Al Capone, but his persona and the actions of the Mafia in general have been placed into the category of compelling American folklore; the repugnance instilled by long-ago shootings of those tied to the mob system cannot rival today's crimes, which we often view live on television. The Columbine High School massacre in Littleton, Colorado in April 1999 represents one of the most well-known examples of such broadcast moments. In the 1920s and 1930s, one might view a black and white photograph of a deceased gangster in the evening newspaper or in a book on Al Capone. In 1999, we watched, disturbed yet transfixed, as students ran out of their formerly safe school building, a few crumpling to the ground as they exited, overcome by gunshot injuries. In 2001, we watched in absolute horror and disbelief as New York City's World Trade Center towers fell to the ground. The deep pain of such events perhaps makes us nostalgic for the urban problems of the past.

However remote the earlier violent episodes may be from our present day experiences, it remains true that in understanding our past fears we better understand where the United States is today. The destination cannot be comprehended without a clear sense of the voyage. Now, as suburbs sprawl outward so far from their urban hosts that they meet or overlap with the suburbs of other cities, and when workers typically face long commutes from their suburban homes to their suburban worksites, Americans expend considerable energy contemplating issues of lifestyle. Now, when what were once thought of as inner-city problems filter into suburban outposts, we should readdress the subject of anti-urbanism. Retreating to a life in the suburbs or the country cannot mean an escape from "urban" problems. At present, the nation and indeed the world grows increasingly linked and increasingly vulnerable through the proliferation of information technologies, widely available means of transportation, and growing populations settling on less and less remaining space. We have failed to erase the challenges of poverty, and racism and ethnic hatreds have taken a new and perhaps stronger hold among some groups of citizens. These prejudices have surfaced despite the economic upsurge of the 1990s and the greater acceptance of difference by the bulk of Americans. Given these changes, we must understand that the problems formerly assigned to "others" or a "faraway" city like Chicago, actually affect everyone in the United States. The "infamous city" did not disappear, but rather engulfed us.

Notes

NOTES TO THE INTRODUCTION

1. From Nelson Algren, *Chicago: City on the Make* (Chicago: University of Chicago Press, 1987), n.p. The poem was originally published as part of Baudelaire's *Petits Poemes en Prose* collection.
2. Kevin Lynch, *The Image of the City* (Cambridge, Massachusetts: The MIT Press, 1960), 3.
3. Anselm Strauss, *Images of the American City* (New Brunswick, New Jersey: Transaction Books, 1976), 8; and Kevin McNamara, *Urban Verbs: Arts and Discourses of American Cities* (Stanford, California: Stanford University Press, 1996), 12.
4. Michael Kammen, *Mystic Chords of Memory: The Transformation of Tradition in American Culture* (New York: Vintage Books, 1991), 7.
5. Morton and Lucia White, *The Intellectual Versus the City: From Thomas Jefferson to Frank Lloyd Wright* (Cambridge, Massachusetts: Harvard University Press and the M.I.T. Press, 1962), 1.
6. David Harvey, *The Condition of Postmodernity: An Enquiry into the Origins of Cultural Change* (Cambridge, Massachusetts: Blackwell Publishers, 1990), 5.
7. Strauss, *Images of the American City*, 49.
8. Michael Parenti, *Make-Believe Media: The Politics of Entertainment* (New York: St. Martin's Press, 1992), 3-4.
9. See Mike Davis, *City of Quartz: Excavating the Future in Los Angeles* (New York: Vintage Books, 1992), 6-88.

NOTES TO CHAPTER ONE

1. Robert Cromie, *A Short History of Chicago* (San Francisco: Lexikos, 1984), 35, and Campbell Gibson, "Population of the 100 Largest Cities and Other Urban Places in the United States: 1790 to 1990," (Washington: U.S. Government, Population Division, June 1998), accessed at http://www.census.gov/population/www/documentation/twps0027.html#citypop June 24, 2003.
2. *The Detroit Free Press*, October 10, 1871, p. 3.

3. Karen Sawislak, *Smoldering City: Chicagoans and the Great Fire, 1871–1874* (Chicago: The University of Chicago Press, 1995), 2 and 28; and *The Chicago Tribune*, October 12, 1871, p. 2.

4. Frank Luzerne, *The Lost City!* (New York: Wells & Company, 1872), 83; "A Terribly Destructive Conflagration Last Night," *The Chicago Tribune*, October 8, 1871, p. 3; H.A. Musham, "The Great Chicago Fire, October 8th-10th, 1871," in *Papers in Illinois History And Transactions for the Year 1940* (Springfield, Illinois: The Illinois State Historical Society, 1941), 89-93; *The Atlanta Constitution*, Evening Edition, October 8, 1871, p. 1; and Elias Colbert and Everett Chamberlin, *Chicago and the Great Conflagration* (Chicago: J.S. Goodman & Co., 1871), 196-197.

5. Luzerne, 183; "FIRE! The Destruction of Chicago!," *The Chicago Tribune*, October 11, 1871, p. 1; and Musham, "The Great Chicago Fire," 138.

6. *The Chicago Tribune*, October 12, 1871, p. 2; *The Detroit Free Press*, October 10, 1871, p. 1 and 4; "Dispatch from Washington, D.C.," in Charles Deane, Scrapbook of Clippings Regarding the Chicago Fire, 1871, Chicago Historical Society; *The Atlanta Constitution*, Morning Edition, October 11, 1871, p. 2; and "The Effect of the Disaster in the Metropolis: A Lively Day in Wall Street—The General Effect Upon the City," *The New York Herald*, October 10, 1871 in *The Ruined City: Or, The Horrors of Chicago* (New York: Ornum and Company Publishers, 1871), 24.

7. *The Ruined City*, 24; and *The Doomed City!: Chicago During An Appalling Ordeal!* (Detroit: Michigan News Company, 1871), 35.

8. See Christi Parsons, "Historian Finds a New Suspect For Chicago Fire," *The Chicago Tribune*, January 7, 1997, News Section, p. 1; and Steve Mills, "Uncowed Aldermen Clear Mrs. O'Leary," *The Chicago Tribune*, October 7, 1997, Metro Chicago Section, p. 1. Northwestern University professor Carl Smith and I are in agreement that Bales' assertions cannot be proven definitively.

9. "Chicago in Ashes," *Harper's Weekly*, October 28, 1871, p. 1010; Colbert, *Chicago and the Great Conflagration*, 202; "The World's Fire: The Great Conflagration in the City of Chicago, Oct. 8 and 9, '71," in *The Chicago Evening Post*, October 18, 1871, p. 2; and "The World's Fire," *The Chicago Weekly Post*, October 29, 1871, p. 4.

10. James W. Sheahan and George P. Upton, *The Great Conflagration. Chicago: Its Past, Present, and Future* (Chicago and Philadelphia: Union Publishing Company, 1871), 64; and Luzerne, *The Lost City!*, 91-92.

11. Michael Ahern, "Mrs. O'Leary Cow Story Refuted by Old Reporter. Michael Ahern Also 'Nails' Yarn That Owner Has Just Died in Michigan. Hay Started Big 1871 Fire," *Chicago Tribune*, January 21, 1915, in Deane, Scrapbook of Clippings Regarding the Chicago Fire, 1871. In part Ahern wrote this article to dispute the claim that Mrs. O'Leary had just died in Escanaba, Michigan. He claimed to have attended her funeral twenty years earlier.

12. "The Fire," *The Chicago Times*, October 18, 1871, p. 1, Newberry Library. Over the years this cow acquired the name of "Gwendolyn." See clipping in Deane, Scrapbook of Clippings Regarding the Chicago Fire, 1871.

13. Perry R. Duis and Glen E. Holt, "Chicago As It Was: Kate O'Leary's Sad Burden," in *Chicago*, October 1978, 220.

14. Duis, "Kate O'Leary's Sad Burden," 222; and Ahern, "Mrs. O'Leary's Cow," in Deane, Scrapbook of Clippings Regarding the Chicago Fire, 1871.

15. *The Atlanta Constitution*, Morning Edition, October 10, 1871, p. 1; *The Detroit Free Press*, Second Edition, October 10, 1871, p. 3; and *The Chicago Tribune*, October 11, 1871, p. 2.

16. Edgar Johnson Goodspeed, *The Great Fires in Chicago and the West* (Chicago: J.W. Goodspeed Publishers, 1871), 29 and 82; Colbert and Chamberlin, *Chicago and the Great Conflagration*, 9; *The Ruined City*, 9; and *Chicago Burned: An Authentic, Concise and Graphic Account* (Elkhart, Indiana: John F. Funk & Bro., n. d.), 4.

17. Luzerne, *The Lost City!*, 89.

18. *The Doomed City!*, 35; and "A Graphic Story. Statement of Ex-Lieut.-Gov. Bross of the Chicago Tribune—Scenes During and After the Fire—What Chicago Has, What She Needs, and What She Will Be," in *Chicago Burned*, 19.

19. *The Chicago Tribune*, October 12, 1871, p. 1; *The Atlanta Constitution*, Morning Edition, October 11, 1871, p. 2; and *The Doomed City!*, 36.

20. *The Ruined City*, 11.

21. Ross Miller, *American Apocalypse: The Great Fire and the Myth of Chicago* (Chicago: The University of Chicago Press, 1990), 93.

22. *New York Herald Tribune*, October 19, 1871; and quoted in *The Ruined City*, 31.

23. *The Chicago Tribune*, October 11, 1871, p. 1; and *The Atlanta Constitution*, Morning Edition, October 10, 1871, p. 1.

24. James W. Sheahan and George T. Upton, *The Great Conflagration*, in "The Great Chicago Fire and The Web of Memory," Chicago Historical Society and Northwestern University, www.chicagohs.org/fire/index.html; and Goodspeed, *The Great Fires in Chicago and the West*, 10.

25. *The Chicago Tribune*, October 12, 1871, p. 3; *Chicago Burned*, 19-20; and Sawislak, *Smoldering City*, 22.

26. *Chicago Burned*, 19; *The Chicago Tribune*, October 11, 1871, p. 2; *The New York Times*, October 10, 1871, p. 8; and *The Ruined City*, 48.

27. *The New York Times*, October 9, 1871, p. 1; *The Detroit Free Press*, Second Edition, October 8, 1871, p. 4; *The Detroit Free Press*, October 11, 1871, p. 1; "Thrilling Incidents of the Great Disaster," *The New York Sun*, in *The Great Fire. Leading Newspaper Accounts of the Terrible Chicago Conflagration* (St. Louis: St. Louis Book and News Company, 1871), 13; *The New York Herald Tribune*, October 12, 1871, in Sawislak, *The Smoldering City*, 80; and Colbert, *Chicago and The Great Conflagration*, 214.

28. Luzerne, *The Lost City!*, 69.

29. Goodspeed, *The Great Fires of Chicago and the West*, 40; "A Thrilling Scene: A Lady Braving the Flames with Her Child," from the *Telegram*, October 10, 1871, in *The Ruined City*, 28; Luzerne, *The Lost City!*, 153 and 164.

30. Luzerne, *The Lost City!*, 122 and 126; and "Chicago in Ashes," *Harper's Weekly*, October 28, 1871, p. 1010, from Collection of Newspapers on Chicago Conflagration of October 1871, Case Collection, Newberry Library, Chicago.

31. *The Ruined City*, 42.

32. Goodspeed, *The Great Fires in Chicago and the West*, 49; and Colbert, *Chicago and The Great Conflagration*, 217.

33. "Chicago in Ashes," *Harper's Weekly*, October 28, 1871, p. 1010, from Collection of Newspapers on Chicago Conflagration of October 1871, Case Collection, Newberry Library, Chicago; and *The Chicago Tribune*, October 12, 1871, in *The Great Fire*, 14.

34. "Chicago in Ashes," *Harper's Weekly*, October 28, 1871, p. 1010; *The Lakeside Memorial of the Burning of Chicago* (Chicago: The University Publishing Company, 1872), 31; "The World's Fire: The Great Conflagration in the City of Chicago, Oct. 8 and 9, '71," in *The Chicago Evening Post*, October 18, 1871, p. 5; and Carl Smith, *Urban Disorder and the Shape of Belief: The Great Chicago Fire, the Haymarket Bomb, and the Model Town of Pullman* (Chicago: University of Chicago Press, 1995), 55. Contemporary observer Frank Luzurne also thought the claims of incendiarism to be a hoax. See Luzurne, *The Lost City!*, 100.

35. Goodspeed, *The Great Fires in Chicago and the West*, 48; "Fire! Destruction of Chicago!" in *The Chicago Tribune*, October 11, 1871, p. 1; *The Doomed City!*, 25; and Luzurne, *The Lost City!*, 100.

36. "The World's Fire: The Great Conflagration in the City of Chicago, Oct.8 and 9, '71," in *The Chicago Evening Post*, October 18, 1871, p. 5; *The Chicago Tribune*, October 12, 1871, p. 1; "Proclamation!" Graff Collection, Newberry Library, Chicago; and Sawislak, *Smoldering City*, 49-63.

37. Colbert, *Chicago and The Great Conflagration*, 217; Goodspeed, *The Great Fires in Chicago and the West*, 7-8; "Thrilling Incidents of the Great Disaster," *The New York Sun*, in *The Great Fire*, 12; *The Ruined City*, 19; and Luzerne, *The Lost City!*, 199.

38. *The Atlanta Constitution*, October 10, 1871, Morning Edition, p. 1; *The Detroit Free Press*, October 10, 1871, p. 1; Goodspeed, *The Great Fires in Chicago and the West*, 81; Goodspeed, *The Great Fires in Chicago and the West*, 64; and Colbert, *Chicago and The Great Conflagration*, 195.

39. *Chicago Burned*, 32; and Alfred L. Sewell, *"The Great Calamity!" Scenes, Incidents, and Lessons of the Great Chicago Fire of the 8th and 9th of October, 1871* (Chicago: Alfred L. Sewell, Publisher, 1871), 77.

40. *The Chicago Times*, October 18, 1871, p. 1; and *Chicago Burned*, 32.

41. "The Chicago Calamity," *The Cincinnati Commercial*, October 10, 1871, in *The Chicago Tribune*, October 12, 1871, p. 1; and Luzerne, *The Lost City!*, 135.

42. Sawislak, *Smoldering City*, 37; and Smith, *Urban Disorder and the Shape of Belief*, 25.

43. E.P. Roe, *Barriers Burned Away* (New York: Dodd, Mead, and Company, 1886), 22.

44. Roe, *Barriers Burned Away*, frontispiece and 138.

45. "The World's Fire: The Great Conflagration in the City of Chicago, Oct. 8 and 9, '71," *The Chicago Evening Post*, October 18, 1871, p. 2; J.W. Foster, "What Remains," *The Lakeside Memorial of the Burning of Chicago*, 85; *The Chicago Times*, October 18, 1871, p. 1; and *The Chicago Tribune*, October 11, 1871, p. 2.

46. *The Chicago Weekly Post*, October 29, 1871, p. 1; *The Great Fire*, 19; and "Chicago Delenda Est," *The Inter-Ocean* (Chicago), October 10, 1872, p. 1.

47. *The Chicago Tribune*, October 12, 1871, p. 2; and "The Great Calamity," *St. Louis Democrat*, October 10, 1871 in *The Chicago Tribune*, October 12, 1871, p. 2.

48. *The New York Herald*, October 10, 1871, in *The Ruined City*, 36.

49. *The Ruined City*, 25 and 31-33.

50. Deane, Scrapbook of Clippings Regarding the Chicago Fire, 1871; and "Chicago Insurance Companies," *The Chicago Weekly Post*, October 29, 1871, p. 3.

51. *The Chicago Tribune*, October 12, 1871, p. 2; *The Chicago Evening Post*, October 18, 1871, p. 1; and Luzurne, *The Lost City!*, 211.

52. "The World's Fire: The Great Conflagration in the City of Chicago, October 8 and 9, '71," *The Chicago Evening Post*, October 18, 1871, p. 2; and Luzurne, *The Lost City!*, 237-238.

53. Sawislak, *Smoldering City*, 81 and 119.

54. *The Detroit Free Press*, October 11, 1871, p. 2; Henry M. Look, "Rescue of Chicago, in *Chicago Burned*, back cover; N. S. Emerson, "The Burning City," in Luzurne, *The Lost City!*, 117; and William Bross, *History of Chicago. Historical and Commercial Statistics, Sketches, Facts and Figures Republished from the "Daily Democratic Press"* (Chicago: Jansen, McClurg & Co., Booksellers, Publishers, Etc., 1876), 99.

55. *The Chicago Tribune*, October 11, 1871, p. 2; *Chicago Burned*, 19; and back cover, and *The Chicago Tribune*, October 11, 1871, p. 2.

56. Bross, *History of Chicago*, 83 and 123; and Lloyd Lewis and Henry Justin Smith, *Chicago: The History of Its Reputation* (New York: Harcourt, Brace and Company, 1929), 120.

57. *Chicago Burned*, 15.

58. Bross, *History of Chicago*, 94-97.

59. Bross, *History of Chicago*, 98-101; Sawislak, *Smoldering City*, 166; and Lewis, *Chicago*, 65.

60. Goodspeed, *The Great Fires in Chicago and the West*, 49.

NOTES TO CHAPTER TWO

1. Arthur M. Schlesinger, *The Rise of the City: 1878–1920* (New York: Hill and Wang, 1967), 67-76 in Reid Badger, *The Great American Fair: The World's Columbian Exposition and American Culture* (Chicago: Nelson Hall, 1979), 29.

2. Alan Trachtenberg, *The Incorporation of America: Culture and Society in the Gilded Age* (New York: Hill and Wang, 1982), 7, 15, and 114.

3. Nash, *Virgin Land*, 159, 187, and 192-3.

4. See Henry Nash Smith, *Virgin Land: The American West as Symbol and Myth* (Cambridge: Harvard University Press, 1970), 3, 128, and 123-4. For more on Native American patterns of land usage, see William Cronon, *Changes in the Land: Indians, Colonists, and the Ecology of New England* (New York: Hill and Wang Division of Farrar, Strauss, and Giroux, 1983).

5. Nash, *Virgin Land*, 159, 187, and 192-3.

6. See Josiah Strong, *Our Country* (Cambridge, Massachusetts: The Belknap Press of Harvard University Press, 1963), 171 and 174; Trachtenberg, *The Incorporation of America*, 101; and T.J. Jackson Lears, *No Place of Grace: Antimodernism and The Transformation of American Culture, 1880–1920* (New York: Pantheon Books, 1981), 26 and 32.

7. Carl Smith, *Urban Disorder and the Shape of Belief: The Great Chicago Fire, the Haymarket Bomb, and the Model Town of Pullman* (Chicago: The University of Chicago Press, 1995), 5.

8. Henry Loomis Nelson, "The Clubs of Chicago," *Harper's Weekly*, August 20, 1892, 806-7.

9. Lawrence W. Levine, *Highbrow/Lowbrow: The Emergence of Cultural Hierarchy in America* (Cambridge, Massachusetts: Harvard University Press, 1988), 177 and 206; and Robert H. Wiebe, *The Search for Order, 1877–1920* (New York: Hill and Wang, 1967), 12.

10. Frank Luzurne, *The Lost City!* (New York: Wells & Company, 1872), 230; and William Bross, *History of Chicago. Historical and Commercial Statistics, Sketches, Facts and Figures Republished from the "Daily Democratic Press"* (Chicago: Jansen, McClurg & Co., Booksellers, Publishers, Etc., 1876), 91.

11. *Chicago Burned: An Authentic, Concise and Graphic Account* (Elkhart, Indiana: John F. Funk & Bro., n.d), 5, Newberry Library, Chicago.

12. *The Chicago Tribune*, October 12, 1871, p. 2 and *Chicago Evening Post*, October 18, 1871, p. 1, from Collection of Newspapers on Chicago Conflagration of October 1871, Case Collection, Newberry Library, Chicago.

13. Ross Miller, *American Apocalypse: The Great Fire and the Myth of Chicago* (Chicago: The University of Chicago Press, 1990), 91 and 111; and *A Complete Guide to the Great Inter-State Industrial Exposition of 1873: Also the Art Catalogue and a Critical & Valuable Review of the Pictures in the Art Gallery* (Chicago: D. & C.H. Blakely, Book, Job and Commercial Printers, 1873), 30, Chicago Historical Society, Chicago.

14. *A Complete Guide to the Great Inter-State Industrial Exposition*, 5.

15. *Inter-State Industrial Exhibition of Chicago: Programme for the Fair of 1873* (Chicago: Tinker & Gibson, Publishers, 1873), 10, Chicago Historical Society, Chicago; John E. Findling, *Chicago's Great World's Fairs* (Manchester: Manchester University Press, 1994), 4; *Programme for the Sixth Annual Exhibition of the Inter-State Industrial Exposition of Chicago* (Chicago: Jameson & Morse, Printers, 1878), 3, Chicago Historical Society, Chicago; *A Complete Guide to the Great Inter-State Industrial Exposition*, 63; and Perry R. Duis and Glen E. Holt, "Chicago As It Was: Chicago's Lost Exposition," *Chicago*, July 1977, 74. Chicago perhaps learned its lesson by

the 1990s, when plans for a World's Fair in Chicago to mark the 100th birthday of the World's Columbian Exposition were eventually dropped.

16. *A Complete Guide to the Great Inter-State Industrial Exposition,* 5.

17. *A Complete Guide to the Great Inter-State Industrial Exposition,* 6-15; *The Exposition Guide to Chicago* (Chicago: Walworth Books, 1873), 3; and *Inter-State Industrial Exhibition of Chicago),* 7, Chicago Historical Society, Chicago.

18. *A Complete Guide to the Great Inter-State Industrial Exposition,9,* and 29-33.

19. Duis, "Chicago as It Was," 190 and David Lowe, *Lost Chicago* (New York: Wings Books, 1975), 135.

20. *The Exposition Guide to Chicago,* 4.

21. *Inter-State Industrial Exhibition,* 8-16.

22. *A Complete Guide to the Great Inter-State Industrial Exposition,* 34-5.

23. *A Complete Guide to the Great Inter-State Industrial Exposition,* 62-4; and Duis, "Chicago As It Was," 74.

24. John D. Kysela, "Sara Hallowell Brings 'Modern Art' to the Midwest," *Art Quarterly* 27, no. 2 (1964): 150-165; and *A Complete Guide to the Great Inter-State Industrial Exposition,* art guide supplement within guide, 20.

25. Lowe, *Lost Chicago,* 126-135.

26. Henry Steele Commager, *The American Mind* (New Haven, Connecticut: Yale University Press, 1950), 41 in David F. Burg, *Chicago's White City of 1893* (Lexington, Kentucky: The University Press of Kentucky, 1976), xiii.

27. Hubert Howe Bancroft, *The Book of the Fair, and Historical and Descriptive Presentation of the World's Science, Art, and Industry, as Viewed Through the Columbian Exposition at Chicago in 1893,* Fin-de-Siecle Edition (Chicago and San Francisco: The Bancroft Company, Publishers, 1893), 37, Newberry Library, Chicago; Badger, *The Great American Fair,* 44; *The Chicago Record's History of the World's Fair, Copiously Illustrated* (Chicago: Chicago Daily News Co., 1893), 3, Newberry Library, Chicago, 3; and Hon. DeWitt C. Creiger, Thomas B. Bryan, and Edward T. Jeffrey, *Arguments Before a Special Committee of the United States Senate, In Support of the Application of the Citizens of Chicago for the Location In Their City of the World's Exposition of 1892, January 11, 1890* (Washington: Government Printing Office, 1890), 12, Newberry Library, Chicago.

28. *The Chicago Record's History of the World's Fair,* 3; *World's Columbian Exposition Souvenir, Containing a Story of Christopher Columbus and His Discoveries* (Chicago: North American Engraving and Publishing Company, 1895), 29-30, Newberry Library, Chicago; and Bancroft, *The Book of the Fair,* 37.

29. Edward C. Shankland, "Designers and Organizers of the Fair," *The Engineering Magazine: An Industrial Review, World's Fair in Retrospect, Souvenir Number,* January 1894, 509, Harold Washington Public Library, Chicago; and *World's Columbian Exposition Souvenir,* 30.

30. J.B. Campbell, editor, *Campbell's Illustrated History of the World's Columbian Exposition,* vol. 1 (Chicago: J.B. Campbell, 1894), 38, Newberry

Library, Chicago; and Francis A. Walker, "America's Fourth Centenary," *Forum*, February 1890, 618.

31. Wim de Witt, "Building an Illusion: The Design of the World's Columbian Exposition," in Neil Harris, Wim de Wit, James Gilbert and Robert W. Rydell, *Grand Illusions: Chicago's World Fair of 1893* (Chicago: Chicago Historical Society, 1893), 51; and Captain Charles King, "The City of the World's Fair," *Cosmopolitan*, November 1891, 50.

32. *Chicago Record's History*, 4; and Andrew Carnegie, "Its Value to the American People," *Engineering Magazine: An Industrial Review, World's Fair in Retrospect, Souvenir Number*, January 1894, 417, Harold Washington Public Library, Chicago.

33. *World's Columbian Exposition Souvenir*, 34.

34. Charles H. Jones and Hon. E.O. Stannard, *Reasons Why the World's Fair of 1892 Should be Located at St. Louis, Arguments Made Before the Senate World's Fair Committee* (Washington: Government Printing Office, 1890), 3, 7, 12, and 17.

35. Alex D. Anderson, Myron M. Parker, John W. Powell, and Felix Agnus, *Arguments Before the Quadro-Centennial Committee of the United States Senate, In Support of Senate Bills Nos. 1839 and 1135, Each Entitled "A bill to provide for Three Americas and World's Exposition at the National Capital in 1892," January 10, 1890* (Washington: Government Printing Office, 1890), 3 and 5, Newberry Library, Chicago.

36. Creiger, *Arguments Before a Special Committee*, 4 and 15-25.

37. Creiger, *Arguments Before a Special Committee*, 3. In all his apparent generosity, Creiger did not mention Washington, D.C. at all.

38. Badger, *The Great American Fair*, 48; Emmett Dedmon, *Fabulous Chicago* (Atheneum: New York, 1981), 221; and Creiger, *Arguments Before a Special Committee*, 9.

39. *Hearings Before the Quadro-Centennial Committee of the United States Senate With Respects to the Commemoration of the Four-Hundredth Anniversary of the Discovery of America, January 11, 1890* (Washington: Government Printing Office, 1890), 9, Newberry Library, Chicago.

40. *Hearings Before the Quadro-Centennial Committee*, 21.

41. *World's Columbian Exposition Souvenir*, 34; and J.E. Chamberlin, "Chicago and the Fair," *Youth's Companion*, May 4, 1893, 6, Harold Washington Public Library, Chicago.

42. Bancroft, *The Book of the Fair*, 40.

43. Department of Publicity and Promotion, *After Four Centuries: The World's Fair* (Chicago: J.M.W. Jones Stationery and Printing Co., 1891), 2, Lilly Library, Bloomington, Indiana; and Bancroft, *The Book of the Fair*, 41-42.

44. "The World's Columbian Exposition," *Harper's Weekly*, November 22, 1890, p. 914.

45. "The Chicago Parks and the Fair," *Harper's Weekly*, May 10, 1890, p. 372; "The World's Columbian Exposition," *Harper's Weekly*, November 22, 1890, p. 915; and Badger, *The Great American Fair*, 65.

46. "The Organization of the World's Fair, *Harper's Weekly*, July 26, 1890, p. 578.

47. Badger, *The Great American Fair*, 59; and "The World's Fair," *Harper's Weekly*, October 4, 1890, p. 779.
48. "The Organization of the World's Fair," *Harper's Weekly*, July 26, 1890, p. 578.
49. "The World's Fair," *Harper's Weekly*, October 4, 1890, p. 779.
50. J.B. Campbell, editor, *The World's Columbian Exposition Illustrated*, March 1892, 2, Lilly Library, Bloomington, Indiana; and "A Midway Review," *Dial*, September 1, 1893, 105-7.
51. Bancroft, *The Book of the Fair*, 45-6.
52. J.B Campbell, editor, *The World's Columbian Exposition Illustrated*, Vol. 1, no. 1, February 1891, 3-5, Newberry Library, Chicago; and "Mr. Flower on the World's Fair, *New York Times*, November 14, 1890, p. 1.
53. *Chicago by Day and Night: The Pleasure Seeker's Guide to the Paris of America* (Chicago: Thomson and Zimmerman, 1892), 226, Newberry Library, Chicago; *The Chicago Record History of the World's Fair*, 4; and de Wit, "Building an Illusion," in Harris, *Grand Illusions*, 47.
54. "The World's Fair," *Harper's Weekly*, October 4, 1890, p. 779; "Regarding the World's Fair," *Harper's Weekly*, February 13, 1892, p. 161; Badger, *The Great American Fair*, 74-5; and J. B. Campbell, editor, *World's Columbian Exposition Illustrated*, March 1892, 70, Lilly Library, Bloomington, Indiana.
55. *Official Minutes of the Fourth and Fifth Sessions of the World's Columbian Commission Held in the City of Chicago, April 1st to 4th, 1891, Inclusive, and September 2nd to 8th, Inclusive* (Chicago: Knight, Leonard & Company, 1891), 64 and 6 (Fifth Session new pagination), Lilly Library, Bloomington, Indiana.
56. "The Last Day of the Fair," *Harper's Weekly*, November 11, 1893, p. 1074; and Rossiter Johnson, *A History of the World's Columbian Exposition, Held in Chicago in 1893* (New York: D. Appleton and Company, 1897), 361, Newberry Library, Chicago.
57. Campbell, *Campbell's Illustrated History*, 38.
58. Questions to Specialists, *Our Day*, December 1890, 468-70.
59. For more on Gompers, see Alonzo T. Jones, *The Captivity of the Republic. A Report of the Hearing By House Committee on Columbian Exposition, January 101-13, 1893, And the Present Status and Effect Of the Legislation On Sunday Closing Of The World's Fair* (n.p: International Liberty Association, 1893), 115, Newberry Library, Chicago; Trachtenberg, *The Incorporation of America*, 218; and Burg, *Chicago's White City of 1893*, 90.
60. J.B. Campbell, editor, *The World's Columbian Exposition Illustrated*, July 1892, 91, Lilly Library, Bloomington, Indiana; *World's Fair Puck*, May 15, 1893, 14, *World's Fair Puck*, May 1, 1893, 5, and *World's Fair Puck*, June 5, 1893, 54-55, Harold Washington Public Library, Chicago; and Rev. Henry C. Kinney, *Why the Columbian Exposition Should Be Opened on Sunday: A Religio-Social Study* (Chicago: Rand, McNally & Company, Printers, 1892), 29.
61. Bishop J.L. Spaulding, "Why the World's Fair Should be Opened on Sunday," *Arena*, December 1892, 45-7.

62. "Bishop Potter on Sunday Opening," *Nation*, September 29, 1892, 236-7; and Henry C. Potter, "Sunday and the Columbian Exposition," *Forum*, October 1892, 194-200.

63. James De Normandie, *"Sunday and the Columbian Fair." A Sermon Preached to the First Church, Roxbury, Boston, July 24, 1892* (Boston: Damrell & Upham, The Old Corner Bookstore, 1892), 6 and 14, Newberry Library, Chicago.

64. Elder Frederick W. Evans, *The World's Fair! Shall it Be Closed One Day in the Week to Please a Certain Sect* (Pittsfield, Massachusetts: Press Eagle Publishing Company, 1891), 5, Newberry Library, Chicago.

65. Johnson, *A History of the World's Columbian Exposition*, 361; and Badger, *The Great American Fair*, 94.

66. "A Clash of Authority: Two World's Fair Committees in Juxtaposition," *New York Times*, November 15, 1890, p. 1.

67. Butterworth, Honorable Benjamin, "The World's Columbian Exposition," Speech presented in the House of Representatives, Friday, February 6, 1891, 3, Newberry Library, Chicago; and Teleford Burnham and James F. Gookins, *Chicago: The Site of the World's Fair of 1892. The Main Expositions on the Lake Front, and Special Exhibitions at the Principal Parks, Connected by a Railroad Circuit With All Other Lines of Transportation, and the Heart of the City* (Chicago: Rand, McNally & Co., 1889), 17, Newberry Library, Chicago.

68. "Literary Tributes to the World's Fair," *Dial*, October 1, 1893, 177; J.B. Campbell, *Campbell's Illustrated History of the World's Columbian Exposition*, 18; "The Midway Plaisance," *Harper's Weekly*, May 13, 1983, p. 442; and Carnegie, "Its Value to the American People," *Engineering Magazine: An Industrial Review, World's Fair in Retrospect, Souvenir Number, January 1894*, 417, Harold Washington Public Library, Chicago.

69. J.B. Campbell, editor, *World's Columbian Exposition Illustrated*, March 1893, 309, Newberry Library, Chicago; and *Harper's Weekly*, August 20, 1892, p. 806.

70. "A Midway Review," *Dial*, September 1, 1893, 106.

71. Julian Ralph, "Exploiting the Great Fair," *Harper's Weekly*, August 20, 1892, p. 806; and *Official Minutes of the Fourth and Fifth Sessions of the World's Columbian Commission*, 29, Lilly Library, Bloomington, Indiana.

72. Henry Van Brunt, "The Architectural Event of Our Times," and Bar Ferree, "Architecture," *Engineering Magazine: An Industrial Review, World's Fair in Retrospect, Souvenir Number*, January 1894, 430, Harold Washington Public Library, Chicago; and M.A. Lane, "The Chicago Fair," *Harper's Weekly*, July 2, 1892, p. 643.

73. Chronicle and Comment, *Dial*, May 16, 1893, 299; *World's Fair Puck*, May 15, 1893, cover, Harold Washington Public Library, Chicago; "Music at the World's Fair," *Dial*, June 1, 1893, 330.

74. "Music at the World's Fair," *Dial*, June 1, 1893, 330; Burg, *Chicago's White City of 1893*, 17; C. Norman Fay, "The Theodore Thomas Orchestra," *Outlook*, January 22, 1910, 160 in Levine, *Highbrow/Lowbrow*, 116, Levine, *Highbrow/Lowbrow*, 115; "A Midway Review," *Dial*, September 1,

1893, 107; and Clara Louise Burnham, *Sweet Clover: A Romance of the White City*, edited by Donna Winters (Caledonia, Michigan: Big Water Publishing, 1992), 98.

75. "A Midway Review," *Dial*, September 1, 1893, 106.

76. "The Columbian Exposition at Chicago," *Harper's Weekly*, April 30, 1892, 421-22; and Badger, *The Great American Fair*, 80-1.

77. Donna Carlton, *Looking for Little Egypt* (Bloomington: IDD Books, 1994), 2-3; and James Gilbert, *Perfect Cities: Chicago's Utopias of 1893* (Chicago: The University of Chicago Press, 1991), 44.

78. *Official Minutes of the Fourth and Fifth Sessions of the World's Columbian Commission*, 91 (Fifth session new pagination).

79. Gilbert, *Chicago's Utopias of 1893*, 95.

80. "The Midway Plaisance," *Harper's Weekly*, May 13, 1893, p. 442.

81. Gilbert, *Chicago's Utopias of 1893*, 210; *Street In Cairo, Columbian Exposition* (Chicago: The Winters Art Litho. Co., n.d.), 15, Harold Washington Public Library, Chicago; Carnegie, "Its Value to the American People," *Engineering Magazine: An Industrial Review, World's Fair in Retrospect, Souvenir Number, January 1894*, 421, Harold Washington Public Library, Chicago; and Frederic Remington, "A Gallop Through the Midway," *Harper's Weekly*, October 7, 1893, p. 963.

82. Carlton, *Looking for Little Egypt*, ix; and Julian Hawthorne, *Humors of the Fair* (Chicago: E.A. Weeks & Company, 1893), 178 and 191, Newberry Library, Chicago.

83. Frederic Remington, "A Gallop Through the Midway," *Harper's Weekly*, October 7, 1893, p. 963; Jones, Calista Webster to Harlow S. and Mary June Black Webster, Chicago, June 10, 1893, Lilly Library, Bloomington, Indiana; and Burnham, *Sweet Clover*, 71. Jones quoted courtesy of the Lilly Library, Bloomington, Indiana.

84. Carlton, *Looking for Little Egypt*, 46 and 49-50.

85. Carlton, *Looking for Little Egypt*, 80- 82.

86. Julian Ralph, "Chicago—The Main Exhibit," *Harper's New Monthly Magazine*, February 1892, 425.

87. Edmund Mitchell, "International Effects of the Fair," 472, *Engineering Magazine: An Industrial Review, World's Fair in Retrospect, Souvenir Number*, January 1894, Harold Washington Public Library, Chicago; and William Dean Howells, "Letters of an Alturian Traveler," *Cosmopolitan*, December 1893, 218.

88. J.B.Campbell, editor, *World's Columbian Exposition Illustrated*, April 1892, 26, Lilly Library, Bloomington, Indiana.

89. Captain Charles King, "The City of the World's Fair," *Cosmopolitan*, November 1891, 49; and *World's Fair Puck*, May 22, 1893, 33, Harold Washington Public Library, Chicago.

90. Henry B. Fuller, *With the Procession* (Chicago: The University of Chicago Press, 1965), 203; and William T. Stead, *If Christ Came to Chicago!: A Plea for the Union of All Who Love in the Service of All Who Suffer*, 1894 Reprint, Chicago Historical Bookworks, 1990), 123.

91. Henry Loomis Nelson, "The Clubs of Chicago," *Harper's Weekly*, August 20, 1892, p. 806.

92. Julian Ralph, "Chicago's Gentle Side," *Harper's New Monthly Magazine*, July 1893, 288; and *World's Fair Puck*, October 2, 1893, 257, Harold Washington Public Library, Chicago.

93. "The Last Day of the Fair," *Harper's Weekly*, November 11, 1893, p. 1074; Johnson, *A History of the World's Columbian Exposition*, 462-3; and Smith, *Urban Disorder and the Shape of Belief*, 268.

94. "The Last Day of the Fair," *Harper's Weekly*, November 11, 1893, p. 1074; Smith, *Urban Disorder and the Shape of Belief*, 268; and Burg, *Chicago's White City of 1893*, 287-8.

NOTES TO CHAPTER THREE

1. Kenan Heise, Introduction to William T. Stead's *If Christ Came to Chicago: A Plea for the Union of All Who Love in the Service of All Who Suffer*, 1894 (Reprint, Chicago Historical Bookworks, 1990), no page; Judith Walkowitz, *City of Dreadful Delight: Narratives of Sexual Danger in Late-Victorian London* (Chicago: The University of Chicago Press, 1992), ix, 81, and 95-96; and Herbert Asbury, *Gem of the Prairie: An Informal History of the Chicago Underworld*, 1940 (Reprint, Northern Illinois University Press, 1986), 155.

2. Stead, *If Christ Came to Chicago!*, 123.

3. Asbury, *Gem of the Prairie*, 157.

4. Civic Federation of Metropolitan Chicago Manuscript Records, Box 1, Folder 2, Chicago Historical Society, Chicago. (Hereafter collection known as Civic Federation.)

5. Civic Federation, Box 1, Folder 1A.

6. James Weber Linn, "Chicago," *New Republic*, January 4, 1919, 279.

7. Henry B. Fuller, "The Upward Movement in Chicago," *Atlantic Monthly*, October 1897, 534.

8. Lincoln Steffens, "Chicago: Half-Free and Fighting On," *McClure's Magazine*, October 1903, 563-77. For more on the Civic Federation, see Emmett Dedmon, *Fabulous Chicago* (New York: Atheneum, 1981), 241-269.

9. Civic Federation, Box 1, Folder 1A, page 19.

10. Commercial Club of Chicago Papers, Box 1, Folder 1, Chicago Historical Society, Chicago. (Hereafter known solely as Commercial Club.)

11. Commercial Club, Emmett Dedmon, "A Short History of the Commercial Club," September 25, 1968, pages 1-39, Box 1, Folder 1. The John W. Candler with whom Macfarland lunched in Boston would later be responsible for congressional inquiry into the Columbian Exposition. The Candler Commission is described in Chapter Two.

12. Commercial Club, Dedmon, page 14, Box 1, Folder 1; and Commercial Club, Box 17, Folder 5.

13. George E. Hooker, "A Plan for Chicago," *Survey*, September 4, 1909, 778-90.

14. Charles H. Wacker, "The Plan of Chicago," *American City*, October 1909, 52-3; Commercial Club, Box 1, Folder 1; and Dedmon, *Fabulous Chicago*, 301.

15. Harold M. Mayer and Richard C. Wade, *Chicago: Growth of a Metropolis* (Chicago: The University of Chicago Press, 1969), 312.

16. Lloyd Lewis and Henry Justin Smith, *Chicago: The History of Its Reputation* (New York: Harcourt, Brace and Company, 1929), 325.

17. Elliott Flower, "Campaigning for Trade," *Harper's Weekly*, May 22, 1909, 11-31.

18. Elia W. Peattie, "The Artistic Side of Chicago," *Atlantic Monthly*, December 1899, 833.

19. Editor's Table, *New England Magazine*, March 1901, 108-9.

20. George Fitch, "Seeing Chicago Through a Megaphone," *Ladies Home Journal*, March 1907, 17.

21. L. B. Knox, "Impressions of Chicago Faces," *Atlantic Monthly*, January 1906, 33.

22. Henry B. Fuller, *The Cliff-Dwellers, A Novel* (New York: Harper and Brothers Publishers, 1893), 1.

23. Frank Norris, *The Pit: The Epic of Wheat* (New York: Penguin Books, 1994), viii and 39; and *Pit*, 1904, Lilly Library, Bloomington, Indiana.

24. Knox, "Impressions of Chicago Faces," *Atlantic Monthly*, January 1906, 31.

25. George Fitch, "Seeing Chicago Through a Megaphone," *Ladies Home Journal*, March 1907, 17.

26. Franklin H. Head, "The Heart of Chicago," *The New England Magazine*, July 1892, 561.

27. Julian Ralph, "A Recent Journey Through the West: IX.—Chicago Since the Fair," *Harper's Weekly*, November 16, 1895, 1088; Charles Whibley, "Chicago," *Living Age*, February 16, 1907, 390; George Fitch, "Seeing Chicago Through a Megaphone," March 1907, 17; and Lewis Mumford, "Reflections on Chicago," *New Republic*, February 27, 1929, 45.

28. Marshall Everett, *The Great Chicago Theater Disaster: The Complete Story Told By the Survivors*, Memorial Edition (n.p: n.d.), n.p. Lilly Library, Bloomington, Indiana; and "Chicago Theatre Fire," *Harper's Weekly Supplement*, January 9, 1904, 74.

29. Franklin Matthews, "Chicago as a Storm Centre," *Critic*, February 1904, 175.

30. Robert Gottesman, "Introduction," in Upton Sinclair, *The Jungle* (New York: Penguin Books, 1985), xiv-xxvii; and Carl Smith, *Chicago and the American Literary Imagination, 1880–1920* (Chicago: University of Chicago Press, 1984), 164-170.

31. Sinclair, *The Jungle*, 31.

32. William M. Tuttle, *Race Riot: Chicago in the Red Summer of 1919* (New York: Antheneum, 1970), 3-10.

33. Herbert Asbury, *Gem of the Prairie: An Informal History of the Chicago Underworld* (Dekalb: Northern Illinois University Press, 1986), 95-6; Walter C. Reckless, *Vice in Chicago* (Chicago: The University of Chicago Press, 1933), 15; Stead, *If Christ Came to Chicago*, 260; and Lewis, *Chicago*, 203.

34. Charles Washburn, *Come Into My Parlor: A Biography of the Aristocratic Everleigh Sisters of Chicago* (New York: Knickerbocker Publishing Company, 1936), 15-79.
35. Washburn, *Come Into My Parlor*, 194 and 209-210.
36. Asbury, *Gem of the Prairie*, 117; and Reckless, *Vice in Chicago*, 3.
37. Vice Commission of Chicago, *The Social Evil in Chicago: A Study of Existing Conditions* (Chicago: Gunthorp-Warren Printing Company, 1911), 1-3 and 6; Asbury, *Gem of the Prairie*, 285; and Lewis, *Chicago*, 343.
38. Vice Commission, *The Social Evil*, 10 and 25-26.
39. Vice Commission, *The Social Evil*, 3.
40. Reckless, *Vice in Chicago*, 1-2; and Julian Street, "Chicago: Chapter VI—Abroad at Home—American Ramblings, Observations, and Adventures," *Collier's*, August 1, 1914, 25.
41. See for example "Vice as a Nuisance," *Survey*, June 21, 1919, 464; "Putting out the Red-Lights," *Literary Digest*, November 13, 1915, 1086-7; "Fighting Vice Segregation in Chicago," *Literary Digest*, November 9, 1912, 848; and "Chicago, 'The Cleanest City,'" *Survey*, November 9, 1918, 164.
42. Barbara C. Schaaf, *Mr. Dooley's Chicago* (Garden City, New York: Anchor Press/Doubleday, 1977), 20, 22, and 379.
43. Finley Peter Dunne, *Mr. Dooley at His Best* (n.p.: Archon Books, 1969), 119-121.
44. William L. Chenery, "Turbulent Mistress of the West," *Collier's*, March 22, 1930; Frederick Matthews, "Chicago as a Storm Centre," *Critic*, February 1904, 174; and Lewis, *Chicago*, 33.
45. Andrew A. Bruce, "Introduction," in John Landesco, *Organized Crime in Chicago, Part III of the Illinois Crime Survey, 1929* (Chicago: University of Chicago Press, 1929), ix-xii and 2-4.
46. Asbury, *Gem of the Prairie*, 205, 172, 177, and 196.
47. Asbury, *Gem of the Prairie*, 312-373; Laurence Bergreen, *Capone: The Man and the Era* (New York: Touchstone Books, 1994), 82 and 605; and John Kobler, *Capone: The Life and World of Al Capone* (New York: Da Capo Press, 1971), 33-34
48. Merwin, "Chicago, the American Paradox," *Saturday Evening Post*, October 26, 1929, 8.
49. "Why is Chicago," *World Tomorrow*, December 7, 1932, 534.
50. Lewis Mumford, "Reflections on Chicago," *New Republic*, February 27, 1929, 44-5.
51. Henry Stone to William E. Dever, June 15, 1926, File 52, General Correspondence, June to December 1926, William E. Dever—Mayoralty Papers, Chicago Historical Society, Chicago.
52. Jack Lait, "Chicago," *American Magazine*, January 1918, 27.
53. Franklin Matthews, "Chicago as a Storm Centre," *Critic*, February 1904, 172.
54. Norris, *Pit*, 57-8.
55. Elia W. Peattie, "The Artistic Side of Chicago," *Atlantic Monthly*, December 1899, 831.

NOTES TO CHAPTER FOUR

1. Aida Hozic, *Hollyworld: Space, Power, and Fantasy* (Ithaca: Cornell University Press, 2001), 4-7; and Andrew Ross, *The Celebration Chronicles: Life, Liberty, and the Pursuit of Property Value in Disney's New Town* (New York: Ballantine Books, 1999), 5 and 54.

2. Harriet Monroe, "Defending the World's Fair," *New Republic*, July 19, 1933, 265.

3. John E, Findling, *Chicago's Great World Fairs*, (Manchester: Manchester University Press, 1994), 45.

4. "'Clean' Chicago Promised for World's Fair: Crimeless City by 1933 Assured on Anniversary of Valentine's Day Murders," *Washington Herald*, February 14, 1930, no page, Lenox Lohr's Clipping Scrapbook, folder 14-252, box 29, Century of Progress Papers, University of Illinois-Chicago Special Collections, Chicago, Illinois; Robert Isham Randolph, as told to Forrest Crissey "Business Fights Crime in Chicago," *Saturday Evening Post*, August 16, 1930, 12. (Century of Progress Papers hereafter referred to as COPP); and "Lone Crusader for Dry Reform Visits Chicago; Wars on Gangs/Percy L. Crosby Will Be Guest of Honor at Dinner Tonight," *Chicago Post*, March 6, 1931 in personal scrapbook of Lenox Lohr, no folder, Box 29, COPP.

5. Lenox Lohr, *Fair Management: The Story of the Century of Progress Exposition/A Guide for Future Fairs*, (Chicago: The Cuneo Press, Inc., 1952), 29; Findling, *Chicago's Great World Fairs*, 47; and Robert W. Rydell, *World of Fairs: The Century-of-Progress Expositions*, (Chicago: The University of Chicago Press, 1993), 97 and 120-1.

6. "Address of Major L.R. Lohr Delivered Over Radio Station WGN, July 10, 1929," second personal scrapbook of Lenox Lohr, no folder, Box 29, COPP.

7. Lee Alexander Stone, "Chicago: Greatest Advertised City in the World, Not the Wickedest," 1929, 1 and 5, Reprinted from *Chronicle of Chicago*, Folder 16-207, Box 14, COPP.

8. "Approval Predicted for State Fair Fund: Dawes Says Senate Committee Will Recommend Appropriation of $500,000," *Journal of Commerce*, February 7, 1931, page 3.

9. AHK, Untitled Speech, February 8, 1933, Folder 14-3, Box 1, COPP.

10. Harold M. Mayer and Richard C. Wade, *Chicago, Growth of a Metropolis* (Chicago: The University of Chicago Press, 1969), 364; "World Fair Has Qualified for 'N-R-A' Honor: Maj. Lohr Points Out How It Has Helped National Recovery," Lenox Lohr's Second Clipping Scrapbook, Promotion Department Collections, no folder, Box 29, COPP; Lohr, *Fair Management*, n.p..

11. Myron E. Adams to Mayor William Dever, August 17, 1923, Fair History, folder 12-19, Box 2, COPP; "Resume of the History of the Chicago Centennial," Fair History, folder 15-19, Box 2, COPP; and Myron E. Adams, Temporary Secretary, "Launching the Chicago Centennial," Fair History, folder 15-13, Box 2, COPP.

12. Findling, *Chicago's Great World Fairs*, 41; and Lohr, *Fair Management*, 8-12 and 15.

13. "Lohr Outlines Work Ahead in World's Fair: Admonishes Chicago to Make 1933 More Than Great Show for Visitors," *Chicago Journal of Commerce and La Salle Street Journal*, January 17, 1930, no page, Lenox Lohr's Clipping Scrapbook, Folder 14-252, Box 29, COPP.

14. Press release, March 3, 1933, Folder 14-4, Box 1; and Press Release, March 4, 1933, Box 1, COPP.

15. "The Bargain of the Century," *Chicago Tribune*, May 21, 1933, pg. 1; and *The Official Pictures of A Century of Progress Exposition Chicago 1933* (Coral Springs, Florida: B. Klein Publications, 1933).

16. For language regarding the "sale" of Chicago, see "Address of Samuel Insull Before the Association of Commerce," November 21, 1928, 1, Chicago Historical Society, Chicago; and P.J. Byrne, "Will the Fair be Ready?," *Commerce: Official World's Fair Magazine*, April 1933, 15, Chicago Historical Society, Chicago.

17. "Minutes of Regular Meeting of the Board of Trustees of A Century of Progress," 4, folder 3-30, Box 3 COPP, Press Release, February 26, 1933, folder 14-2, Box 1 COPP; Press Release February 1, 1933, folder 14-3, Box 1, COPP; Press Release, February 24, 1933, folder 14-2, Box 1, COPP; and Press Release, March 4, 1933, folder 14-4, Box 1, COPP.

18. "'Let's Go Chicago!' Week Proclaimed," *Chicago Tribune*, May 18, 1933, pg. 1; "City Launches It's Prosperity Parade Today," *Chicago Tribune*, May 22, 1933, pg. 1; and "'Let's Go' Week Wins Backing of City's Business," *Chicago Tribune*, May 19, 1933, pg. 5.

19. Rufus Dawes, News Release, October 31, 1934, folder 14-238, Box 27, COPP.

20. Lohr, *Fair Management*, n.p; and Jack Dearborn, "The Truth about a Century of Progress: 1933 World's Fair," *Real America*, October 1933, 25.

21. Jerome Beatty, "Did I meet you at the FAIR?," *American Magazine*, September 1933, 65-6; "Is It Progress?" *Christian Century*, June 28, 1933, 838-9; and "The Commercial Note and the Hall of Religion," *Christian Century*, November 22, 1933, 1459.

22. Forrest Crissey, "Chicago's Century of Progress Exposition," *Saturday Evening Post*, March 28, 1931, 53; Forrest Crissey, "Why the Century of Progress Architecture?" *Saturday Evening Post*, June 10, 1933, 16-17; and Findling, *Chicago's Great World's Fairs*, 110.

23. Bruce Bliven, "A Century of Treadmill: A Few Funeral Flowers for the Chicago Fair," *New Republic*, November 15, 1933, 10; Press Release, January 19, 1933, Promotion Department, Folder 14-1, Box 1, COPP; and Crissey, "Why the Century of Progress Architecture," 16-17.

24. Ely Jacques Kahn, "Close-Up Comments on the Fair," *Architectural Forum, Special Edition: A Century of Progress Exposition*, July 1933, 23 and from same issue, Albert Kahn, "A Pageant of Beauty," 26, and Buckminster Fuller, "Profit Control and the Pseudo-Scientific," 27, Chicago Historical Society, Chicago.

25. "The Lay Critics Speak," *Architectural Forum, Special Edition: A Century of Progress Exposition*, July 1933, 28; and Jerome Beatty, "Did I Meet You at the FAIR?," *American Magazine*, September 1933, 67.

26. Louis Skidmore, "Planning and Planners," *Architectural Forum, Special Edition: A Century of Progress Exposition,* July 1933, 29; and Findling, *Chicago's Great World Fairs,* 60.

27. Lewis Mumford, "Two Chicago Fairs," *New Republic,* January 21, 1931, 272; Tom Mead, *Chicago News,* February 27, 1931, n.p., Lenox Lohr's second clipping scrapbook, Promotion Department, no folder, Box 29, COPP; and "Wright Fights Fair Protest," *Chicago Evening American,* February 26, 1931, no page, Lenox Lohr's second clipping scrapbook, Promotion Department, no folder, Box 29, COPP.

28. Llewellyn Jones, "Chicago Interlude," *New Republic,* July 5, 1933, 204-5; and Bliven, "A Century of Treadmill," 12.

29. Julian Jackson, "A Century of What?," unpublished speech read before Literary Club of Chicago, 1950, Chicago Historical Society, Chicago; and Jess Kreuger, "Fair Nights," (n.p.: n.d.), 16, Chicago Historical Society, Chicago.

30. Crissey, "Chicago's Century of Progress Exposition," 5.

31. "A Century of Nudity," (Chicago: n.p., 1933), n.p., Chicago Historical Society, Chicago; and *World's Fair News: A Century of Progress,* July 9, 1933, pg. 1, July 30, 1933, pg. 1, September 3, 1933, pg. 1, September 10, 1933, pg. 1, and September 17, 1933, pg. 1, folder 14-208, Box 26, COPP.

32. John S. Van Gilder, "Outline for A Quick Two or Three Day Visit to the Cream of A Century of Progress Exposition," Century of Progress Papers, File 68, Chicago Historical Society, Chicago; and "Is It Progress?" *Christian Century,* June 28, 1933, 839.

33. Vicki Kirkland, "40 years of plumes: Taking a fan-cy to Sally Rand," *Chicago Tribune,* January 13, 1973, Section 001, pg. 11; *Chicago Tribune,* May 28, 1933, section 1, pg. 9; and William Leonard, "At 71, Sally keeps on fanning and bubbling," *Chicago Tribune,* September 14, 1975, Section 6, pg. 12.

34. "Fair Official Sanction Given to Girl Shows: Lohr Tours Cabarets, Finds None Offends Good Taste, Censorship is Ruled Out," no publication information, Lenox Lohr's second clipping scrapbook, Promotion Department, no folder, Box 29, COPP. Taxi dancers were hired by fair concessions. See "200 Girls Hired as Taxi Dancers for C.H. Weber," *Chicago Tribune,* May 27, 1933, 4.

35. "Fair's Manager Sees the Nudes: Is Not Shocked," *Chicago Tribune,* July 21, 1933, pg. 6.

36. *Chicago Tribune,* July 10, 1933, pg. 5.

37. Jack Dearborn, "The Truth about a Century of Progress: 1933 World's Fair," *Real America,* October 1933, 23, Chicago Historical Society, Chicago; and T.R. Carskadon, "Sally Rand Dances to the Rescue," *American Mercury,* July 1935, 355-7.

38. Emmett Dedmon, *Fabulous Chicago,* enlarged edition, (New York: Atheneum, 1981), 338; "'Dress 'Em Up Or Close Up,' Mayor's Order," n.p., pg. 1, Lenox Lohr's second clipping scrapbook, Promotion Department, no folder, Box 29, COPP; and Jackson, "A Century of What?, n.p.

39. Kirkland, "40 years of plumes," pg. 11.

40. Rydell, *World of Fairs*, 92; William Leonard, "Vaudeville's dead, 'twas rightly said," *Chicago Tribune*, January 12, 1973, section 2, pg. 3; Leonard, "At 71, Sally keeps on fanning and bubbling," pg. 12; and "The fan dance is over," *Chicago Tribune*, September 1, 1979, section 2, pg. 10.

41. Brenda Stone, "Sally Rand reveals her religious side," *Chicago Tribune*, January 15, 1973, Section 1A, pg. 3; and Kirkland, "40 years of plumes: Taking a fan-cy to Sally Rand," pg. 11.

NOTES TO CHAPTER FIVE

1. The title of this chapter is influenced by an article by John Bodnar entitled "Reworking Reality: Oral Histories and the Meaning of the Polish Immigrant Experience," in *International Annual of Oral History*, 1990. "In Old Chicago," Twentieth Century Fox, 1938.

2. Alson J. Smith, *Syndicate City: The Chicago Crime Cartel and What to Do About It* (Chicago: Henry Regnery Company, 1954), 281, Chicago Historical Society, Chicago.

3. Armitage Trail, *Scarface* (New York: Dell, 1959), n.p.

4. *Scarface*, The Caddo Company, 1932 and The Hughes Tool Company, 1960, Indiana University Media Collections, Bloomington, Indiana.

5. *Public Enemy*, Warner Brothers, 1931.

6. *Does Crime Pay? No! Life Story of Al Capone in Pictures, as Shown by the Uncensored Photos in this Book*, n.p., n.d., Chicago Historical Society, Chicago.

7. *Life of Al Capone in Pictures! and Chicago's Gang Wars* (Lake Michigan Printing Company, 1931), Chicago Historical Society, Chicago.

8. John Roeburt, *Al Capone, a Novel* (New York: Pyramid Books, 1959), 6, Chicago Historical Society, Chicago.

9. Fred Pasley, *Al Capone: The Biography of a Self-Made Man* (New York: Ivest Washburn, 1930), 9.

10. Eliot Ness and Oscar Fraley, *The Untouchables* (New York: Barnes & Noble Books, 1996), 253.

11. Ness, *The Untouchables*, 11 and 131.

12. Ness, *The Untouchables*, 207-8 and 252.

13. *The Untouchables*, First and Second Episodes, Desilu Playhouse, Museum of Television and Radio Showcase, MCMLIX, and *The Untouchables*, "The Takeover," Desilu Productions, Museum of Broadcast History, Chicago, n.d..

14. "The Chicago Rackets: Capone's Heirs Have Brought His Methods Up To Date," *Life*, November 29, 1948, 95 and 97; Lester Velie, "The Capone Gang Muscles Into Big-Time Politics," *Collier's*, September 30, 1950, 18; Gene Cook and Robert Hagy, "*Life's* Reports: Gangland Stirs Again," *Life*, May 15, 1944, 14; and Carey McWilliams, "Chicago's Machine Gun Politics," *Nation*, March 15, 1952, 245-6.

15. Smith, *Syndicate City*, xiii.

16. Robert J. Casey, "The Bullet Barons: The Gang Wars and the Incredible Big Shots Who Led Them, Covered For You By Chicago's Most Famous Crime Reporter," *Holiday*, October 1951, 90 and 94.

17. Nelson Algren, *Never Come Morning* (New York: Four Walls Eight Windows, 1987), n.p.; and Nelson Algren, *Chicago: City On the Make* (Chicago: The University of Chicago Press, 1987), 23 and 25.

18. Algren, *Never Come Morning*, 70.

19. Nelson Algren, *The Man With the Golden Arm* (New York: Doubleday & Company, Inc., 1949), 17.

20. Saul Below, *The Adventures of Augie March* (New York: Penguin Books, 1953), 82.

21. Richard Wright, *Native Son* (New York: Harper and Row, 1987), 101; and Richard Wright, *Black Boy (American Hunger): A Record of Childhood and Youth* (New York: HarperPerennial, 1993), 307.

22. Alan Whitney, "*Playboy*: Sex on a Skyrocket," *Chicago*, October 1955, 32, Chicago Historical Society, Chicago; and Hugh M. Hefner, Editor, *The Playboy Annual: Entertainment for Men* (New York: Waldorf Publishing Company, 1957), n.p, Chicago Historical Society, Chicago.

23. See Joanne Meyerowitz, editor, *Not June Cleaver: Women and Gender in Postwar America, 1945–1960* (Philadelphia: Temple University Press, 1994). *Hugh Hefner: American Playboy*, (Twentieth Century Fox Film Corporation, 1996), videocassette.

24. Whitney, "*Playboy*: Sex on a Skyrocket," 35 and 37; and Jon Anderson, "A Hefner Dossier," *Chicagoan*, June 1974, 49, Chicago Historical Society, Chicago.

25. Frank Brady, *Hefner* (New York: Macmillian Publishing Company, 1974), 3, 4, and 6, Chicago Historical Society, Chicago.

26. Brady, *Hefner*, 5, *The Playboy Club*, pamphlet, 1960, Chicago Historical Society, Chicago; and *Hugh Hefner: American Playboy*.

27. *Playboy After Dark*, 1969, Museum of Broadcast History, Chicago.

28. Fanny Butcher, "National Bazaar: How do Chicago merchants entice billions of dollars out of your pockets every year?" *Holiday*, October 1951; and Albert Halper, "It's the Giant of America's Heartland," *Holiday*, October 1951, 45.

29. Fanny Butcher, "Chicago," *Holiday*, May 1954, 14.

30. Stanley Walker, "Our Far Flung Correspondents: Return of a Non-Native," *New Yorker*, April 6, 1946, 90 and 93.

31. A.J. Liebling, "Profiles: Second City. I—So Proud to Be Jammy-Jammy," *The New Yorker*, January 12, 1952, 30.

32. A.J. Liebling, "Profiles: Second City. II—At Her Feet the Slain Deer," *The New Yorker*, January 19, 1952, 32, 39-40, and 51.

33. Edgar Lee Masters, *The Tale of Chicago* (New York: G.P. Putnam and Sons, 1933), 339, Chicago Historical Society, Chicago; "Mayor Kelly's Chicago: A Strong Democratic Boss Runs a Lusty City," *Life*, July 17, 1944, 67; and Smith, *Syndicate City*, xvi.

NOTES TO CHAPTER SIX

1. See Howard Zinn, *A People's History of the United States, 1492-Present* (New York: HarperCollins Publishers, 1995), 450.
2. See Tom Hayden, *Rebellion in Newark: Official Violence and Ghetto Response* (New York: Random House, 1967).
3. Frank. B. Woodford and Arthur M. Woodford, *All Our Yesterdays: A Brief History of Detroit* (Detroit: Wayne State University Press, 1969); "Cities: The Fire This Time," *Time*, August 4, 1967, 13-18; and "Politics: After Detroit," *Time*, August 4, 1967, 18-9.
4. "The Nation," *Time*, August 4, 1967, 12; and "An American Tragedy, 1967," *Newsweek*, August 7, 1967, 18.
5. "An American Tragedy, 1967," *Newsweek*, August 7, 1967, 18.
6. David Farber, *Chicago '68* (Chicago: The University of Chicago Press, 1988), 116.
7. Roger Biles, *Richard J. Daley: Politics, Race, and the Governing of Chicago* (Dekalb: Northern Illinois University Press, 1995), 20-22.
8. Mike Royko, *Boss: Richard J. Daley of Chicago* (New York: E.P. Dutton and Co., Inc., 1971), 58.
9. Biles, *Richard J. Daley*, 184. According to Biles, New York faced the worst economic disaster in American urban history during John Lindsey's time in office (1966–1973).
10. Richard G. Stern, "A Valentine for Chicago," *Harper's Magazine*, February 1962, 68; "'Police State' or Model City? Chicago in Perspective," *U.S. News and World Report*, September 16, 1968, 64; and "Chicago's Blitzkrieg," *Christian Century*, September 11, 1968, 1127.
11. James Dugan, "Mayor Daley's Chicago," *Holiday*, December 1963, 84; Biles, *Richard J. Daley*, 80; John Bartlow Martin, "My Chicago," *Holiday*, March 1967, 98; and "'Police State' or Model City? Chicago in Perspective," *U.S. News and World Report*, September 16, 1968, 64.
12. George A. Larson and Jay Pridmore, *Chicago Architecture and Design* (New York: Harry N. Abrams, Inc., 1993), 186-8, 178, and 180.
13. Biles, *Richard J. Daley*, 78.
14. Stevenson Swanson, editor, *Chicago Days: 150 Defining Moments in the Life of a Great City* (Wheaton, Illinois: Cantigny First Division Foundation, 1997), 202; and Arnold R. Hirsch, *Making the Second Ghetto: Race & Housing in Chicago, 1940–1960* (New York: Cambridge University Press, 1983), 265.
15. "Crime: Return of the Rub-Out," *Time*, March 8, 1963, 28; and Biles, *Richard J. Daley*, 79.
16. Biles, *Richard J. Daley*, 146-7.
17. Biles, *Richard J. Daley*, 65; Sandy Smith, "You can't expect police on the take to take orders," *Life*, December 6, 1968, 40 and 42; and "Chicago's Blitzkrieg," *Christian Century*, September 11, 1968, 1127.
18. "Crime: Cops and/or Robbers," *Time*, February 1, 1960, 16.
19. "Crime: Cops and/or Robbers," *Time*, February 1, 1960, 16.
20. "Two Views of Chicago," *Harper's Magazine*, April 1964, 140-1.

21. Farber, *Chicago '68*, 100 and 115; and Biles, *Richard J. Daley*, 148.
22. "Chicago: Vigilantes and Visigoths," *Newsweek*, February 26, 1968, 26.
23. "Stalag '68," *Time*, August 23, 1968, 12; "Hippies, Yippies, and Mace," *Newsweek*, September 2, 1968, 25-6; and "Down to the Barbed Wire," *Newsweek*, August 26, 1968, 17-18.
24. "Daley City Under Siege," *Time*, August 30, 1968, 19.
25. "Daley City Under Siege," *Time*, August 30, 1968, 18.
26. Farber, *Chicago '68*, xiii, xvi, and 72.
27. Farber, *Chicago '68*, 17.
28. Farber, *Chicago '68*, 112; "An April Shower of Billy Clubs and a May Victory," *Christian Century*, May 15, 1968, 639; and "Down to the Barbed Wire," *Newsweek*, August 26, 1968, 17.
29. "An April Shower of Billy Clubs and a May Victory," *Christian Century*, May 15, 1968, 639; and Biles, *Richard J. Daley*, 149.
30. "Chicago Trying Hard to Keep the Lid On," *Business Week*, August 17, 1968, 25; "Daley City Under Siege," *Time*, August 10, 1968, 19; and Farber, *Chicago '68*, 153.
31. "'Police State' or Model City? Chicago in Perspective," *U.S. News and World Report*, September 16, 1968, 65.
32. "Aftermath of Chicago Riots: Attack and Counter Attack," *U.S. News and World Report*, December 16, 1968, 50; "Hippies, Yippies, and Mace," *Newsweek*, September 2, 1968, 26; and Farber, *Chicago '68*, 165.
33. Keith Wheeler, "'This is Daley's Chicago—he doesn't dig anything else,'" *Life*, September 6, 1968, 29; "Daley City Under Siege," *Time*, August 30, 1968, 18; and Biles, *Richard J. Daley*, 159.
34. Biles, *Richard J. Daley*, 161.
35. Biles, *Richard J. Daley*, 163; Loudon Wainwright, "The View from Here," *Life*, September 13, 1968, 33; and "'Police State' or Model City? Chicago in Perspective," *U.S. News and World Report*, September 16, 1968, 64.
36. "Bypassing Chicago?" *Business Week*, September 7, 1968, 32.
37. "Walker Report: Chicago Cops Rioted," *Life*, December 6, 1968, 35; and "Aftermath of Chicago Riots: Attack and Counter Attack," *U.S. News and World Report*, December 16, 1968, 49.
38. Biles, *Richard J. Daley*, 175-7.
39. "Battle of Chicago—And the Consequences," *U.S. News and World Report*, September 9, 1968, 43.
40. Alfred Bester, "Chicago Sights and Delights," *Holiday*, March 1967, 134; Richard Atcheson, "The Spirit of Old Town," *Holiday*, March 1967, 67; and Richard Dunlop, "Chicago for the Fun of It," *Holiday*, March 1967, C6.
41. Arno Karlen, "The New Chicago," *Holiday*, March 1967, 48.

NOTES TO THE AFTERWORD

1. Alice Sinkevitch, ed. *AIA Guide to Chicago* (San Diego: A Harvest Original/ Harcourt Brace and Company, 1993), 123.
2. Mike Davis, "Foreword," in Marco D'Eramo, *The Pig and the Skyscraper—Chicago: A History of Our Future* (London: Verso, 2002), viii.

3. Marco D'Eramo, *The Pig and the Skyscraper—Chicago: A History of Our Future* (London: Verso, 2002), 8, 14, and 440.

4. Thomas H. Pauly, "Introduction," in Maurine Watkins, *Chicago* (Carbondale: Southern Illinois University Press, 1997), vii-xxvii.

5. Roger Avery, accessed May 28, 2003, available from http://www.avary.com/rogeravary/journal/archive/2002_10_01_journalarchive.php.

Bibliography

SECONDARY SOURCES

Abrahamson, Mark. *Urban Enclaves: Identity and Place in America.* New York: St. Martin's Press, 1996.

Allen, Robert C. *Horrible Prettiness: Burlesque and American Culture.* Chapel Hill: The University of North Carolina Press, 1991.

Anderson, Benedict. *Imagined Communities: Reflections on the Origin and Spread of Nationalism.* Revised Edition. London: Verso, 1991.

Anderson, Jon. "A Hefner Dossier." *Chicagoan*, June 1974, 48-51. Chicago Historical Society, Chicago.

Andrews, Clarence A. *Chicago In Story: A Literary History.* Iowa City, Iowa: Midwest Publishing Company, 1982.

Angle, Paul. "The Inter-State Exposition Building, 1873-1892." *Chicago History* (Spring 1966): 321-33.

Asbell, Bernard. "Unlocking the Key Clubs." *Chicago*, June 1955, 28-33. Chicago Historical Society, Chicago.

Asbury, Herbert. *Gem of the Prairie: An Informal History of the Chicago Underworld.* DeKalb: Northern Illinois University Press, 1986.

Badger, R. Reid. *The Great American Fair: The World's Columbian Exposition and American Culture.* Chicago: Nelson Hall, 1979.

Bender, Thomas. *Towards an Urban Vision: Ideas and Institutions in Nineteenth Century America.* Baltimore: The Johns Hopkins University Press, 1991.

Bergreen, Laurence. *Capone: The Man and the Era.* New York: Touchstone, 1994.

Biles, Roger. *Big City Boss in Depression and War: Mayor Edward J.Kelly of Chicago.* Dekalb: Northern Illinois University Press, 1984.

Biles, Roger. *Richard J. Daley: Politics, Race, and the Governing of Chicago.* Dekalb: Northern Illinois University Press, 1995.

Bluestone, Daniel. *Constructing Chicago.* New Haven, Conn.: Yale University Press, 1991.

Bodnar, John. *Remaking America: Public Memory, Commemoration, and Patriotism in the Twentieth Century.* Princeton: Princeton University Press, 1992.

Bodnar, John. "Reworking Reality: Oral Histories and the Meaning of the Polish Immigrant Experience." *International Annual of Oral History*, 1990.

Boyer, Paul. *Urban Masses and Moral Order in America, 1820-1920.* Cambridge: Harvard University Press, 1978.

Bowron, Bernard R., Jr. *Henry B. Fuller of Chicago: The Ordeal of a Genteel Realist in Ungenteel America*. Westport, Conn.: Greenwood Press, 1974.

Brady, Frank. *Hefner*. New York: Macmillian Publishing Company, 1974. Chicago Historical Society, Chicago.

Brown, Julie K. *Contesting Images: Photography and the World's Columbian Exposition*. Tucson: The University of Arizona Press, 1994.

Burg, David F. *Chicago's White City of 1893*. Lexington: The University Press of Kentucky, 1976.

Cahan, Cathy and Richard Cahan. "The Lost City of the Depression." *Chicago History 5* (Winter 1976-7): 233-42.

Cappetti, Carla. *Writing Chicago: Modernism, Ethnography, and the Novel*. New York: Columbia University Press, 1993.

Carlton, Donna. *Looking for Little Egypt*. Bloomington, Indiana: IDD Books, 1994.

Chafets, Ze'ev. *Devil's Night and Other True Tales of Detroit*. New York: Vintage Books, 1991.

Chauncey, George. *Gay New York: Gender, Urban Culture, and the Making of the Gay Male World, 1890-1940*. New York: Basic Books, 1994.

Chicago Tribune, January to December 1997.

Conforti, Joseph A. *Imaging New England: Explorations of Regional Identity from the Pilgrims to the Mid-Twentieth Century*. Chapel Hill: The University of North Carolina Press, 2001.

Cronon, William. *Changes In the Land: Indians, Colonists, and the Ecology of New England*. New York: Hill and Wang, 1983.

Cronon, William. *Nature's Metropolis: Chicago and the Great West*. New York: W.W. Norton & Company, 1991.

D'Eramo, Marco. *The Pig and the Skyscraper—Chicago: A History of Our Future*. London: Verso, 2002.

Davidson, Guy. "James Donald, *Imaging the Modern City*: a review." *Australian Humanities Review*. (June 2000) Accessed On-line at www.lib.la-trobe.edu.au/AHR/Issue-June-2000/davidson.html, May 22, 2003.

Davis, Mike. *City of Quartz: Excavating the Future in Los Angeles*. New York: Vintage Books, 1992.

Dedmon, Emmett. *Fabulous Chicago*. New York: Atheneum, 1981.

Donald, James. *Imaging the Modern City*. Minneapolis: University of Minnesota Press, 1999.

Douglas, Ann. *Terrible Honesty: Mongrel Manhattan in the 1920s*. New York: The Noonday Press, 1995.

Drew, Bettina. *Nelson Algren: A Life on the Wild Side*. New York: G.P. Putnam's Sons, 1989.

Duis, Perry R. and Glen E. Holt. "Chicago As It Was: Chicago's Lost Exposition." *Chicago*, July 1977.

Duis, Perry R. "Chicago As It Was: Kate O'Leary's Sad Burden." *Chicago*, October 1978.

Duncan, Hugh Dalziel. *The Rise of Chicago as a Literary Center from 1885 to 1920*. Totowa, New Jersey: The Bedminster Press, 1964.

Dunlap, M.H. *Gilded City: Scandal and Sensation in Turn-of-the-Century New York*. New York: William Morrow, 2000.

Dybwad, G.L. and Joy V. Bliss. *Annotated Bibliography: World's Columbian Exposition. Chicago, 1893, with Illustrations and Price Guide*. Albuquerque: The Book Stops Here, 1992.

Ehrenhalt, Alan. *The Lost City: Discovering the Forgotten Virtues of Community in the Chicago of the 1950s*. New York: Basic Books, 1995.

Einhorn, Robin. *Property Rules: Political Economy in Chicago, 1833-1872*. Chicago: University of Chicago Press, 1991.

Fairfield, John. *The Mysteries of the Great City: The Politics of Urban Design, 1877-1937*. Columbus: Ohio State University Press, 1993.

Findling, John E. *Chicago's Great World Fairs*. Manchester, U.K.: Manchester University Press, 1994.

Gilbert, James. *Perfect Cities: Chicago's Utopias of 1893*. Chicago: University of Chicago Press, 1991.

Gilfoyle, Timothy J. *City of Eros: New York City, Prostitution, and the Commercialization of Sex, 1790-1920*. New York: W.W. Norton &Company, 1992.

Gillette, Howard, Jr. and Zane L. Miller, eds. *American Urbanism: Historiographical Review*. New York: Greenwood Press, 1987.

Ghent Urban Studies Team, eds. *Post Ex Sub Dis: Urban Fragmentations and Constructions*. Rotterdam: 010 Publishers, 2002.

Ginger, Ray. *Altgeld's America: The Lincoln Ideal Versus Changing Realities*. New York: Markus Wiener Publishing, 1958.

Gottesman, Robert. Introduction to *The Jungle,* by Upton Sinclair. New York: Penguin Books, 1985.

Grossman, James R. *Land of Hope: Chicago, Black Southerners, and the Great Migration*. Chicago: University of Chicago Press, 1991.

Harvey, David. *The Condition of Postmodernity: An Enquiry into the Origins of Cultural Change*. Cambridge, Mass.: Blackwell, 1990.

Harris, Neil, Wim de Wit, James Gilbert, and Robert W. Rydell. *Grand Illusions: Chicago's World's Fair of 1893*. Chicago: Chicago Historical Society, 1993.

Hayden, Dolores. *The Power of Place: Urban Landscapes as Public History*. Cambridge: MIT Press, 1995.

Hirsch, Arnold R. *Making the Second Ghetto: Race & Housing in Chicago, 1940-1960*. Cambridge, U.K.: Cambridge University Press, 1990.

Holt, Barbara. "An American Dilemma On Display: Black Participation at the Chicago Century of Progress Exposition, 1933-1934." Unpublished Paper. Chicago Historical Society, Chicago.

Hozic, Aida. *Hollyworld: Space, Power, and Fantasy in the American Economy*. Ithaca: Cornell University Press, 2001.

Hugh Hefner: American Playboy. Twentieth Century Fox Film Corporation, 1996. Videocassette.

Jacoby, Tamar. *Someone Else's House: American's Unfinished Struggle for Integration*. New York: The Free Press, 1998.

Jaffe, Harry S. and Tom Sherwood. *Dream City: Race, Power, and the Decline of Washington, D.C.* New York: Simon and Schuster, 1994.

Jackson, Julian J. "A Century of What?" Paper read November 30th, 1970 to the Literary Club of Chicago. Chicago Historical Society, Chicago.

Johnson, Curt and R. Craig Sautter. *Wicked City: Chicago: From Kenna to Capone.* Highland Park, Illinois: December Press, 1994.

Kirkland, Joseph. *The Story of Chicago.* Chicago: Dibble Publishing Company, 1892.

Kobler, John. *Capone: The Life and World of Al Capone.* New York: Da Capo Press, 1971.

Kogan, Harman and Rick Kogan. *Yesterday's Chicago.* Miami: E.A. Seeman Publishing, Inc., n.d.

Krabbendam, Hans, Marja Roholl, and Tity De Vries, eds. *The American Metropolis: Image and Inspiration.* Amsterdam: VU University Press, 2001.

Kysela, John D. "Sara Hallowell Brings 'Modern Art' to the Midwest." *Art Quarterly* 27, no. 2 (1964): 150-167.

Larson, Erik. *The Devil in the White City: Murder, Magic, and Madness at the Fair That Changed America.* New York: Crown Publishers, 2003.

Larson, George A. and Jay Pridmore. *Chicago Architecture and Design.* New York: Harry N. Abrams, Inc., 1993.

Lawson, Robert. *The Great Wheel.* New York: Viking Press, 1957.

Lears, T.J. Jackson. *No Place of Grace: Antimodernism and the Transformation of American Culture, 1880-1920.* New York: Pantheon Books, 1981.

Lemann, Nicholas. *The Promised Land: The Great Black Migration and How it Changed America.* New York: Vintage Books, 1992.

Levine, Lawrence W. *Highbrow/Lowbrow: The Emergence of Cultural Hierarchy in America.* Cambridge: Harvard University Press, 1988.

Levy, David. W., Introduction to *A Traveler from Alturia,* by William Dean Howells. Boston: Bedford Books of St. Martin's Press, 1996.

Lewis, Lloyd and Henry Justin Smith. *Chicago: The History of Its Reputation.* New York: Harcourt, Brace and Company, 1929.

Lindberg, Richard. *Chicago By Gaslight: A History of Chicago's Netherworld, 1880-1920.* Chicago: Academy Chicago Publishers, 1996.

Lofland, Lyn H. *The Public Realm: Exploring the City's Quintessential Social Territory.* New York: Aldine De Gruyter, 1998.

Lowe, David. *Lost Chicago.* New York: Wings Books, 1975.

Marx, Leo. *The Machine in the Garden: Technology and the Pastoral Ideal in America.* New York: Oxford University Press, 1964.

Mayer, Harold M. and Richard C. Wade. *Chicago: Growth of a Metropolis.* Chicago: University of Chicago Press, 1969.

Meier, August and Elliott M. Rudwick. "Negro Protest at the Chicago World's Fair, 1933-34." *Journal of the Illinois State Historical Society* LIX (Summer 1966): 161-71.

Meyerowitz, Joanne J. *Women Adrift: Independent Wage Earners in Chicago, 1880-1930.* Chicago: University of Chicago Press, 1988.

Miller, Donald L. *City of the Century: The Epic of Chicago and the Making of America.* New York: Simon & Schuster, 1996.

Miller, Ross. *America Apocalypse: The Great Fire and the Myth of Chicago.* Chicago: University of Chicago Press, 1990.

1992 World's Fair Forum Papers. Volume I: Legacies From Chicago's World Fairs: A Background for Fair Planning. Chicago Historical Society, Chicago.

Pauly, John J. "The Great Chicago Fire as a National Event." *American Quarterly* 36 (1984) : 668-673.

Prasch, Thomas. "Race and Commerce at the Columbian Exposition." Paper presented at the Annual Meeting of the Popular Culture Association, Chicago, Illinois, April 9, 1994.

Regnery, Henry. *Creative Chicago: From The Chap-Book to the University*. Chicago: Chicago Historical Bookworks, 1993.

Rosen, Ruth. *The Lost Sisterhood: Prostitution in America, 1900-1918*. Baltimore: Johns Hopkins University Press, 1982.

Ross, Andrew. *The Celebration Chronicles: Life, Liberty and the Pursuit of Property Value in Disney's New Town*. New York: Ballantine Books, 1999.

Royko, Mike. *Boss: Richard J. Daley of Chicago*. New York: E.P. Dutton and Company, Inc., 1971.

Ruth, David E. *Inventing the Public Enemy: The Gangster in American Culture, 1918-1934*. Chicago: University of Chicago Press, 1996.

Rydell, Robert W. *All the World's a Fair: Visions of Empire at American International Expositions, 1876-1916*. Chicago: University of Chicago Press, 1984.

Rydell, Robert W. *World of Fairs: The Century-of-Progress Expositions*. Chicago: University of Chicago, 1993.

Sawislak, Karen. *Smoldering City: Chicagoans and the Great Fire, 1871-1874*. Chicago: University of Chicago Press, 1995.

Sennett, Richard. *The Fall of Public Man*. New York: W.W. Norton, 1976.

Schaaf, Barbara C. *Mr. Dooley's Chicago*. Garden City, New York: Anchor Press/ Doubleday, 1977.

Shortridge, James R. *The Middle West: Its Meaning in American Culture*. Lawrence, Kansas: University Press of Kansas, 1989.

Alice Sinkevitch, ed. *AIA Guide to Chicago*. San Diego: A Harvest Original/Harcourt Brace and Company, 1993.

Smith, Carl J. *Chicago and the American Literary Imagination, 1880-1920*. Chicago: University of Chicago Press, 1894.

Smith, Carl J. *Urban Disorder and the Shape of Belief: The Great Chicago Fire, the Haymarket Bomb, and the Model Town of Pullman*. Chicago: University of Chicago Press, 1995.

Smith, Henry Nash. *Virgin Land: The American West as Symbol and Myth*. Cambridge: Harvard University Press, 1978.

Sorkin, Michael, ed. *Variations on a Theme Park: The New American City and the End of Public Space*. New York: Hill and Wang, 1992.

Spies, Kathleen. "'Masked Beyond Recognition': The Danse du Ventre and the Female Grotesque at the 1893 World's Columbian Exposition." Paper presented at the NCSA conference, April 1998.

Sugrue, Thomas J. *The Origins of the Urban Crisis: Race and Inequality in Postwar Detroit*. Princeton: Princeton University Press, 1996.

Swanson, Stevenson, editor. *Chicago Days: 150 Defining Moments in the Life of a Great City*. Wheaton, Ill.: Cantigny First Division Foundation, 1997.

Teaford, Jon C. *Cities of the Heartland: The Rise and Fall of the Industrial Midwest*. Bloomington: Indiana University Press, 1993.

Terkel, Studs. *Chicago*. New York: Pantheon Books, 1986.

Trachtenberg, Alan. *The Incorporation of America: Culture and Society in the Gilded Age.* New York: Hill and Wang, 1982.

William M. Tuttle. *Race Riot: Chicago in the Red Summer of 1919.* New York: Antheneum, 1970.

Walkowitz, Judith. *City of Dreadful Delight: Narratives of Sexual Danger in Late-Victorian London.* Chicago: The University of Chicago Press, 1992.

Wallace, Irving. "Call Them Madam: The High Life and Times of Chicago's Legendary Everleigh Sisters Who Once Held Court in America's Most Opulent Palace of Pleasure." *Playboy Magazine,* September 1965. Chicago Historical Society, Chicago.

Warner, Sam Bass Jr. *The Urban Wilderness: A History of the American City.* Berkeley: University of California Press, 1995.

Weimann, Jeanne Madeline. *The Fair Women: The Story of The Woman's Building, World's Columbian Exposition, Chicago, 1893.* Chicago: Academy Chicago, 1981.

White, Morton and Lucia White. *The Intellectual Versus the City: From Thomas Jefferson to Frank Lloyd Wright.* Cambridge: Harvard University Press and the MIT Press, 1962.

Whitney, Alan. "Playboy: Sex on a Skyrocket." *Chicago,* October 1955, 32-37. Chicago Historical Society, Chicago.

Wiebe, Robert H. *The Search for Order, 1877-1920.* New York: Hill and Wang, 1967.

Williams, Kenny J. *A Storyteller and a City: Sherwood Anderson's Chicago.* DeKalb: Northern Illinois University Press, 1988.

Williams, Kenny J. *Prairie Voices: A Literary History of Chicago from the Frontier to 1893.* Nashville, Tenn.: Townsend Press, 1980.

Williams, Kenny J. and Bernard Duffey, eds. *Chicago's Public Wits: A Chapter in the American Comic Spirit.* Baton Rouge: Louisiana State University Press, 1983.

Woodford, Frank B. and Arthur M. Woodford. *All Our Yesterdays: A Brief History of Detroit.* Detroit: Wayne State University Press, 1969.

Zukin, Sharon. *The Cultures of Cities.* Cambridge: Blackstone Publishers, 1995.

Zukin, Sharon. *Landscapes of Power: From Detroit to Disney World.* Berkeley: University of California Press, 1991.

SOURCES

Abbot, Willis J. "The Harrison Dynasty in Chicago." *Munsey's Magazine,* September 1903, 809-15.

Abbott, Edith. "Poor People in Chicago." *New Republic,* October 5, 1932, 209.

Ackerberg, Robert E. Jr. "Chicago Cares a Little." *Nation,* February 19, 1938, 227.

Addams, Jane. "A Decade of Prohibition." *Survey,* October 1, 1929.

Addams, Jane. "Miss Addams." *Ladies Home Journal,* July 1913, 19.

Addams, Jane. "Woman's Work for Chicago." *Municipal Affairs* 2 (September 1898): 502-8.

Ade, George. *Artie and Pink Marsh.* Chicago: University of Chicago Press, 1963.

Ade, George. *Bang! Bang!* New York: J.H. Sears & Co., 1928.

Ade, George. *Chicago Stories*. Chicago: Henry Regnery Company, 1963.

Ade, George. *Doc' Horne: A Story of the Streets and Town*. Chicago: Herbert S. Stone and Company, 899.

"Aftermath of Chicago Riots: Attack and Counterattack." *U.S. News and World Report*, December 16, 1968, 49-50.

Akers, Milburn. "Chicago Dumps Kelly." *Nation*, January 4, 1947, 7-9.

Akers, Milburn. "Chicago's Un-American Guests." *Nation*, May 26, 1945, 597-8.

Akers, Milburn. "Twilight of Boss Kelly." *Nation*, April 13, 1946, 425-6.

"Al Capone's Victory." *New Republic*, July 1, 1931, 167.

Algren, Nelson. *Chicago: City on the Make*. Chicago: University of Chicago Press, 1979.

Algren, Nelson. "City Against Itself." *Nation*, February 13, 1954, 135-6.

Algren, Nelson. *The Man with the Golden Arm*. New York: Doubleday & Company, Inc., 1949.

Algren, Nelson. *Never Come Morning*. New York: Four Walls Eight Windows, 1987.

Algren, Nelson. "One Man's Chicago." *Holiday*, October 1951.

"All Roads Lead to Chicago's Rainbow City: The Century of Progress is Already a Magnet for Summer Travel—and Other Resorts Beckon." *Literary Digest*, June 3, 1933, 29-34.

Anderson, Alex D., Myron M. Parker, John W. Powell, and Felix Agnus. *Arguments Before the Quadro-Centennial Committee of the United States Senate, In Support of Senate Bills Nos. 1839 and 1135, Each Entitled "A bill to provide for Three Americas and World's Exposition at the National Capital in 1892." January 10, 1890*. Washington: Government Printing Office, 1890. Newberry Library, Chicago.

Anderson, Sherwood. *Windy McPherson's Son*. Urbana: University of Illinois Press, 1993.

"An Appeal to the People of Otoe and Adjoining Counties." Nebraska City Proclamation, October 11, 1871. Newberry Library, Chicago.

"An April Shower of Billy Clubs and a May Victory." *Christian Century*, May 15, 1968, 639.

Architectural Forum. Special Edition: Century of Progress Exposition. July 1933. Chicago Historical Society, Chicago.

Atcheson, Richard. "The Spirit of Old Town." *Holiday*, March 1967.

Atlanta Constitution, October 1871.

Baker, Helen Cody. "A Century of Progress in Welfare." *Survey*, July 1933, 251-2.

Baker, Helen Cody. "Chicago's Mrs. Bowen." *Survey*, April 1939, 106-7.

Baker, Helen Cody. "The Things We Do Together." *Survey*, May 1938, 165-7.

Baker, Ray Stannard. "Capital and Labor Hunt Together: Chicago and the Victim of the New Industrial Conspiracy." *McClure's Magazine*, September 1903, 451-463.

Baker, Ray Stannard. "Seeing America: Letters From the Field. The New Chicago and Its Progressive People." *American Magazine*, March 1914, 52-4.

Bancroft, Hubert Howe. *The Book of the Fair, and Historical and Descriptive Presentation of the World's Science, Art, and Industry, as Viewed Through the Columbian Exposition at Chicago in 1893*. Fin de Siecle Edition. Chicago and San Francisco: The Bancroft Company, Publishers, 1893. Newberry Library, Chicago.

Bannister, Herbert. "The Commercial and Industrial Growth of Chicago." *Harper's Monthly*, December 28, 1912, p. 18.

"'Battle of Chicago' And the Consequences." *U.S. News and World Report*, September 9, 1968, 42-3.

Beale, Betty, James J. Kilpatrick, and Peregrine Warsthorne. "The Other Side of the Chicago-Police Story." *U.S. News and World Report*, September 16, 1968, 60-2.

Beatty, Jerome. "Did I Meet You at the FAIR?" *American Magazine*, September 1933.

Beatty, Jerome. "Making Police Commissioner Allman's Tough Job (sic) in Chicago." *American Magazine*, April 1933.

Bellow, Saul. *The Adventures of Augie March*. New York: Penguin Books, 1984.

Bellow, Saul. *It All Adds Up: From the Dim Past to the Uncertain Future*. New York: Penguin Books, 1994.

Bent, Silas. "Newspapermen—Partners in Crime?" *Scribner's Magazine*, November 1930, 520-6.

Bester, Alfred. "Chicago Sights and Delights." *Holiday*, March 1967.

"Big Bill and Al." *Newsweek*, December 26, 1938, 10.

Bishop, Glenn and Paul T. Gilbert. *Chicago's Progress: A Review of the World's Fair City*. Chicago: Bishop Publishing Company, 1933. Chicago Historical Society, Chicago.

"Bishop Potter on Sunday Opening." *Nation*, September 29, 1892, 236-7.

Bliven, Bruce. "A Century of Treadmill: A Few Funeral Flowers for the Chicago Fair." *New Republic*, November 15, 1933, 10-12.

Bolitho, William. "The Gangster Traumatism." *Survey*, March 1, 1930.

Bolitho, William. "The Natural History of Graft." *Survey*, May 1, 1930.

Bolitho, William. "The Psychosis of the Gang." *Survey*, February 1, 1930.

Borders, Karl. "Cashless Chicago." *Survey*, February 15, 1930.

"Branding the Buildings at the Chicago Fair: Exposition Architects Call Attention to Ingenuity of Design and Use of Color in Answer to Charges of Imitation and Ugliness." *The Literary Digest*, August 12, 1933, 36.

Brennan, G.A. "A Hero of the Great Fire: How William Haskell Saved a Large Part of the South Side in 1871." *World's Chronicle*, October 9, 1910, 206-207. Chicago Historical Society, Chicago.

Brewster, K.L. "Chicago." *Ladies Home Journal*. June 1929.

Brewster, Kate Lancaster. "The Ryerson Gift to the Art Institute of Chicago." *American Magazine of Art*, February 1938, 94-100.

Bross, William. "Chicago and the Sources of Her Past and Future Growth." A Paper Read Before the Chicago Historical Society, January 20, 1880. Chicago: Jansen, McClurg & Co., 1880. Chicago Historical Society, Chicago.

Bross, William. *History of Chicago*. Chicago: Jansen, McClurg & Co., Booksellers, Publishers, Etc., 1876.

Bross, William. Papers. Chicago Historical Society, Chicago.

Bross, William. *The Railroads, History and Commerce*. Chicago: Democratic Press Job and Book Steam Printing Office, 1854.

Buckley, Martin E. "Mrs. O'Leary's Cow." Chicago Historical Society, Chicago, n.d.

Buffalo Bill's Wild West and Congress of Rough Riders of the World. Chicago: The Blakely Printing Company, 1893. Harold Washington Public Library, Chicago.

Burgess, O.A. "The Late Chicago Fire! A Homily On the Great Fire in Chicago," in *History of Indianapolis From 1818: A Record of Events Occurring During a Period of Over Fifty Years, From the Foundation of the State Government of Indiana, Indianapolis*. Indianapolis: W. H. Drapier, 1871. Newberry Library, Chicago.

Burnham, Daniel. "How Chicago Finances Its Exposition." *Review of Reviews*, October 1932, 37-38.

Burnham, Clara Louise. *Sweet Clover: A Romance of the White City*. Edited by Donna Winters. Caledonia, Mich.: Big Water Publishing, 1992.

Burnham, Teleford and James F. Gookins. *Chicago: The Site of the World's Fair of 1892. The Main Expositions on the Lake Front, and Special Exhibitions at the Principal Parks, Connected by a Railroad Circuit With All Other Lines of Transportation, and the Heart of the City*. Chicago: Rand, McNally & Co., Printers, 1889. Newberry Library, Chicago.

"The Burning of the World's Fair Buildings." *Harper's Weekly*, July 21, 1894, p. 687.

Burns, Walter Noble. *The One-Way Ride: The Red Trail of Chicago Gangland from Prohibition to Jake Lingle*. Garden City, New York: Doubleday, Doran & Company, Inc., 1931. Chicago Historical Society, Chicago.

Busch, Francis X. *Enemies of the State*. New York: Bobbs-Merrill Company, Inc., 1954. Chicago Historical Society, Chicago.

"Business in Bronzeville." *Time*, April 18, 1938, 70-2.

Butcher, Fanny. "Chicago." *Holiday*, May 1954.

Butcher, Fanny. "National Bazaar: How Do Chicago Merchants Entice Billions of Dollars Out of Your Pockets Every Year?" *Holiday*, October 1951.

Butterworth, Honorable Benjamin. "The World's Columbian Exposition." Speech presented in the House of Representatives, Friday, February 6, 1891. Newberry Library, Chicago.

"Bypassing Chicago?" *Business Week*, September 7, 1968, 32.

"Calling in a Minister to Help the Chicago Police." *Literary Digest*, May 27, 1922.

Campbell, J.B., editor. *Campbell's Illustrated History of the World's Columbian Exposition*. 2 vols. Chicago: J.B. Campbell, 1894. Newberry Library, Chicago.

Campbell, J.B., editor. *The World's Columbian Exposition Illustrated*. Vol. 1- 3. Chicago: James B. Campbell, 1892. Newberry Library, Chicago and Lilly Library, Bloomington, Indiana.

Casey, Robert J. "The Bullet Barons: The Gang Wars and the Incredible Big Shots Who Led Them, Covered For You By Chicago's Most Famous Crime Reporter." *Holiday*, October 1951, 90-5.

Carskadon, T.R. "Sally Rand Dances to the Rescue." *American Mercury*, July 1935, 355-8.

Cave, Albert. "The Newest Journalism." *Living Age*, February 16, 1907, 393-404.

"A Century of Nudity." Chicago Historical Society, Chicago.

"A Century of Progress: Chicago International Exposition of 1933. A Statement of Its Plan and Purposes and of the Relation of States and Foreign Governments to Them." Chicago Historical Society, Chicago.

Century of Progress Collection. Chicago Historical Society Collections, Chicago.

Century of Progress Collection. University of Illinois at Chicago.

"The Century of Progress Takes Its 1932 Inventory." *Chicago Visitor*, January 1932. Chicago Historical Society, Chicago.

Chatfield-Taylor, H.C. "The Age of Uproar: A Final Paper of Midland Memories." *Century Magazine*, November 1925, 27-35.

Chatfield-Taylor, H.C. "Memories of Chicago: I.—Pristine Days." *Century Magazine*, July 1925, 285-91.

Chatfield-Taylor, H.C. "Memories of Chicago: II.—The Age of Gentility." *Century Magazine*, August 1925, 459-65.

Chatfield-Taylor, H.C. "Memories of Chicago: III.—The Gods of the Market Place and Others." *Century Magazine*, September 1925, 539-47.

Chatfield-Taylor, H.C. "When the World Came to Chicago: Further Memories of the Midland." *Century Magazine*, October 1925, 679-88.

Chenery, William L. "Turbulent Mistress of the West." *Collier's*, March 22, 1930.

Chenery, William L. "Politics in Chicago." *New Republic*, March 15, 1919, 213-5.

Chenery, William L. "Why We Have Gangs." *Collier's*, August 9, 1930, 58.

"Chicago." *New Republic*, January 26, 1918, 384-5.

"Chicago." *Putnam's Monthly*, October 1906, 12-14.

"Chicago About to Honor the Poet Who Lampooned Her." *Literary Digest*, February 5, 1921, 29-30.

Review of *Chicago and the Old Northwest, 1673-1835: A Study of the Evolution of the Northwestern Frontier with a History of Fort Dearborn*, by Milo Milton Quaife. *Nation*, December 25, 1913, 620-1.

"Chicago and the Railroad System of the Middle West." *Scientific American*, December 11, 1909.

"Chicago As the Literary Capital of the United States." *Current Opinion*, August 1920, 242-243.

Chicago Association of Commerce, editors. *Chicago: The Great Central Market. Brief Story of the Second Largest City in the United States, Showing its Phenomenal Growth in One Crowded Century, with Emphasis Upon its Position As a Center of Commerce, Industry, Recreation, and Culture.* Chicago: R.L. Polk & Co., 1923.

Chicago By Day and Night: The Pleasure Seeker's Guide to the Paris of America. Chicago: Thomson and Zimmerman, 1892. Newberry Library, Chicago.

"Chicago Brings a Dead Law to Life." *Literary Digest*, October 23, 1915, 889.

Chicago Burned. An Authentic, Concise and Graphic Account. The Great Chicago Fire, October 8, 9 & 10, 1871. As seen by Eye Witnesses, together with Startling Heartrending Incidents. Also a Graphic Description of the Fires and Loss of Life in Wisconsin, Michigan and Minnesota. Elkhart, Ind.: John F. Funk & Bro., n.d. Newberry Library, Chicago.

"Chicago: City Names Worst Gangsters, and Starts Clean-up." *Newsweek*, September 2, 1933, 10.

Chicago Daily News, 1893. Chicago Historical Society, Chicago.

"Chicago: Ed Kelly Comes Through With an All Time Record Majority: Gets to Work on Patronage." *Newsweek*, April 13, 1935, 7-8.

"Chicago Election." *Life*, March 31, 1947, 38-41.

"Chicago Epidemic." *New Republic*, February 28, 1931, 62.

"The Chicago Fire." *Nation*, January 7, 1904, 7-8.

"Chicago Fire." *Commonweal*, June 1, 1934, 131.

Chicago Fire Cyclorama Pamphlets. Chicago Historical Society, Chicago.

"Chicago Fire: $10,000,000 Loss Is a Tragic 'Big Event.'" *Newsweek*, May 26, 1934, 11.

"Chicago: Hobo Capital of America." *Survey*, June 1, 1923.

"The Chicago Hussars." *Harper's Weekly*, May 13, 1898, p. 443.

"Chicago In Composite Photographs." *Literary Digest*, March 2, 1912, 426-27.

"Chicago: Law and Disorder." *Business Week*, August 31, 1968, 16.

"Chicago Marks Time." *New Republic*, February 8, 1919, 53-4.

"Chicago on Fire!" *Chicago Post Extra*, October 9, 1871. Newberry Library, Chicago.

"The Chicago Parks and the Fair." *Harper's Weekly*, May 10, 1890, p. 372.

"Chicago Passes the 3,000,000 Mark." *Literary Digest*, September 5, 1925, 15.

"Chicago: Philanthropic Ward Boss Explains an Embezzlement." *Newsweek*, December 19, 1936, 16-18.

"Chicago Project." *Time*, August 8, 1938, 34.

Chicago Provincial Council and Board School Sisters of St. Francis. "The Daley Lessons." Correspondence. *Commonweal*, October 11, 1968.

"The Chicago Rackets: Capone's Heirs Have Brought His Methods Up to Date." *Life*, November 29, 1948, 95-109.

"Chicago Replies." *Journal of Social Hygiene* 19 (May 1933): 277-8.

"Chicago Supplement." *Harper's Weekly*, January 18, 1890.

"Chicago 'The Cleanest City.'" *Survey*, November 9, 1918, 164.

Chicago Times, 1882-1893. Chicago Historical Society, Chicago.

Chicago Tribune, October 1871-August 1999.

"Chicago Trying Hard to Keep the Lid On." *Business Week*, August 17, 1968, 24-5.

Chicago Weekly Post, October 1871. Newberry Library, Chicago.

"Chicago's Battle Against Crime." *Literary Digest*, January 17, 1925, 12.

"Chicago's Blitzkrieg," *Christian Century*, September 11, 1968, 1127.

"Chicago's Crusade." *Commonweal*, January 2, 1929, 249-50.

"Chicago's Gangs." *Literary Digest*, November 6, 1926, 28-29.

"Chicago's Higher Evolution." *Dial*, October 1, 1892, 205-6.

"Chicago's Machine Runs on Gratitude." *Life*, October 21, 1940, 94.

"Chicago's 'Morals Court.'" *Literary Digest*, May 31, 1913, 1228-9.

"Chicago's New Use for Gunmen." *Literary Digest*, June 16, 1928, 9.

"Chicago's New Club of the Arts: The Appropriate Location of the 'Cliff-Dwellers.'" *Harper's Weekly*, May 15, 1909, p. 30.

"Chicago's Recent Growth as a Financial Center." *Literary Digest*, September 22, 1928, 72-73.

The Chicago Record's History of the World's Fair. Chicago: Chicago Daily News Co., 1893. Newberry Library, Chicago.

"Chicago's State Street Fun-Time Shopping." *Holiday*, March 1967.

"Chicago Swaps Bosses." *New Republic*, April 22, 1931, 260-2.

"Chicago: The Gang's All Here." *Newsweek*, June 22, 1964, 34-36.

"Chicago: Vigilantes and Visigoths." *Newsweek*, February 26, 1968, 26.

"Chicago's Theatre Fire." *Harper's Weekly Supplement*, January 9, 1904, 73-6.

"Chicago's War on Labor Terrorism." *Literary Digest*, May 27, 1992, 7-9.

"Chicago's Worst." *Time*, December 16, 1935, 51-2.

Churchill, Allen. *A Pictorial History of American Crime, 1849-1929*. New York: Holt, Rinehart, and Winston, 1964. Chicago Historical Society, Chicago.

Chronicle and Comment. *Dial*, May 16, 1893, 299.

"Cities: The Fire Next Time." *Time*, August 4, 1967, 13-18.

Civic Federation of Metropolitan Chicago Records. Chicago Historical Society, Chicago.

Close, Kathryn. "Women Alone." *Survey*, September 1938, 281.

"Columbian Exposition at Chicago," *Harper's Weekly*, April 20, 1892, p. 417-21.

"Columbian Exposition—IV: The Ensemble." *Nation*, August 24, 1893, 132-3.

Commerce: Official World's Fair Magazine. February 1932-January 1934. Chicago Historical Society, Chicago.

Compton, Arthur H. "Oxford and Chicago: A Contrast." *Scribner's Magazine*, June 1936, 355-7.

Cook, Gene and Robert Hagy. "Life's Reports: Gangland Stirs Again." *Life*, May 15, 1944, 13-15.

Cook, Joel. *The World's Fair at Chicago. Described in a Series of Letters to "The London Times."* World's Columbian Exposition, Department of Publicity and Promotion, Chicago. Chicago: Rand, McNally & Company, 1891. Newberry Library, Chicago.

Cooley, T.M. "The Lessons of the Recent Civil Disorders." *Forum*, September 1894, 1-19.

Crawford, T.C. "The Pullman Company and Its Striking Workmen." *Harper's Weekly*, July 21, 1894, p. 686-7.

Creiger, Hon. DeWitt C., Thomas B. Bryan, and Edward T. Jeffrey. *Arguments Before a Special Committee of the United States Senate, In Support of the Application of the Citizens of Chicago for the Location In Their City of the World's Exposition of 1892. January 11, 1890*. Washington: Government Printing Office, 1890. Newberry Library, Chicago.

Cressey, Paul Frederick. "Population Succession in Chicago: 1893-1930." *American Journal of Sociology* 44 (June 1938): 59-69.

"Crime in Chicago: A Resident of the Windy City Relieves His Mind." *New Republic*, August 29, 1928, 36-9.

"Crime: Cops and/or Robbers." *Time*, February 1, 1960.

"Crime: Return of the Rub-Out." *Time*, March 8, 1963, 28.

"Crime: The Untouchables." *Newsweek*, April 22, 1963, 25-6.

"Criminal Shoots it Out With Police," *Life*, August 15, 1949, 32-3.

"The Crisis in the States." *Spectator*, July 14, 1894, 36-7.

Crissey, Forrest. "Chicago's Century of Progress Exposition." *Saturday Evening Post*, March 28, 1931.

Crissey, Forrest. "Chicago's Encore." *Saturday Evening Post*, July 14, 1934.

Crissey, Forrest. "Why the Century of Progress Architecture?" *Saturday Evening Post*, June 10, 1933.

Cronan, Jeremiah. "Line8 [*sic*] Written Out on the Mo8t [*sic*] Dreadful Fire That Broke out in Chicago in America." Dublin: P. Brereton Printer, 1871. Newberry Library, Chicago.

Colbert, Elias and Everett Chamberlin. *Chicago and the Great Conflagration*. Chicago: J.S. Goodman & Company, 1871.

Collection of Newspapers on the Chicago Conflagration. Newberry Library, Chicago.

Commercial Club of Chicago Records. Chicago Historical Society, Chicago.

"The Compleat Delegate." *Time*, August 30, 1968, 19.

A Complete Guide to the Great Inter State Industrial Exposition of 1873: Also the Art Catalogue and a Critical & Valuable Review of the Pictures in the Art Gallery. Chicago: D. & C.H. Blakely, Book, Job, and Commercial Printers, 1873. Chicago Historical Society, Chicago.

"Conflagration!" *Telegraph-Extra* (Kenosha, Wisconsin), October 9, 1871. Newberry Library, Chicago.

Courtney, Thomas J. "The Shakedown: Racket Busting in Chicago." *Forum*, April 1938, 223-8.

Cunningham, R.M. Jr. "Borderline Breakfast." *New Republic*, December 17, 1945, 836-7.

"Daley under Siege." *Time*, August 30, 1968, 18-19.

Dawes, Charles G. Address of the Honorable Charles G. Dawes Before the Association of Commerce, Chicago Illinois, November 21, 1928. Chicago Historical Society, Chicago.

Dawes, Rufus. *A Century of Progress: Report of the President to the Board of Trustees*. Chicago: n.p., 1936. Chicago Historical Society, Chicago.

Dayton, Thaddeus S. *Harper's Weekly*, December 28, 1912, p. 11-12.

De Koven Bowen, Louise. "When Chicago Was Very Young." *Atlantic Monthly*, February 1926, 195-203.

De Koven Bowen, Louise. "When Chicago Was Very Young." *Atlantic Monthly*, March 1926, 343-350.

De Normandie, James. "Sunday and the Columbian Fair." A Sermon Preached to the First Church, Roxbury, Boston, July 24, 1892. Boston: Damrell & Upham, The Old Corner Bookstore, 1892.

Dearborn, Jack. "The Truth About a Century of Progress: 1933 World's Fair." *Real America*, October 1933. Chicago Historical Society, Chicago.

Deane, Charles. Scrapbook of Clippings Regarding the Chicago Fire, 1871. Chicago Historical Society, Chicago.

"The Decorations at Chicago." *Nation*, August 8, 1892, 84-5.

Department of Publicity and Promotion, World's Columbian Exposition. *After Four Centuries: The World's Fair. The Discovery of America to Be Commemorated By An International Exposition.* Chicago: J.M.W. Jones Stationery and Printing Co., 1891. Lilly Library, Bloomington, Ind.

Depew, Honorable Chauncey M. *The Columbian Oration: Delivered at the Dedication Ceremonies of the World's Fair at Chicago, October 21, 1892.* n.p.: n.d. Newberry Library, Chicago.

Detroit Free Press, October 1871-February 1998.

Detroit News, 1968.

Dever, William E.—Mayoralty Papers. Chicago Historical Society, Chicago.

Does Crime Pay? No! Life Story of Al Capone in Pictures, as Shown By the Uncensored Photos in this Book. n.p., n.d. Chicago Historical Society, Chicago.

Donnelley, Thomas. "Industrial War in Chicago." *New Republic,* August 23, 1922, 359-60.

Dougherty, Mary. "Lake Shore Elite." *Holiday,* October 1951.

Douglas, Paul H. "Ickes of Chicago." *New Republic,* May 3, 1933, 331-3.

"Down to the Barbed Wire." *Newsweek,* August 26, 1968, 17-9.

Dreiser, Theodore. *Jennie Gerhardt.* New York: Penguin Books, 1994.

Dreiser, Theodore. *Sister Carrie.* New York: Bantam Books, 1992.

Dreiser, Theodore. *The Titan.* New York: Meridian Classic, A Division of Penguin Books, 1984.

Drury, John. "Chicago." *World's Fair Supplement. Chicago International Market. A Guide to A Century of Progress and the City of Chicago.* Chicago: The Chicago Association of Commerce, 1934. Chicago Historical Society, Chicago.

"Dry Sundays in Chicago—The Fight Won." *Survey,* October 23, 1915, 80-1.

"Drying Up Chicago." *Literary Digest,* December 15, 1923, 16.

Dugan, James. "Mayor Daley's Chicago." *Holiday,* December 1963.

Dunlop, Richard. "Chicago for the Fun of It." *Holiday,* March 1967.

Dunne, Finley Peter. *Dissertations by Mr. Dooley.* New York: Harper Brothers, 1906.

Dunne, Finley Peter. *Mr. Dooley At His Best.* n.p.: Archon Books, 1969.

Editor's Table. *New England Magazine,* March 1901, 107-116.

Edward J. Kelly Papers. Chicago Historical Society, Chicago.

Ellis, Dr. Horace. "Chicago, the Centenarian: This Famous Metropolis of the Midwest Is Getting Ready to Celebrate One Hundred Years of Existence—How the City Originated." *National Republic.* October 1930, v. 18, 26-27, 42.

"The End of the Fair." *The Christian Century,* November 22, 1933, 1459.

The Engineering Magazine: An Industrial Review. World's Fair in Retrospect, Souvenir Number. January 1894. Harold Washington Public Library, Chicago.

Evans, Elder Frederick W. *The World's Fair! Shall it Be Closed One Day in the Week to Please a Certain Sect.* Pittsfield, Massachusetts: Press Eagle Publishing Company, 1891. Newberry Library, Chicago.

The Everleigh Club Illustrated. n.p., n.d. Chicago Historical Society, Chicago.

Everett, Marshall. *The Great Chicago Theater Disaster: The Complete Story Told By the Survivors*. Memorial Edition. n.p: n.d. Lilly Library, Bloomington, Ind.

Everts, Rev. W.W. "The Lessons of Disaster." *Chicago Pulpit: A Weekly Publication*. October 19, 1872. Chicago: Carpenter & Sheldon, Publishers, vol. II, no. 43, 159-166.

The Exposition Guide to Chicago. Chicago: Walworth, Brooks, & Co., 1873. Chicago Historical Society, Chicago.

"The Exposition Souvenir." *Sixth Annual Inter-State Industrial Exposition of Chicago*. n.p.: 1878. Chicago Historical Society, Chicago.

Farr, Finis. *Chicago: A Personal History of America's Most American City*. New Rochelle, New York: Arlington House, 1973.

"Fashionable Chicago." *Harper's Weekly*, May 22, 1903, p. 875.

"The Fated City." *Sentinel Extra* (Chicago), July 14, 1874. Newberry Library, Chicago.

Favill, Henry B. M.D., et al. "The Chicago Vice Commission." *Survey*, May 6, 1911, 215-218.

"Fighting Vice Segregation in Chicago." *Literary Digest*, November 9, 1912, 848.

"The Fire." *Chicago Times*, October 18, 1871, p. 1. Newberry Library, Chicago.

Fitch, George. "'Seeing Chicago' Through a Megaphone." *Ladies Home Journal*, March, 1907, 17.

Flinn, John J. *Marvelous City of the West. A History, An Encyclopedia, and A Guide*. Second Edition. Chicago: The Standard Guide Co., 1892. Newberry Library, Chicago.

Flinn, John J. *Official Guide to the World's Columbian Exposition*. Chicago: The Columbian Guide Company, 1893. Newberry Library, Chicago and Lilly Library, Bloomington, Indiana.

Flower, Elliott. "Campaigning for Trade." *Harper's Weekly*, May 22, 1909.

"The Flowery End of a Chicago Gangster." *Literary Digest*, December 6, 1924, 39-48.

Flynn, John T. "Other People's Money." *New Republic*, June 16, 1937, 157-8.

"Ford and a Century of Progress." *World's Fair Archival Video*, Vol. One. Corrales, New Mexico: New Deal Films, Inc.

"Forty-ninth Annual." *American Magazine of Art*, November 1938, 659-60.

Fuller, Henry B. "Chicago." *Century Magazine*, May 1912, 25-33.

Fuller, Henry B. *The Cliff-Dwellers, A Novel*. The Gregg Press, Ridgewood, N.J., 1968.

Fuller, Henry B. "Development of Arts and Letters." In Ernest Ludlow Bogart and Charles Manfred Thompson, eds., *The Centennial History of Illinois*, vol. 4, *The Industrial State, 1870-1893* (Chicago: A.C. McClurg & Co., 1922), 188-216

Fuller, Henry B. "The Upward Movement in Chicago." *Atlantic Monthly*, October 1897, 534-547.

Fuller, Henry B. *With the Procession*. Chicago: The University of Chicago Press, 1965.

Gardner, Albert Teneyck. "Art for the Public," *American Magazine of Art*, September 1938.

Garrett, Oliver H.P. "Politics and Crime in Chicago." *New Republic*, June 9, 1926, 78-80.

Gates, Gary Paul. "Chicago After Dark." *Holiday*, March 1967.

Gifford, Anna. "Complete Correct Chapter Concerning Chicago's Conflagration, 1871." 1872. Chicago Historical Society, Chicago.

Goodspeed, Edgar Johnson. *The Great Fires in Chicago and the West. History and Incidents, Losses and Sufferings, Benevolence of the Nations, &c., &c. By a Chicago Clergyman. To Which is Appended a Record of the Great Conflagrations of the Past. Illustrated with Map and Scenes.* Chicago: J.W. Goodspeed, Publishers, 1871.

Gosnell, Harold F. "The Chicago 'Black Belt' As a Political Battleground." *American Journal of Sociology* 39 (November 1933): 329-41.

"Governor Altgeld and the President." *Nation*, July 12, 1894, 22-3.

Granger, Alfred. *Chicago Welcomes You.* Chicago: A. Kroch, 1933. Chicago Historical Society, Chicago.

Gray, John H. "City Government of Chicago." Review of *Municipal History and Present Organization of the City of Chicago*, by S. E. Sparling and *The Charters of the City of Chicago*, by E.J. James. *Municipal Affairs* 2 (September 1898), 539-41.

Gray, John H. "Franchises and Taxation in Chicago." *Municipal Affairs* 1 (December 1897): 766-767.

"The Great Calamity of the Age!" *Evening Journal-Extra* (Chicago), October 9, 1871.

"Great Chicago Fire." *Daily-Gazette Extra*, October 10, 1871. Newberry Library, Chicago.

The Great Fire. Leading Newspaper Accounts of the Terrible Chicago Conflagration, Including Descriptions of the Origin and Progress of the Fire, By Eyewitnesses, Correspondents, Etc., Harrowing Incidents, Hairbreadth Escapes, with a Correct Map. St. Louis: St. Louis Book and News Co., 1871. Newberry Library, Chicago.

"The Growing World's Fair." *Chicago Visitor*, February 1931, 14-5. Chicago Historical Society, Chicago.

Gruenberg, Robert. "Chicago Fiddles While Trumbull Park Burns." *Nation*, May 22, 1954, 441-3.

Gruenberg, Robert. "Trumbull Park: Act II. Elizabeth Wood Story." *Nation*, September 18, 1954, 230-2.

"Gunners and Targets In Chicago's Crime War." *Literary Digest*, October 30, 1926, 40-46.

Gutheim, F.A. "Buildings for Beasts: Our Zoos in Transition." *American Magazine of Art*, July 1936.

Halper, Albert. "It's the Giant of America's Heartland." *Holiday*, October 1951.

Hartley, Roland, "Chicago As a Distributing Point." *Harper's Weekly*, January 25, 1913, p. 12.

Hartman, Donald K., ed. *Fairground Fiction: Detective Stories of the World's Columbian Exposition.* New York: Motif Press, 1992.

Hartshorne, Richard. "Reply to Lewis Mumford." *New Republic.* April 3, 1929, 201-202.

Haskell, Douglas. "Architecture. 1933: Looking Forward at Chicago." *Nation*, January 24, 1934, 109-10.

Hawthorne, Julian. *Humors of the Fair*. The Marguerite Series, No. 12, September 15, 1893. Chicago: E.A. Weeks & Company, 1893. Newberry Library, Chicago.

Hayes, Frank L. "Chicago's Rent Riot." *Survey*, September 15, 1931, 548-9.

Head, Franklin H. "The Heart of Chicago." *New England Magazine*, July 1892, 550-67.

Hearings Before the Quadro-Centennial Committee of the United States Senate With Respects to the Commemoration of the Four-Hundredth Anniversary of the Discovery of America. January 11, 1890. Washington: Government Printing Office, 1890. Newberry Library, Chicago.

Hecht, Ben. "'How's Chicago Now?'" *Forum*, August 1918, 181-8.

Hefner, Hugh M., editor. *The Playboy Annual: Entertainment for Men*. New York: Waldorf Publishing Company, 1957. Chicago Historical Society, Chicago.

Hepner, Arther. "'Call Me Jake.'" *New Republic*, March 24, 1947, 20-3.

"Hippies, Yippies and Mace." *Newsweek*, September 2, 1968, 25-6.

Holman, Charles T. "Chicago Fair Breaks Record." *Christian Century*, August 23, 1933.

Holman, Charles T. "Chicago's Fair Near Opening." *Christian Century*, January 13, 1933, 98.

Hooker, George E. "Industrial War in Chicago." *New Republic*, June 7, 1922, 39-42.

Hooker, George E. "A Plan for Chicago." *Survey*, September 4, 1909, 778-90.

Hostetter, Gordon L. "Gangsterized Industry." *Survey*, January 1933, 16-17.

"How a Negro Feels When Chased by a Mob." *Literary Digest*, October 28, 1922, 43-45.

"How Chicago's Fair simulates Business Recovery: Crowded Trains, Airplanes, Automobiles and Lake Steamers Carry Visitors to the Century of Progress Exposition and Chicago Profits from Their Spendings." *Literary Digest*, August 12, 1933, v. 116, 36.

Howe, Frederic C. *The City: The Hope of Democracy*. New York: Charles Scribner's Sons, 1905.

Howells, William Dean. "Letters of an Alturian Traveler." *Cosmopolitan*, November 1893, 110-116 and December 1893, 218-232.

Hughes, Emmet John. "The Great Disgrace." *Newsweek*, August 7, 1967, 17-18.

Hungerford, Edward. "The New Chicago: What is Signified By the Passing of 'The Big Girl and the Motto'—The New Ideals and Aspirations that are Now Cherished in the City by Lake Michigan." *Harper's Weekly*, July 22, 1911, 10.

Husband, Joseph. "Chicago: An Etching." *New Republic*, November 20, 1915, 70-1.

Hutchinson, Paul. "Progress on Parade." *Forum*, June 1933, 370-3.

Hyde, Henry M. "A New Era of Building in Chicago." *Harper's Weekly*, September 7, 1901, 893.

Ickes, Harold L. "Harold L. Ickes: Stealing the Middle West Blind." *New Republic*, February 12, 1951.

"Illinois Abatement Law Held Constitutional." *Survey*, November 18, 1916, 173.

"Illinois, Crossroads of the Continent." *National Geographic Magazine*, May 1931, 562-94.

"Illinois Goes to the Polls." *New Republic,* April 29, 1936, 331.

"Illinois Vote: Kelly-Nash Machine's Defeat Chiefly of Local Significance." *Newsweek,* April 23, 1938, 13-4.

The Illustrated World's Fair, 1890–1891. Harold Washington Public Library, Chicago.

"In Old Chicago." *Time,* April 25, 1938, 13.

Insull, Samuel. Address of Samuel Insull Before the Association of Commerce, November 21, 1928. Chicago Historical Society, Chicago.

Inter-State Exhibition of Chicago. Programme for the Fair of 1873. Chicago: Tinker & Gibson, Publishers, 1873. Chicago Historical Society, Chicago.

Inter-Ocean (Chicago), 1883. Chicago Historical Society, Chicago.

"Is It Progress?" *Christian Century,* June 28, 1933, 838-840.

Jack, Homer A. "Chicago Violent Armistice." *Nation,* December 10, 1949, 571-2.

Jack, Homer A. "The New Chicago Fires." *Nation,* November 22, 1947, 551-3.

Jack, Homer A. "Trumbull Park Riots." *Nation,* June 19, 1954.

"The Javanese Dancers." *Harper's Weekly,* October 28, 1893, p. 1038-9.

"Jewels of American Gods for Chicago." *Literary Digest,* June 17, 1933, 28.

Johnson, Bascom. "An Open Letter to Journal Readers." *Journal of Social Hygiene* 19 (March 1933): 172-4.

Johnson, Martyn. "Chicago's Renaissance: An Old Italian Pageant in a New-World Setting." *Putnam's Monthly,* April 1909, 41-47.

Johnson, Rossiter. *A History of the World's Columbian Exposition, Held in Chicago in 1893.* New York: D. Appleton and Company, 1897. Newberry Library, Chicago.

Jones, Alonzo. *The Captivity of the Republic. A Report of Hearing By House Committee On Columbian Exposition, January 10-13, 1893. And the Present Status and Effect Of The Legislation On Sunday Closing Of The World's Fair.* International Liberty Association, 1893. Newberry Library, Chicago.

Jones, Calista Webster to Harlow S. and Mary June Black Webster, Chicago, June 6, 10, 11, and 15th, 1893. Lilly Library, Bloomington, Indiana.

Jones, Charles H. and Hon. E.O. Stanard. *Reasons Why the World's Fair of 1892 Should Be Located At St. Louis. Arguments Made Before the Senate World's Fair Committee.* Washington: Government Printing Office, 1890. Newberry Library, Chicago.

Jones, Llewellyn. "Chicago Interlude." *New Republic.* July 5, 1933, vol. 75, 203-5.

"Juvenile Crime and Community Morale." *Common Welfare,* July 27, 1918, 479.

Karlen, Arno. "The New Chicago." *Holiday,* March 1967.

Kearney, John. "Mayor Daley: Decision-Maker in Chicago." *Commonweal,* August 9, 1968, 518-9.

Keith, John. "The Strangle-hold of Labor: II. The Problem of Transportation." *Harper's Weekly,* December 5, 1903, 1940-1.

Keith, John. "The Strangle-hold of Labor: I. The Rent Rack." *Harper's Weekly,* November 28, 1903, 1902-4.

Key, V.O. Jr. "Police Graft." *American Journal of Sociology* 40 (March 1935): 624-35.

King, Captain Charles. "The City of the World's Fair." *Cosmopolitan*, November 1891, 37-63.

Kinney, Rev. Henry C. *Why the Columbian Exposition Should Be Opened On Sunday: A Religio-Social Study.* Chicago: Rand, McNally & Company, Printers, 1892. Newberry Library, Chicago.

Kirkwood, Edith Brown. "The Business Woman's Lunch." *Good Housekeeping*, May 1911, 555-9.

Knox, Loren H.B. "Impressions From Chicago Faces." *Atlantic Monthly*, January 1906, 28-34.

Kogan, Herman. "Report from Chicago." *New Republic*, April 14, 1947, 21.

Kreuger, Jess. *Fair Nights.* n.p., 1933. Chicago Historical Society, Chicago.

"L.B.J.'s Man in Chicago." *Time*, August 23, 1968, 12-14.

Lahey, Edwin A. "Anything Can Happen in Chicago." *Nation*, January 1, 1936, 12-4.

Lait, Jack. "Chicago." *American Magazine*, January 1918.

Lait, Jack and Lee Mortimer. *Chicago Confidential: The Lowdown on the Big Town.* New York: Crown Publishers, 1950.

The Lakeside Memorial of The Burning of Chicago. Chicago: The University Publishing Company, 1872. Newberry Library, Chicago.

Landesco, John. *Organized Crime in Chicago: Part III of the Illinois Crime Survey, 1929.* Chicago: The University of Chicago Press, 1929.

Lane, M.A. "The Chicago Fair." *Harper's Weekly*, July 2, 1892, p. 643.

Lane, M.A. "The Exposition as it Will Be." *Harper's Weekly*, December 19, 1891, p. 1018-9.

Lane, M.A. "In a Chicago Pool-Room." *Harper's Weekly*, September 10, 1892, p. 878.

Lane, M.A. "The Lake Front, Chicago." *Harper's Weekly*, November 12, 1892, p. 1091.

Lane, M.A. "On The Exposition Grounds." *Harper's Weekly*, April 9, 1892, p. 341.

Lane, M.A. "The Strike." *Harper's Weekly*, July 21, 1894, p. 687-8.

Lane, M.A. "One View of World's Fair." *Harper's Weekly*, August 6, p. 1892.

Lane, M.A. "The Woman's Building, World's Fair." *Harper's Weekly*. January 9, 1892.

Lane, M.A. "The World's Fair. *Harper's Weekly*, February 20, 1892, p.190.

"The Last Day of the Fair." *Harper's Weekly*, November 11, 1893, p.1074.

Leach, Paul R. "Strong Mayor vs. City Manager." *Survey*, October 1931.

Leibling, A.J. "Profiles: Second City. II—At Her Feet the Slain Deer." *New Yorker*, January 19, 1952.

Leibling, A.J. "Profiles: Second City. III—The Massacre." *New Yorker*, January 26, 1952.

Leibling, A.J. "Profiles: Second City. I—So Proud to Be Jammy-Jammy." *New Yorker*, January 12, 1952.

"Letters to the Editors." *Life*, December 27, 1948, 2.

Lewis, Lloyd. "Chicago's Booze War." *New Republic*, March 31, 1929, 88-90.

Life of Al Capone in Pictures! and Chicago's Gang Wars. Lake Michigan Printing Company, 1931. Chicago Historical Society, Chicago.

"The Light Turned on a Race Riot." *Literary Digest*, October 28, 1922, 11-12.

Lindsey, Almont. "Paternalism and the Pullman Strike." *American Historical Review* 44 (January 1939): 272-89.

Linn, James Weber. "Chicago." *New Republic*, January 4, 1919, 278-80.

Linn, James Weber. "What Kind of Boston is Chicago?" *World's Work*, July 1906, 7766-71.

Lippincott, Sara Jane. *New Life in New Lands: Notes of Travel.* New York: J.B. Ford and Company, 1873.

"Literary Tributes to the World's Fair." *Dial*, October 1, 1893, 176-78.

"Literature At the Columbian Exposition." *Dial*, February 1, 1893, 67-68.

Lohr, Lenox R. *Fair Management: The Story of A Century of Progress Exposition/ A Guide for Future Fairs.* Chicago: The Cuneo Press, Inc., 1952.

Lovett, Robert Morss. "'Big Bill' Thompson of Chicago." *Current History*, June 1931, 379-83.

Lovett, Robert Morss. "Chicago: 'Gigantic, Willful, Young.'" *New Republic*, April 20, 1927, 243-6.

Lovett, Robert Morss. "Chicago, the Phenomenal City." *Current History*, November 1929, 328-34.

Luzerne, Frank. *The Lost City! Drama of the Fire-Fiend of Chicago, As It Was, and As It Is! And Its Glorious Future! A Vivid and Truthful Picture of All of Interest Connected with the Destruction of Chicago And the Terrible Fires of the Great North-West. Startling, Thrilling Incidents, Frightful Scenes, Hair Breadth Escapes, Individual Heroism, Self-Sacrifices, Personal Anecdotes, &c.* New York: Wells & Company, 1872. Newberry Library, Chicago.

"Machine Guns Now—What Next?" *Literary Digest*, May 15, 1926, 12.

Mackintosh, Charles Herbert. *The Doomed City! Chicago During An Appalling Ordeal! The Fire Demon's Carnival. The Conflagrations in the West, South, and North Divisions. Graphic Sketches from the Scene of the Disaster.* Detroit: Michigan News Company, 1871. Newberry Library, Chicago.

Madison, Randolph. "Letter from Chicago." *New Republic*, April 23, 1945, 549-51.

"The Management of the World's Fair," *Harper's Weekly*, December 6, 1890, 951.

March, Rev. Septimus, B.A. "The Burning of Chicago: A Lesson of Dependence. Being a Sermon Preached in Albion Chapel, Southhampton." Southhampton: Gutch & Cox, 1871. Chicago Historical Society, Chicago.

Martin, John Bartlow. "My Chicago." *Holiday*, March 1967.

Mason, Edward G. "Chicago." *Atlantic Monthly*, July 1892, 33-40.

Mason, Edward G. "Early Visitors to Chicago." *New England Magazine*, April 1892, 188-206.

Masters, Edgar Lee. "Chicago: Yesterday, To-Day and To-Morrow." *Century Magazine*, July 1928, 283-94.

Masters, Edgar Lee. "Introduction to Chicago." *American Mercury Magazine*, January 1934, 49-59.

Masters, Edgar Lee. *Spoon River Anthology.* New York: Dover Publications,1992.

Masters, Edgar Lee. *The Tale of Chicago.* New York: G.P. Putnam's Sons, 1933. Chicago Historical Society, Chicago.

Matthews, Franklin. "Chicago as a Storm Centre." *Critic*, February 1904, 172-5.

Mayer, Milton S. "Chicago—City of Unrest. Even There Communism Has Made No Headway." *Forum*, January 1933, 46-51.

Mayer, Milton S. "Chicago Is Broke." *Nation*, February 13, 1937, 177-9.

Mayer, Milton S. "How to Wreck Your Schools: The Destruction of Education in Chicago." *Forum*, May 1937, 259.

Mayer, Milton S. "It's Hell to Be a Chicago Liberal." *Nation*, February 25,1939, 223-4.

"Mayor Kelly's Chicago: A Strong Democratic Boss Runs a Lusty City." *Life*, July 17, 1944, 67-77.

McCormick, Robert. "Star-Spangled Town: An Outstanding Chicagoan Interprets His City as a Stronghold of Rugged Americanism." *Holiday*, October 1951, 70.

McDermott, William F. "Chicago Strikes Back." *North American Review*, July 1931, 56-64.

McDonald, R.H. *R.H. McDonald's Illustrated History and Map of Chicago With a History of the Great Fire: A Record of All the Great Fires of the World.* New York: R.B. Thompson & Co., 1872. Chicago Historical Society, Chicago.

McClure, J.B., editor. *Stories and Sketches of Chicago.* Chicago: Rhodes & McClure, Publishers, 1880.

McWilliams, Carey. "Chicago's Machine-Gun Politics." *Nation*, March 15, 1952, 245-7.

Merriam, C.E. "Cleaning Up Chicago." *New Republic*, April 24, 1929, 272-3.

Merwin, Samuel. "Chicago, the American Paradox." *Saturday Evening Post*, October 26, 1929, v. 209, 8-9, 118, 122.

"The Metropolis of the Prairies." *Harper's New Monthly Magazine*, October 1880, 711-31.

"Micro-zoo at Chicago Fair." *Literary Digest*, May 13, 1933, 24.

"The Midway Plaisance." *Harper's Weekly*, May 13, 1898, p. 442.

"A Midway Review." *Dial*, September 1, 1893, 105-7.

Miller, Justin. "Getting Away with Murder: The Illinois Crime Survey Penetrates the Underworld." *Survey*, July 1, 1929.

Miller, Robert A. "The Relation of Reading Characteristics to Social Indexes." *American Journal of Sociology* 41 (May 1936): 738-56.

"Mob Rule in Chicago." *New Republic*, April 10, 1950, 12-3.

Monroe, Harriet. "Defending the World's Fair." *New Republic.* July 19, 1933, 265.

Monroe, Lucy. "The Bentzon on Chicago." *Critic*, August 18, 1894, 109-10.

Mowrer, Ernest. "City Life and Domestic Discord." *Survey*, December 1, 1926, 298-9.

"Mr. Chauncey DePew's Last Oration." *Spectator*, October 29, 1892, 585-7.

"Mr. Mencken's 'Chicagoaid.'" *Literary Digest*, July 24, 1920, 29-30.

Mumford, Lewis. "Reflections on Chicago." *New Republic.* February 27, 1929, 44-5.

Mumford, Lewis. "Two Chicago Fairs." *New Republic.* January 21, 1933, 270-72.

"Murder, Politics and Vice in Chicago." *Survey*, August 8, 1914, 476-7.

Murray, James R. "Pity the Homeless or Burnt Out." Boston: White, Smith & Company, 1871. Newberry Library, Chicago.

Murray, William. "The Troubled Arts." *Holiday*, March, 1967.

Musham, H.A. "The Great Chicago Fire, October 8-10, 1871." In *Papers In Illinois History and Transactions for the Year 1940*. Springfield, Ill.: The Illinois State Historical Society, 1941. Chicago Historical Society, Chicago.

"Music At the World's Fair." *Dial*, June 1, 1893, 329-30.

"Music: A Fourth Opera Company Sprouts Where 3 Died Before." *Newsweek*, November 9, 1935, 37.

"The Nation." *Time*, August 4, 1967, 12-3.

Nelson, Henry Loomis. "The Clubs of Chicago." *Harper's Weekly*, August 10, 1892, p. 806-7.

Ness, Eliot and Oscar Fraley. *The Untouchables*. New York: Barnes & Noble Books, 1996.

New York Times, October 1871-December 1968.

Nicholes, Anna E. "The Chicago City Welfare Exhibits." *American City*, July 1912, 22-5.

"No Federal Mop For Chicago's Crime Wave." *Literary Digest*, March 20, 1926, 7-8.

Norris, Frank. *The Pit: The Epic of The Wheat*. New York: Penguin Books, 1994.

O'Faolin, Sean. "The Three Chicagos." *Holiday*, December 1960.

Official Catalogue of Exhibits, World's Columbian Exposition, Chicago, ILLS (sic) U.S.A. Chicago: W.B. Cokey, 1893. Lilly Library, Bloomington, Ind.

Official Catalogue of the Inter-State Industrial Exposition of Chicago, Ill. Chicago: James Nowlan, Publisher, 1873. Chicago Historical Society, Chicago.

Official Catalogue of the Inter-State Industrial Exposition of Chicago, Ill. Sixth Annual Exhibition. Chicago: Fox, Cole & Co., Publishers, 1878. Chicago Historical Society, Chicago.

Official Minutes of the First Meeting of the World's Columbian Commission, held in The City of Chicago, June 26th to July 3d, 1890. Chicago: Rand, McNally & Co., Printers, 1890. Lilly Library, Bloomington, Ind.

Official Minutes of the Fourth and Fifth Sessions of the World's Columbian Commission Held in the City of Chicago, April 1st to 4th, 1891, Inclusive, and September 2nd and 8th, 1891, Inclusive. Chicago: Knight Leonard & Company, 1891. Lilly Library, Bloomington, Ind.

The Official Pictures of A Century of Progress Exposition Chicago 1933. Coral Springs, Florida: B. Klein Publications, 1933 and 1993.

Official Souvenir Program of Chicago Day at the World's Fair. Chicago: Thos. Knapp Printing and Binding Co., 1893. Newberry Library, Chicago.

Official Views of the World's Columbian Exposition, 1893. Chicago: Press Chicago Photogravure, Co., 1893. Lilly Library, Bloomington, Ind.

"On the Firing-Line During the Chicago Race-Riots." *Literary Digest*, August 23, 1919, 45-6.

"The Opening of the Chicago Exhibition." *Spectator*, May 6, 1893, 594-5.

"The Opening of the Great Exhibition." *Dial*, May 16, 1893, 297-8.

"Opening of the University of Chicago." *Dial*, October 1, 1892, 206.

Oppenheim, J.H. "Autopsy on Chicago." *American Mercury*, April 1937, 454-61.

"The Organization of the World's Fair." *Harper's Weekly*, July 26, 1890, p. 578.

Our Rostrum. *Forum*, December 1927, 943-5.

Paige, Clara Paul. "Chicago's Unemployables." *Survey*, December 1937, 373-5.
Pasley, Fred. *Al Capone: The Biography of a Self-Made Man*. New York: Ives Washburn, 1930.
"The Passing of the White City. *Harper's Weekly*, January 20, 1894, p. 54.
"Pastimes." *Time*, April 4, 1938, 51.
Patterson, W.R. "Tenement-Houses in Chicago." Review of *Tenement Conditions in Chicago*, by Robert Hunter, editor. *Municipal Affairs* 6 (June 1902): 285-7.
Payne, Will. "Chicago! All Change!" *Saturday Evening Post*. November 15, 1930, v. 203, 22-3, 92-97.
Pearson, Ralph M. "The Artist's Point of View: Big Things Are Happening in Chicago." *Forum*, August 1937, 95.
Peattie, Elia W. "The Artistic Side of Chicago." *Atlantic Monthly*, December 1899, 828-834.
"Permanent Impress of the Chicago Fair: America's Insistence on Still Higher Standards of Living, and Its Receptivity to Cultural Influences Revealed at Exposition." *Literary Digest*, November 25, 1933, 29.
Peters, William. "Race War in Chicago." *New Republic*, January 9, 1950, 10-2.
Pickett, Montgomery Breckenridge. "Opening of the Great Fair." *Harper's Weekly*, May 13, 1898, p. 442.
Playboy: Entertainment for Men. December 1956. Chicago Historical Society, Chicago.
Playboy After Dark. Playboy. 1969. Museum of Broadcast History, Chicago.
The Playboy Club. Chicago, 1960. Chicago Historical Society, Chicago.
"A Pleasure, Indeed!" *Chicago Visitor*, February 1931, 3. Chicago Historical Society, Chicago.
Plum, Mary. *Murder at the World's Fair*. New York: Harper and Brothers, 1933. Chicago Historical Society, Chicago.
"'Police State' or Model City? Chicago in Perspective." *U.S. News & World Report*, September 16, 1968, 64-6.
"Police: Through a Fine Screen." *Time*, September 13, 1968, 69.
"Politics: After Detroit." *Time*, August 4, 1967, 18-9.
Potter, Henry C. "Sunday and the Columbian Exposition." *Forum*, October 1892, 194-200.
"The Power Plant." *Harper's Weekly*, May 13, 1893, p. 442.
Programme for the Sixth Annual Exhibition of the Inter-State Industrial Exposition of Chicago. Chicago: Jameson & Morse Printers, 1878. Chicago Historical Society, Chicago.
Programme of the Inter-State Industrial Exposition of Chicago, 1874. Chicago: 1874. Chicago Historical Society, Chicago.
Progress: A Century of Progress. April 1, 1931 to April 15, 1934. Chicago Historical Society, Chicago.
"The Progress of Progress." *Nation*, May 31, 1933, 602.
The Public Enemy. Warner Brothers, 1931.
Pullen, Clarence. "The Parks and Parkways of Chicago." *Harper's Weekly*, June 6, 1891, p. 413-16.
"The Pullman Boycott." *Nation*, July 5, 1894, 4-5.

Putnam, Samuel. "Chicago: An Obituary." *American Mercury*, August 1926, 417-25.

"Putting Out the Red Lights." *Literary Digest*, November 13, 1915, 1086-1087.

"Questions to Specialists." *Our Day*, December 1890, 468-74.

Ralph, Julian. "Building Our Great Fair." *Harper's Weekly*, September 17, 1892, p. 897-8.

Ralph, Julian. "Chicago's Argonauts." *Harper's Weekly*, November 12, 1892, p. 1091.

Ralph, Julian. "Chicago's Gentle Side." *Harper's New Monthly Magazine*, July 1893, 286-98.

Ralph, Julian. "Chicago—The Main Exhibit." *Harper's New Monthly Magazine*, February 1892, 425-36.

Ralph, Julian. "Exploiting the Great Fair." *Harper's Weekly*, August 10,1892, p. 806.

Ralph, Julian. "A Recent Journey Through the West." *Harper's Weekly*, November 16, 1895, p. 1088.

Randolph, Robert Isham and Forrest Crissey. "Business Fights Crime in Chicago." *Saturday Evening Post*, August 16, 1930.

Reckless, Walter C. *Vice in Chicago*. Chicago: University of Chicago Press, 1933.

"Reconstruction Chicago." *Survey*, March 22, 1919, 896-7.

"Regarding the World's Fair." *Harper's Weekly*, February 13, 1892, p. 161.

"Relentless War Against Vice in Chicago." *Survey*, June 9, 1917, 249.

"Remember Chicago!" *Nation*, January 15, 1938, 62.

Remington, Frederic. "The Affair of the -th of July." *Harper's Weekly*, February 2, 1895, p. 103-105.

Remington, Frederic. "Chicago Under the Mob." *Harper's Weekly*, July 21, 1894, 680-1.

Remington, Frederic. "A Gallop Through the Midway." *Harper's Weekly*, October 7, 1893, p. 963.

Remington, Frederic. "The Withdrawal of the U.S. Troops." *Harper's Weekly*, August 11, 1894, p. 748.

Review of *Reminiscences of Early Chicago and Vicinity*, by Edwin O. Gale. *Nation*, March 5, 1903, 199.

"The Report on the Chicago Strike." *Nation*, November 22, 1894, 376.

Reynolds, Wilfred S. "Chicago Takes the Next Step." *Survey*, August 15, 1931, 471.

Rich, Adena M. "1854 Mary E. McDowell 1936." *Survey*, November 1936, 332.

Richberg, Donald. "The Spoils of Normalcy." *Survey*, July 1, 1929.

Richey, Elinor. "What Chicago Could Be Proud Of." *Harper's Magazine*, December 1961, 34-9.

"The Right to Criticize Chicago." *Literary Digest*, October 29, 1921, 13-14.

"Riots: Summer Stock." *Newsweek*, February 26, 1968, 26.

The Road to Perdition. Dreamworks, 2002. DVD.

Robson, William. "Chicago's 'Century of Progress.'" *New Statesman and Nation*, July 29, 1933, 132-3.

Roe, E.P. *Barriers Burned Away*. Upper Saddle River, New Jersey: Literature House/ Gregg Press, 1970.

Roeburt, John. *Al Capone, a Novel.* New York: Pyramid Books, 1959. Chicago Historical Society, Chicago.

Root, George F. *Passing Through Fire: Song and Chorus.* Chicago: Root & Cady, 1871. Newberry Library, Chicago.

Ross, Leonard. "Peep Show." *American Mercury*, June 1939, 183-9.

Ross, Robert. *The Trial of Al Capone.* Chicago: Robert Ross, publisher, 1933. Chicago Historical Society, Chicago.

The Ruined City: Or, The Horrors of Chicago. New York: Orum and Company Publishers, 1871. Newberry Library, Chicago.

Runnion, Ray. "Chicago the Beautiful." *Nation*, July 21, 1945, 61-2.

Sandburg, Carl. "Introduction to Chicago." *Holiday*, October, 1951, 32-33.

Sancton, Thomas. "Gone to Chicago." *New Republic*, November 12, 1945, 647-50.

Scarface. The Caddo Company, 1932.

"Seven in Chicago." *Time*, August 5, 1935, 42.

Sewell, Alfred. *"The Great Calamity!" Scenes, Incidents, and Lessons of the Great Chicago Fire of the 8th and 9th of October, 1871.* Chicago: Alfred L. Sewell, Publisher, 1871. Chicago Historical Society, Chicago.

"Sharpshooting." *Survey*, November 1935, 340.

"The Shattered Illusion of Reform." *Nation*, December 22, 1951, inside cover.

Sheahan, James W. and George P. Upton. *The Great Conflagration Chicago: Its Past, Present, and Future.* Chicago: Union Publishing Company, 1871. Chicago Historical Society, Chicago.

Sheperd, William G. "Can Capone Beat Washington too?" *Collier's*, v. 18, 16-17, 42-44.

Sheperd, William G. "If It Isn't Booze, It's Something Else." *Collier's*, November 26, 1932, v. 90, 7-8, 34-37.

Simpson, Herbert. "The Chicago Complex." *Atlantic Monthly*, October 1930, 537-547.

Sinclair, Upton. *The Jungle.* New York: Penguin Classics, 1986.

Smith, Alson J. *Syndicate City: The Chicago Crime Cartel and What to Do About It.* Chicago: Henry Regnery Company, 1954. Chicago Historical Society, Chicago.

Smith, Henry Justin. "Chicago: Her Plans and Her Growing-Pains." *Century Magazine*, March 1927, 607-12.

Smith, Henry Justin. "The Ugly City." *Atlantic Monthly*, July 1919, 27-33.

Smith, Sandy. "You Can't Expect Police on the Take to Take Orders." *Life*, December 6, 1968, 40-4.

Souvenir of A Ride On the Ferris Wheel At the World's Fair, Chicago. Chicago: The American Engraving Company, 1893. Lilly Library, Bloomington, Indiana.

Sparks, Edwin Erle. "The Centennial of Chicago." *Munsey's Magazine*, October 1903, 12-18.

Sparks, Edwin Erle. "This Week's Centennial in Chicago." *Harper's Weekly*, September 26, 1903, p. 1552-1553.

Spaulding, Bishop J.L. "Why the World's Fair Should be Opened on Sunday." *Arena*, December 1892, 45-7.

Speed, Jonathan Gilmer. "The Power Plant." *Harper's Weekly*, May 13, 1898, p. 442-3.

Spitzer, Silas. "Dining in Chicago." *Holiday*, March 1967.

Stead, William T. *If Christ Came to Chicago!: A Plea for the Union of All Who Love in the Service of All Who Suffer*. 1894. Reprint, Chicago Historical Bookworks, 1990.

"Street Corner Sermons for Chicago." *Literary Digest*, April 24, 1926, 31.

Street in Cairo. World's Columbian Exposition. Chicago: The Winters Art Litho. Co., Harold Washington Public Library, Chicago, n.d.

Street, Julian. "Chicago" Chapter VI—Abroad At Home—American Ramblings, Observations, and Adventures." *Collier's*, August 1, 1914, 17-20.

"Street-car Antagonisms that Breed Race Hatred." *Survey*, October 15, 1922, 90-1.

Steffens, Lincoln. "Enemies of the Republic: Illinois: A Triumph of Public Opinion—After an Eight Years' Political War, the Republican Party is Brought to Represent the People—A Missouri Parallel." *McClure's Magazine*, August 1904, 395-408.

Steffens, Lincoln. "Chicago: Half Free and Fighting On." *McClure's Magazine*, October 1903, 563-77.

Stern, Richard G. "A Valentine for Chicago." *Harper's Magazine*, February 1962, 63-9.

Stone, Herbert. *Chicago and the World's Fair: A Popular Guide*. Chicago: n.p., 1892. Newberry Library, Chicago.

Stone, Herbert. *Terra Cotta Guide: Chicago and the World's Fair*. Chicago: Stone & Kimball, 1893.

Strong, Josiah. *Our Country*. Cambridge: The Belknap Press of Harvard University Press, 1963.

Stuart, William H. *The Twenty Incredible Years*. Chicago: M.A. Donohue & Co., 1935.

Sullivan, Edward Dean. "I Know You, Al." *North American Review*, September 1929, 257-64.

"Suspending the Law for New Year's." *Literary Digest*, January 25, 1913, 184-5.

Sutherland, Douglas. "How Chicago Got That Way." *World's Work*, May 1930, 53-5.

"The Tail (sic) of Chicago." *Harper's Weekly*, July 21, 1906, 1020-1.

Taylor, Graham. "Chicago in the Nation's Race Strife." *Survey*, August 9, 1919, 695-7.

Taylor, Graham. "Fighting Vice in Chicago." *Survey*, October 26, 1912, 94-5.

Taylor, Graham. "A Permanent Morals Commission For Chicago." *Survey*, December 12, 1914, 281-282.

Taylor, Graham. "Routing the Segregationists in Chicago." *Survey*, November 30, 1912, 254- 256.

Taylor, Graham. "The Story of the Chicago Vice Commission." *Survey*, May 6, 1911, 230-47.

This Busy World. *Harper's Weekly*, October 7, 1893, p. 963.

"This is Chicago!" *Survey*, November 1, 1929, 160-1.

"The Thompson Defeat In Chicago." *Literary Digest*, July 2, 1921, 17-18.

Thompson, Frederick. "The Sultan and the Chicago Exhibition." *Magazine of American History*, October 1891, 289-295.

Thrasher, Frederic M. "The Gang." *Survey*, October 15, 1921.

Thwaites, J. and M. "Seeing The Shows in Chicago." *American Magazine of Art*, September 1937.

Thwaites, J. and M. "Two Chicago Events." *American Magazine of Art*, January 1938, 39-41.

Times (London), 1933.

"To Kick Out Chicago's Alien Gunmen." *Literary Digest*, March 6, 1926, 13-14.

Trail, Armitage. *Scarface*. New York: Dell, 1959.

"Two Views of Chicago." *Harper's Magazine*, April 1964, 140-9.

"The Unmaking of a Myth: Chicago's Race Riots: an Analysis and a Program." *Survey*, October 1, 1922, 46-9.

The Untouchables. First Episode. Desilu Playhouse, CMLIX.

The Untouchables. "Takeover." Paramount Pictures. 1961. The Museum of Broadcast History, Chicago.

Velie, Lester. "The Capone Gang Muscles Into Big-Time Politics." *Collier's*, September 30, 1950. Chicago Historical Society, Chicago.

"Vice as a Nuisance." *Survey*, June 21, 1919, 464.

Vice Commission of Chicago. *The Social Evil in Chicago: A Study of Existing Conditions*. Chicago: Gunthorp-Warren Printing Company, 1911.

Wacker, Charles H. "The Plan of Chicago." *American City*, October 1909, 48-53.

Wacker, Charles H. and Edward H. Bennett. "Technical Features of the Plan of Chicago." *American City*, October 1909, 54-58.

Wainwright, Loudon. "Alarming Assault on the Young." *Life*, September 13, 1968, 33.

Waldvogel, Merikay and Barbara Brackman. *Patchwork Souvenirs of the 1933 World's Fair: the Sears National Quilt Contest and Chicago's Century of Progress Exposition*. Nashville, Tenn.: Rutledge Hill Press, 1993.

Walker, Francis A. "America's Fourth Centenary." *Forum*, February 1890, 612-21.

"The Walker Report." *Commonweal*, December 30, 1968, 391-2.

"Walker Report: Chicago Cops Rioted." *Life*, December 6, 1968, 35-8.

Walker, Stanley. "Our Far-Flung Correspondents: Return of a Non-Native." *New Yorker*, April 6, 1946.

Walter, Dave, ed. *Today Then: America's Best Minds Look 100 Years Into the Future on the Occasion of the 1893 World's Columbian Exposition*. Helena, Mont.: American & World Geographic Publishing, 1992.

"Ward Boss." *Life*, October 25, 1948, 113-117.

Washburn, Charles. *Come Into My Parlor: A Biography of the Aristocratic Everleigh Sisters of Chicago*. New York: Knickerbocker Publishing Company, 1936.

Waterloo, Stanley. "Who Reads a Chicago Book?" Communications. *Dial*, October 1, 1892, 206-207.

"Weird Lights at Chicago Fair." *Literary Digest*, March 25, 1933, 32.

Wheeler, Keith. "'This is Daley's Chicago—he doesn't dig anything else.'" *Life*, September 6, 1968, 28-9.

Whibley, Charles. "Chicago." *Living Age*, February 16, 1907, 387-93.

"The White City of Chicago." *Spectator*, September 16, 1893, 366-7.

Whiting, F.A. Jr. "Two Versions of American Art: Chicago and Manhattan." *American Magazine of Art*, December 1936.

"Why Chicago Did It." *New Republic*, April 20, 1927, 234-6.

"Why is Chicago?" *World Tomorrow*, December 7, 1932, 534.

"Why the Negro Appeals to Violence." *Literary Digest*, August 9, 1919, 11.

"Will History Repeat Itself?" *Journal of Social Hygiene* 19 (May 1933) 163-4.

Williams, John A. "The Negro: Three Families." *Holiday*, March 1967.

Wilson, Edmund. "Hull House in 1932: I." *New Republic*, January 18, 1933, 260-2.

Wilson, Edmund. "Hull House in 1932: II." *New Republic*, January 25, 1933, 287-90.

Wilson, Edmund. "Hull House in 1932: III." *New Republic*, February 1, 1933, 317-22.

Wonderful Chicago and the World's Fair. Historical and Picturesque. Chicago: George W. Melville, Chicago, 1892. Harold Washington Public Library, Chicago.

"The World's Columbian Exposition." *Harper's Weekly*, November 22, 1890.

"The World's Columbian Exposition." *Harper's Weekly*, May 13, 1893, p. 438.

The World's Columbian Exposition, Department of Publicity and Promotion. *World's Columbian Exposition, Chicago, Ill., May-Oct. 30, 1893: Its Scope, Present Condition, Purposes, and Prospects. Specially Compiled for the Information of the Guests of the Citizens of Chicago, February 22, 1892.* Chicago: Department of Publicity and Promotion, 1892. Harold Washington Public Library, Chicago.

World's Columbian Exposition, 1893. *The Moorish Palace and Its Startling Wonders. The Chief Attraction of the Midway Plaisance.* Chicago: Metcalf Stationery Co., 1893. Newberry Library, Chicago.

World's Columbian Exposition, Official Catalogue, 1893, of Exhibits on the Midway Plaisance. n.p.: n.d. Lilly Library, Bloomington, Ind.

World's Columbian Exposition Pamphlets and Leaflets. Newberry Library, Chicago.

World's Columbian Exposition, Plan and Classification, Department M. Chicago: World's Columbian Exposition, 1892. Lilly Library: Bloomington, Ind.

World's Columbian Exposition Souvenir, Containing a Story of Christopher Columbus and His Discoveries. Chicago: North American Engraving and Publishing Company, 1895. Newberry Library, Chicago.

"The World's Fair." *Harper's Weekly*, October 4, 1890, p. 779.

"The World's Fair and Sunday." *Harper's Weekly*, October 15, 1892, 985-6.

"The World's Fair of 1892—Chicago Favored in the House of Representatives." *Scientific American*, March 8, 1890, 146-7.

World's Fair Puck. May 1, 1893-October 9, 1893. Harold Washington Public Library, Chicago.

Work, Monroe. "Crime Among the Negroes of Chicago: A Social Study." *American Journal of Sociology* 6 (September 1900): 204-223.

"The Wreck of Commercialized Vice." *Survey*, February 5, 1916, 532-3.

Wright, Richard. *Black Boy (American Hunger).* New York: HarperPerennial, 1993.

Wright, Richard. *Native Son.* New York: Harper & Row Publishers, 1966.

Wyatt, Edith. "Chicago's Melting Pot: More Miles of Halsted Street Below Haymarket—Hull House and Its Meaning." *Colliers*, August 27, 1910, 21-2.

Wyatt, Edith. "The Street of Large Trades: Halsted Street's Change from Sordid City Highway to Country Road." *Collier's*, September 3, 1910, 22-3.

Wyatt, Edith. "The Street of Little Trades: Five Miles of Chicago's Halsted Street, from Lake Michigan to the Region of the Penny Arcade." *Colliers*, August 20, 1910, 20-1.

Yarros, Victor S. "Chicago's Surrender." *Survey*, November 20, 1920, 273-275.

Youmans, F. Zeta. "Kindergartens of Crime." *Survey*, September 15, 1928, 581-3.

The Youth's Companion. World's Fair Number. May 4, 1893. Harold Washington Public Library, Chicago.

Zum Andeken, World's Columbian Exposition, Chicago, 1893. In Remembrance of the World's Columbian Exposition, Chicago. New York: American Souvenir & Advertising Co., 1893. Lilly Library, Bloomington, Ind.

Index